RENEW ORLEANS?

Globalization and Community

Susan E. Clarke, Series Editor
Dennis R. Judd, Founding Editor

(series continued on p. 233)

Renew Orleans?

GLOBALIZED DEVELOPMENT AND WORKER RESISTANCE AFTER KATRINA

Aaron Schneider

Globalization and Community, Volume 28

University of Minnesota Press

Minneapolis

London

MINNESOTA

Portions of chapters 6 and 7 were previously published in "New Orleans: Post-Disaster Dual Dualism in Labor Markets and Development," in *Disasters, Hazards, and Law*, ed. Mathieu Deflem, 175–202 (London: Emerald Group Publishing, 2013). Portions of chapter 8 were previously published in "Work, New Orleans, and the Global Shipbuilding Regime," *Work, Organization, Labor, and Globalization* 6, no. 2 (2012): 140–51; reproduced with permission of Pluto Journals via PLSclear.

Published by the University of Minnesota Press
111 Third Avenue South, Suite 290
Minneapolis, MN 55401-2520
http://www.upress.umn.edu

Printed in the United States of America on acid-free paper

The University of Minnesota is an equal-opportunity educator and employer.

Library of Congress Cataloging-in-Publication Data
Names: Schneider, Aaron, author.
Title: Renew Orleans? : globalized development and worker resistance after Katrina / Aaron Schneider.
Description: Minneapolis : University of Minnesota Press, 2018. | Series: Globalization and community ; 28 | Includes bibliographical references and index.
Identifiers: LCCN 2017042761 | ISBN 978-1-5179-0166-0 (pb) | ISBN 978-1-5179-0165-3 (hc)
Subjects: LCSH: Urban renewal–Louisiana–New Orleans. | Elite (Social sciences)–Louisiana–New Orleans. | Working class–Louisiana–New Orleans. | New Orleans (La.)–Economic conditions–21st century. | New Orleans (La.)–Social conditions–21st century.| BISAC: POLITICAL SCIENCE / Public Policy / City Planning & Urban Development. | SOCIAL SCIENCE / Sociology / Urban. | SOCIAL SCIENCE / Disasters & Disaster Relief.
Classification: LCC HT177.N49 S36 2018 | DDC 307.3/4160976335–dc23
LC record available at https://lccn.loc.gov/2017042761

CONTENTS

The week after I arrived in New Orleans in December 2007, the City Council voted to knock down what were known as the Big Four public-housing developments,[1] promising to replace eight thousand public-housing apartments with four thousand mixed-income units. The vote to tear down the Big Four was opposed by protesters, but they were forcibly removed from the council chambers while additional public-housing residents and advocates were prevented from entering City Hall by locked gates and police pepper spray. In 2015, ten years after Hurricane Katrina, only 1,829 replacement units had materialized, and fewer than half of these have public-housing-level rents (Reckdahl 2015).[2] One Louisiana congressman crowed that Hurricane Katrina "finally cleaned up public housing. We couldn't do it, but God did" (Richard Baker quoted in Johnson 2011, 160). Meanwhile, as poor residents were shut out of the city, $71 billion in federal government recovery funding helped pump up property values, and average house prices rose 34 percent overall and 75 percent in the French Quarter tourist district (Sayre 2014).[3]

The transformation of housing should be understood within a particular strategy of economic development—one that takes goods that were public and turns them into an opportunity for the accumulation of private wealth. In New Orleans such strategies have been especially targeted at tourism, which had shared space with other activities prior to Katrina and received only haphazard and isolated support to sports events and conventions, gambling, cruises, music, and heritage. The elites who championed these activities fought for more political and economic command, but for several decades they were blocked by newly ascendant African American political elites, backed by a still-excluded, poor majority African American population. That population depended on traditional sectors that accounted for the bulk of the city's employment, such as commerce, transportation, and manufacturing. Most of these activities were associated with the city's Mississippi River port, connecting the agricultural and manufacturing heartland of the United States to the Gulf of Mexico and the world. The city's position along multiple waterways was strategic, but it was also vulnerable, as highlighted by Katrina, and it was the aftermath of the hurricane that altered the demography of the city and the balance of political power.

This project studies the livelihoods of working people in New Orleans after Hurricane Katrina. The hurricane flooded 80 percent of the city and dislocated hundreds of thousands of residents, creating a chaotic and uncertain social space. Previous equilibria among social and political actors became unbalanced, and the decade after Katrina opened the field for competing interests to lay claim to the city. As the waters receded, victory appears to have been claimed by an emerging elite positioned atop sectors oriented toward global markets. In the halls of power, they have displaced a decayed African American political machine and focused energy on promoting rapidly growing tourism, services, and construction sectors. In these sectors, emerging elites impose highly unequal terms, characterized by a few good jobs and many bad ones, with workers allocated to jobs according to race, gender, and ethnic distinctions. Dynamism for emerging elites in sectors they control leaves out other sectors and segments of the population—a development model characterized by duality.

In resistance to the dual development project, an alternative politics of development appears, and it lingers in the historic victories of workers in sectors that emerging elites neglect, such as manufacturing. These episodes of resistance and the legacies of historic victories promote decent livelihoods and opposition to discrimination by bridging struggles across workplaces and communities.

To explain outcomes of development in New Orleans, this book traces the rise to power of globally oriented elites and explores their project for expansion. Others have described such elites as part of a "transnational capitalist class" that is as comfortable operating in New Orleans as in New South Wales (Robinson 2004). In New Orleans, local members of the globally oriented elites rarely call the shots; instead, they position themselves as the necessary intermediaries for external actors, working together to make New Orleans available to globally integrated production processes. Their strategy to fit New Orleans into global processes has been to segment labor markets according to ascriptive characteristics, such as race, gender, and ethnicity, and pursue dual development strategies in which internationally integrated enclaves leave the rest of the city behind. The book includes comparative and historical analysis that combines quantitative analysis of original surveys in three different sectors, network analysis of an original database of local power structures, and case study of urban political regimes and economic development.

Hurricane Katrina laid bare patterns that appear in all cities: elite factional conflict and capture of local institutions, political determinants of wealth and distribution, and an increasingly exclusionary urban political economy in a rapidly globalizing age. By identifying the local expressions of these processes, this book seeks to tell the story of New Orleans, engage in the political struggle for equitable development, and offer lessons for other urban areas facing political economy questions of how they will develop and for whom.

Of Natural and Human Disasters

Hurricane Katrina hit the Gulf Coast in 2005 as a category 3 storm, with winds over 110 mph and storm surges of five to sixteen feet. While the eye of the hurricane missed the city and the immediate hurricane damage was no more than to be expected, the failure of the levees led to the catastrophic flooding of 80 percent of the city, 1,821 deaths, and damage to 70 percent of all occupied housing units. Katrina remains the most expensive disaster ever to strike the United States, with damages estimated at more than $100 billion and with more than 1.3 million people displaced in Louisiana and similar numbers in neighboring states.[4] As a result of displacement, the pre-Katrina New Orleans population of 455,188 dropped by an estimated 225,000 immediately after the hurricane and had recovered only 75 percent of its original level five years later, to 343,829 (U.S. Census Bureau 2010).

Etched in all of our minds are the cloudy newscast images of the hurricane spiraling toward the city, the awesome power of waters rushing through levee breaches, and sultry boats trolling through water-filled city streets in the aftermath. Most unforgettable of all are the images of people, desperate people, stranded on rooftops. They were families, elderly, children, women, and men, mostly African American and poor, and their appearance in the televised, slow-moving disaster of Katrina shocked viewer consciousness, if only too briefly.[5]

The hurricane also exposed atrocious government response, as Army Corps of Engineers hurricane protections failed and multiple levels of government bungled their relief efforts. Hungry and frustrated evacuees were housed inadequately in the convention center and football stadium never meant for the purpose, police fired shots to prevent survivors from walking across a bridge to neighboring parishes, while on another bridge four survivors were massacred when New Orleans police overreacted to the mistaken assumption that they were armed (*Times-Picayune* Staff 2011). Meanwhile, President George W. Bush famously embraced his Federal Emergency Management Administration director, Michael Brown, to tell him, "You're doing a heckuva job, Brownie." Katrina has since elevated in our lexicon to be coterminous with official failure, used in the same breath as the Iranian hostage crisis or Waterloo (Media Matters for America 2012).

Katrina reminded the rest of the country of a truth that locals long remembered: disasters are as human as they are natural. They do not have to happen the way they do. All along the Mississippi, the Army Corps of Engineers' "levees-only" policy sought to control the river by building ever higher walls, but this led to faster flows and greater sediment and required constant dredging and levee reinforcement. When waters inevitably overflowed their banks or the river sought to change course, past investments limited subsequent options, with ever more disastrous consequences. In the Great Flood of 1927, for example, rising river levels and floods along the upper Mississippi led New Orleans city elites to intentionally destroy a levee, flooding areas of St. Bernard and Plaquemines Parish rather than allow the upriver floods to threaten confidence in downriver protections.[6]

Over subsequent years, disaster was further shaped by human interventions to dig the canals and pipelines that facilitated industrial and oil booms of World War II and afterward. For easier navigation, such constructions were built as straight lines, in contrast to the normal meandering of natural waterways whose bends break storm surges and whose wetlands buffer seawater inflows. In 1965, the two channels of the Mississippi River carved in straight lines, the Gulf Outlet (MR. GO to locals) and the Industrial Canal, channeled ocean water inland during Hurricane Betsy, provoking levee failures in the Lower Ninth Ward. Many local observers continue to believe that the 1965 breaches were as intentional as those of 1927 (Shallat 2001), a mythology that only received greater support when a barge broke free and breached the Industrial Canal levee during Hurricane Katrina in 2005 and once again flooded the Lower Ninth.

Bungling in Katrina's aftermath once again presented the human element of disaster, reinforcing the general feeling of neglect and rejection among survivors. Public figures did little to change the narrative, as the governor of Louisiana, Kathleen Blanco, chose to believe reports of violence and directed her National Guard troops to a wartime footing, "They have M-16s and they're locked and loaded. These troops know how to shoot and kill, and I expect they will" (CNN 2005). Even humanitarian efforts were tinged with disdain, as former first lady Barbara Bush reflected on the survivors she encountered sleeping in a Houston gym, "And so many of the people in the arena here, you know, were underprivileged anyway, so this is working very well for them" (*New York Times* 2005).

These sentiments worked their way into public policy, for example, in the response to housing needs. For those homeowners who wished to return and repair their homes, insurance companies fought every penny, and the government insurer of last resort, the Road Home Program, paid homeowners according to the original value of their homes. This policy had problematic outcomes, especially for those lower-middle-class homeowners who were barely able to get on the property ladder in the first place. While a roof repair in wealthy and poor neighborhoods cost the same, payouts proportion to original values meant that only owners of expensive homes were receiving amounts sufficient to cover the costs.[7]

Also dismal was the situation of those displaced who were not homeowners but renters (Logan 2006a). Evacuated and banned from returning to the flooded city for more than three months, many renters quickly exhausted their savings and had to seek work wherever they were located, making it increasingly difficult to uproot again to return. Representative William Jefferson observed, "This is an example of poor people forced to make choices because they don't have the money to do otherwise" (Byrne 2005). The removal of eight thousand public-housing units intensified the blow.

These policy choices altered the demographic makeup of the city. The percentage of African Americans in the city dropped to 61.3 percent from 66.7 percent.[8] At least in part because so many of the poorest residents have not returned and a new influx of middle-class residents have gentrified certain neighborhoods, average incomes rose from $39,942 to $45,325, and average housing costs increased to $1,200 per month for a family of four (Gabe, Falk, and McCarty 2005; A. Liu, Fellowes, and Mabanta 2006; A. Liu and Plyer 2010). For some, this was the goal all along, a sentiment voiced by uptown businessman James Reiss: "Those who want to see this city rebuilt want to see it done in a completely different way: demographically, geographically and politically. I'm not just speaking for myself here. The way we've been living is not going to happen again, or we're out" (Cooper 2005).

One set of post-hurricane choices holds special relevance for the current study, as these policy choices systematically weakened workplace protections. For the express purpose of "faster and more flexible responses to hazards facing workers involved in the cleanup and recovery," the federal government suspended Occupational Safety and Health Administration

(OSHA) standards, reinstating them in January 2006 for most of the Gulf Coast, though not Orleans Parish (OSHA 2006). The federal government also suspended the Davis-Bacon Act, eliminating requirements for federal contractors to pay prevailing wages, and although the act was reinstated on November 8, all contracts already entered remained grandfathered into the suspension (Whittaker 2005). Further, employers were not required to maintain strict records on wages paid and did not have to verify eligibility to work or identification documents (Wasem 2005). Finally, affirmative action requirements were suspended as were the requirements of open competition for federal contracts, with the suspension of the Competition in Contracting Act (Luckey 2005).

In practice, the weakened regulatory environment has continued long after the temporary period ended, perhaps due to the general weakness of institutions meant to enforce workplace standards.[9] Hurricane Katrina closed the Wage and Hour Division of the New Orleans Department of Labor for four months, and the number of investigations fell by 37 percent in the year after Hurricane Katrina. Even after the office reopened, many post-Katrina violations ended up delayed beyond the two-year statute of limitations that limits Wage and Hour claims (Bernhardt and McGrath 2005).[10]

Working Poor

This project seeks to make sense of the experience of working people and popular sectors after Hurricane Katrina. They were poor before the hurricane, and their poverty has continued afterward. To characterize their experiences, the current project draws on literature on development, where poverty is conceived in ways that are both straightforward and complex. Poverty is straightforward because most observers recognize its outward signs; it is hard to miss. Still, poverty is complex because it includes absolute, multidimensional, probabilistic, and relative considerations. In the context of New Orleans, these varied approaches to poverty, along with the social relations in which poverty is ensconced, offer indicators of the experience of working classes and popular sectors after Katrina.

Most approaches to poverty begin with measures of absolute income, with international organizations setting poverty lines at $1.25 per day in 2005 and the U.S. government setting a national poverty line of approximately $31.00 per day for an individual ($11,344 per year). These thresholds presume a minimum amount of income an individual requires to survive, rooted in a scientifically testable benchmark such as levels of caloric intake and the cost of basic needs (Greeley 1994; Lipton 1997).

For New Orleans, where costs of living are significantly higher than the U.S. average, the national poverty line is probably too low, and an alternative measure is a livable wage, calculated according to average costs of housing, food, transportation, health care, and taxes. Based on these criteria, a living wage in New Orleans is closer to $35,000 per year.[11]

An advantage of absolute definitions of income poverty is that they can be easily compared across time and place. On the other hand, poverty may also have a relative component, taking into account inequality of income (Piketty 2014). In addition to feelings of relative deprivation, inequality can contribute to rising property values and costs of living, making life more difficult even in instances where absolute income goes up. According to the 2014 American Community Survey of the U.S. Census, New Orleans was the second-most-unequal big city, with a gini coefficient of .57, roughly on par with Zambia (McClendon 2014b).

It is also the case that measures that focus on income may miss other aspects of poverty for which monetary income is insufficient, such as those goods for which well-functioning markets may not always exist. For example, income is not always sufficient to purchase goods such as health, education, security, freedom, or political efficacy. Such goods are frequently allocated on a non-market basis, in which access depends on state institutions, social practices, and political processes. To deal with goods that are not necessarily available in the market, multidimensional conceptualizations of poverty set thresholds along a variety of dimensions, such as minimal levels of "income, common property, state-provision, assets, dignity, and autonomy" (Baulch 1996, 1). In measuring human development, for example, the United Nations uses indicators of income, literacy, and life expectancy to construct an index (UNDP 1990).

For the study of New Orleans, it makes sense to consider multiple dimensions, as the city underprovides all manner of public goods. Louisiana ranks last or close to last in health and education statistics, and in many years New Orleans has the highest per capita murder rate in the country, along with police and justice systems that are notoriously corrupt. Further, a number of goods that most people take for granted have been particularly vulnerable since Hurricane Katrina, such as basic working conditions and workplace safety, as well as compliance with labor regulations on minimum wage and overtime laws.[12]

Even if we pay attention to the multidimensional characteristics of poverty, there are additional aspects of poverty that escape observation. For example, some people may not presently be poor but are vulnerable to slip into poverty and spend extended periods in poverty in the course of a year or a lifetime (Devereaux 2003). In the United States, where many families survive just above the poverty line, a crisis can push them under. Also, some professions are highly seasonal, such as tourism, the heart of New Orleans development. People who work in seasonally fluctuating sectors may spend extended periods in poverty in a given year as they wait for their high season to return.

While absolute, multiple, relative, and probabilistic approaches provide rich detail on poverty, it may also be important to consider intersectional measures. Intersectional approaches to poverty focus on interpersonal and intergroup differences, which are of particular importance in places where poverty tends to overlap with other social and political identities. Such an overlap exacerbates the psychological impact of poverty and creates barriers to mobility, as the escape from poverty is blocked by the patterns of exclusion associated with membership in different groups, such as racial, ethnic, and gendered categories. These multiple social processes of exclusion overlap, reinforce, and work together, creating intersectional social categories that are more than the sum of their parts (P. H. Collins 2000).

The intersectional approach does not abstract from economic dimensions of exploitation located in social relations of production. Even as racism, xenophobia, patriarchy, and other forms of exclusion have their own independent history and logic, they are functional to capitalist exploitation. Intersectional exclusion complicates working-class unity and resistance, making it possible for capital to extract surplus from working classes and popular sectors in the workplace and in their communities.[13] The coincidence between class exploitation and other forms of oppression is evident in persistent cross-group differences in patterns of poverty (Aronowitz 2004).[14]

The concept of social exclusion draws further attention to collective, as opposed to individual, experiences of poverty. Social networks provide, or deny, access to resources for collectivities defined by class, racial, ethnic, and gendered dimensions (Fine 2006). Some conceptualize the resources available to collectivities as an alternative form of capital, such as political or social capital (Putnam 1994), embedded in networks useful to exert cultural and political power. In increasingly modern settings, some observers worry about a secular decline of social capital, while others emphasize the unequal distribution of social capital across different groups.[15] For example, Schlozman, Verba, and Brady argue that poor people do not participate in politics "because they can't; because they don't want to; and because nobody asked" (1999, 430). As a result, they never develop the civic skills necessary to engage societal networks. Ultimately, they are isolated from the networks that provide social capital for political engagement (Schlozman, Verba, and Brady 1999).

This project takes a nuanced look at the nature of working-class and popular experience in New Orleans after Hurricane Katrina. It will explore the absolute, multidimensional, and probabilistic dimensions of poverty, and it will pay close attention to the intersection of multiple forms of oppression and patterns of social exclusion.[16] All of these indicators are viewed as a social relation, the product of dynamic and stagnant sectors, privileged and excluded segments of the workforce, and development strategies that express the power relations that evolve over time and appear and are reinforced by local institutions and cultures. Patterns of development as seen in New Orleans are typical of hyper-exploitative social relations: stagnating wages, difficult schedules, limited benefits, and a lack of mobility (Bernhardt et al. 2001). As owners reorganize work and the sectors in which they concentrate their activities, they centralize control, shifting risk onto workers and communities (Lambert 2009), with government providing little capacity or will to curb workplace abuse and violations, and traditional worker organizations such as unions in a weakening position (Fletcher and Gapasin 2009). As indicators of these deteriorating social conditions, Table 1 displays some of the macro-level indicators for the dimensions of poverty considered here.

While some of the indicators have remained stable or even slightly improved, a number of these macro impressions of New Orleans indicate that poverty in various forms continues. Measures of absolute poverty are almost identical to before the storm, and multidimensional poverty is the same or worse in terms of housing (rental costs) and health (infant mortality), if slightly improved in education (percent graduated from high school). Although probabilistic measures of poverty have improved (in terms of weeks of work), a worryingly high number of residents continue to lack year-round employment. Intersectional measures continue to show the complexity of poverty for unique categories of residents, such as poor women (poverty in female-headed households is higher) and African American workers (higher rates of poverty and lower incomes). In terms of social exclusion, simple measures of political access remain low (registered to vote) and there is worse access to safety-net government programs (Social Security).

Such indicators offer a cursory impression of the complex social processes that produce and reproduce poverty. To get a closer look at these processes, the chapters that follow target specific sectors, exploring the way elites attempt to structure production, consumption, and distribution to favor their dual development strategy focused on globally oriented tourism and services. While elites have largely been successful in imposing their will, there are episodes and occasional victories for working classes and

TABLE 1. Indicators of Poverty

Concept of Poverty	Indicator	Before Katrina		After Katrina	
Absolute	% below U.S. poverty line	27.9%	(2000)	27.3%	(2013)
	Average wage as % U.S. average (2013$)	88.8%	(2004)	96.2%	(2013)
Relative	Income ratio of top 5% to bottom 20%, 2000 to 2010	15.1:1		15.4:1	
Multidimensional	% 18 and over without HS diploma	25.4%	(2000)	16.6%	(2011)
	Infant mortality rate per 1,000 births	7.3	(2000)	7.3	(2010)
	Paying > 35% of income on housing	43%	(2004)	51%	(2013)
Probabilistic	< 26 weeks of work per year	48.6%	(2000)	55.4%	(2009–13)
Intersectional	Child poverty in single-mother family	52%	(1999)	58%	(2013)
	% black male unemployment	46%	(2000)	52%	(2015)
	Proportion of black households low income	42%	(1999)	44%	(2013)
	Gap between white and black median income	$25,868	(2005)	$35,451	(2013)
	BA or more 25 and over, black male/white male	35.5%	(2000)	34.3%	(2013)
Social Exclusion	% population 18 and older registered to vote	88.3%	(2004)	66.2%	(2014)
	Population on Social Security	26,654	(2004)	20,325	(2015)
	Per-student state funding to higher education	$8,006	(2004)	$5,127	(2013)

Source: Quigley (2015); www.gnocdc.com; National Center for Health Statistics—www.cbs.gov/nchs/; and U.S. Census—factfinder.census.gov.

popular sectors. The class struggle entailed by the competition between elite and popular interests offers lessons for politics and development in New Orleans and elsewhere.

Overview of the Argument

To make sense of the experience and resistance of working people and popular sectors, this book begins by exploring structural changes in the global economy that have altered the relative power of local factions of capital. In New Orleans, international integration mobilized an emerging elite atop tourism and services sectors, and they consolidated their power through uniquely fragmented local political institutions. In the sectors they operate, they use political power to segment labor markets along ascriptive characteristics of race, gender, and immigration status. Segmentation exaggerates elite control over working conditions and surplus and saddles working people and popular sectors with poverty, inequality, and exclusion. Working people resist, and rare episodes of success are evident in efforts that join organizing in the workplace to resistance in communities, opposing patterns of oppression that operate in both.

New Orleans offers a particularly useful case because its history was punctuated by the devastation of Hurricane Katrina. For a variety of reasons, globally oriented elites had been unable to openly exercise power or capture democratic office in New Orleans. Instead, they accommodated themselves to a competition among rival elite factions and popular actors, enduring stalemated public policy and decades of stagnation (P. Burns and Thomas 2006). This had given the city its characteristic old-world feel, attributed by some to the backward-looking preferences of local notables and by others to the curious mix of popular and elite factions that settled for a corrupt local regime (Baumach and Borah 1981). The hurricane dislocated existing political accommodations and opened an opportunity for globally oriented elites to occupy critical political offices and public institutions.

Their path to power was smoothed by the already fragmented nature of public institutions in the city. Alternative authorities had been invented to manage areas of public policy at multiple points in the city's history. As the entities accumulated and original purposes faded, they left a fragmented patchwork of quasi-public institutions that served as points of access and refuge for rival political and elite factions, contributing to the stalemate and political stagnation of public policy. Katrina allowed globalized elites to surface from their quasi-public entities and openly exercise power with newly won elected offices, through which they could coordinate the bevy of boards, commissions, special districts, and other entities that layer authority in the city.

With political dominance consolidated, they quickly turned to the task of maximizing accumulation in the sectors they controlled. Hurricane Katrina had targeted billions of local, state, and federal funds to the city, funds that emerging elites captured and then used to defeat their rivals and pump dynamism into their preferred sectors: construction, tourism, and services.

The wealth in dynamic sectors has coincided with extreme patterns of inequality and exploitation. Labor conditions are characterized by a few good jobs alongside many bad ones, providing only a few workers with security and decent wages, working conditions, and career trajectories. In general, profits are high, wages low, working conditions abusive, and careers insecure. To preserve such conditions, emerging elites have used their control over public policy to guarantee a minimum of regulation and to stifle worker organization. They infuse class dynamics with race, gender, and ethnic distinctions, reserving the few good jobs for white, male, native-born (but not New Orleanian) workers, and dole out poverty and insecurity to non-white, female, native New Orleanians, and immigrants.

The rapidly growing and highly unequal sectors built by globally oriented elites contrast with those sectors in which popular actors retained a degree of bargaining power. In sectors such as manufacturing, worker efforts over previous decades had remedied discriminatory and highly unequal hiring practices and created jobs with decent wages and lifetime career trajectories. Such work sustained communities and lay at the heart of the culture and social networks that gave New Orleans its distinctive character. Still, despite the importance and the potential for equitable development presented by these sectors, they were well into a several decade decline, starved of the support of local elites. The post-Katrina period accelerated this downward trend, as emerging elites consolidated the local political economy around sectors they controlled and deemphasized sectors in which they might have to share power with worker and popular-sector interests.

Working people and popular sectors experience this deformation of the economy and intensification of exploitation in deepening poverty and inequality. Poverty appears in multiple forms, including substandard wages, denial of public services, intersectional racial-ethnic-gendered exclusion, seasonal insecurity, and the breaking down of social networks. Yet, despite these burdens, people resist. In fact, resistance shows greatest potential and occasional success when it bridges struggles against exploitation in the workplace to struggles for dignity in the community. Struggles that recognize and embrace the overlap between community demands and worker demands show alternative development possibilities rooted in local working classes and community needs. Class conflict pits local working classes and communities against newly dominant globally oriented elites.

Comparative Methodology

This project explores development in New Orleans following Hurricane Katrina. The core argument is that a globally oriented elite has secured leadership among factions of local capital, thereby claiming political leadership over what had been a divided elite and fragmented set of institutions. With political control consolidated, they use government power to invigorate sectors in which they can connect to global actors, such as tourism and construction, and they have neglected traditional sectors such as manufacturing. The principal policy strategy to encourage dynamism is funneling capital into dynamic sectors while selectively deregulating to allow owners to organize production as they wish. The result is a dual model of development, in which globally oriented sectors boom but have little linkage to other sectors. In terms of the resulting poverty experienced by working people and popular sectors, segmentation reserves a few good jobs for white, native-born workers, mostly men, and produces a vast majority of bad jobs, with low wages, insecurity, workplace abuse, and unsafe conditions.

To demonstrate this process, the project applies several different comparative methodologies (see Figure 1). The first comparison is pre-Katrina development and post-Katrina development. New Orleans has always been poor, but the fragmentation of local economic and political elites prior to Katrina meant that there was never a coherent development strategy or consistent set of policies to promote dynamic sectors. This changed after Katrina with the rise of a globally oriented elite who were able to impose a dual development strategy that promoted globally integrated sectors while leaving the rest of the city behind.

The second set of comparisons explores three sectors: construction, tourism and services, and manufacturing. While the first two have been favored by the newly dominant globally oriented elite, manufacturing has been neglected. The result has been growth in construction and services along with segmentation along ascriptive lines of race, ethnicity, and gender. In manufacturing there has been low growth, though workers there

New Orleans Development

	Structure of Elites	Pattern of Development	Impact on Poverty
Pre-Katrina	Fragmented	Stagnant, haphazard	Low growth, steady poverty
Post-Katrina	Globally oriented elites dominant	Dual development	High growth, worsening poverty/ inequality

Post-Katrina Key Sectors

Construction	Globalized large and local small/ medium projects	High growth, low regulation, limited linkages	Segmentation along ethnic lines
Tourism and Services	Fine-dining empires and family/quick-serve	High growth, low regulation, limited linkages	Segmentation by race and gender
Manufacturing	National manufacturing elites shifting to finance	Low growth, outright neglect	Joined-up worker-community struggle

FIGURE 1. Pre- and post-Katrina development and post-Katrina sectorial comparisons.

pursued strategies of joining workplace to community struggle, winning better conditions at work and engagement in communities. While strategies of worker and popular-sector power have not been able to halt the decline in manufacturing, they have begun to appear in emerging sectors of construction and tourism, providing evidence of a uniquely New Orleanian pattern of class formation and struggle.

To provide detail on poverty and resistance in each sector, the project makes use of quantitative and qualitative observations. Quantitative data and qualitative historical tracing describe the evolution of political and economic elites in New Orleans, including a first-of-its-kind interactive mapping of government boards, commissions, public-benefit corporations, and other quasi-governmental entities. Quantitative analysis of surveys of workers in construction, food service, and manufacturing complement qualitative interviews with activists, workers, and observers of each sector. The mix of methods offers both macro impressions of dual development as well as micro understandings of poverty and class struggle occurring in each sector.

Research Approach

Especially in chapters 5, 6, and 7, the project highlights successful episodes of resistance by working classes and popular sectors. In describing these episodes, the focus remains on those elements that give movements of resistance strength. In particular, in construction, services, and manufacturing, the greatest strength comes from movements that tailor their resistance to the intersectional nature of oppression that extends extraction from workplaces to communities. By joining struggles in both sites and drawing on the organic leadership of working people and popular sectors, resistance to the project of elite-led dual development achieves its greatest victories, even if these victories are all too scarce and short-lived.

A description of the short life cycle of many of these episodes might emphasize movement mistakes and inconsistencies as causes of failure. Some of these shortcomings will be addressed, but they do not receive the bulk of attention. The project makes this choice for theoretical and positional reasons. At a theoretical level, the contemporary historical moment gives elites overwhelming structural power, even if movements made no mistakes and exhibited no inconsistencies. Elite agendas are consolidated and biased into political institutions, imposed through policies, and reproduced through the workings of the sectors they control. Quite simply, elites are cohesive and dominant in the current order, and the plight of workers can be explained sufficiently with a focus on elite power and the development model they impose. Mistakes and inconsistencies in the resistance of movements and activists contribute to elite dominance, but they are not the cause of elite dominance, which is structural, nor do momentary lapses invalidate other episodes in which resistance articulates a working-class and popular-sector alternative to elite designs.

The focus on episodes in terms of support for elite projects or articulation of alternatives also recognizes my position. First, I conducted most of the research for this book while I was a professor at Tulane University. Tulane is the leading, exclusive, private university in New Orleans, inaccessible to most of the population and an institution that has consistently sided with globally oriented elites against popular resistance. Second, as a white, male professor at Tulane, I had easy integration with globally oriented elites in New Orleans. This integration only increased in recent years, as I was poached by another university and continued to enjoy the perks of upward mobility within academic circles. In fact, one could argue that my privilege is both advanced by and advances the dominance of a globally oriented elite agenda. In focusing on that agenda, I work to eliminate unjust sources of privilege and put my own privilege in service of resistance.

These factors led me to a methodological focus on episodes as units of analysis. Within any episode of resistance there are mistakes and inconsistencies that align working-class and popular mobilization with elite designs, even as other actions build strength. Rather than attempting to characterize individuals or movements, a characterization of episodes of resistance shifts focus to alternative patterns of development, planted as seeds within movements of resistance and articulated in response to the current dominance of globally oriented elites. Alternative patterns of development remain inchoate, but a focus on episodes of resistance attempts to weave them together to articulate a pattern of development that responds to demands of working classes and popular sectors.

Structure of the Book

The chapters that follow explore the nature of worker and popular-sector experience of poverty and resistance in the face of an emerging globalized elite and their consolidation of control within local political institutions. Chapter 1 develops a framework to make sense of the structural and institutional determinants of development. Chapters 2, 3, and 4 explore the emerging elite's path to power through a close look at the evolution of New Orleans government institutions and their operation in contemporary New Orleans through quantitative analysis of public finance and networks of power. Chapters 5 and 6 explore the popular experience in two sectors dominated by globally oriented elites, construction and tourism, and chapter 7 explores manufacturing, a sector in which workers gained some degree of control over their lives, only to see emerging elites abandon the sector. The conclusion reflects on the implications of New Orleans for popular struggle and development more generally.

In many ways this story is tragic, as the decade since Katrina has consolidated an exclusionary and exploitative development model focused on globally integrated and highly deregulated production processes. Yet, this book also holds a glimmer of hope. Against all odds, even in the sectors most dominated by emerging elites, people resist. As they strive to forge a class identity that confronts the intersection of multiple dimensions of oppression, struggles across workplaces and communities offer an alternative vision of development for the city. It is to this alternative that this book attempts to contribute.

CHAPTER ONE

Dual Development, Segmented Labor Markets, and Urban Regimes

In the aftermath of Hurricane Katrina, the struggle to rebuild New Orleans brought out deeper patterns of social and political struggle. The victors of that struggle have driven an elite agenda through unaccountable institutions to impose intensified patterns of poverty on the working people and popular sectors of the city, especially people of color. This political and economic outcome sheds light on more general social processes related to development, urban politics, and working-class life, relevant to a wide range of cities, both in the United States and internationally.

New Orleans can be understood as a once thriving industrial metropolis that entered relative decline, adding a Deep South flavor to the rust-belt deindustrialized face of U.S. globalization. When the city suffered a disastrous hurricane and failed governmental response in 2005, room opened for an economic transformation led by sectors adapted to globally integrated patterns of accumulation, with unequal and discriminatory results for popular sectors.

This type of economic transformation depended on the political rise of globally oriented elites. Their path to power sheds light on competition among elite and mass actors as shaped by local institutional incentives and constraints. The New Orleans case is of particular interest because in a relatively short time rising elites have left behind African American political machines and accommodations made to a local capitalist class fragmented among rival factions. This shift in the dominant social coalition occurred initially in institutions peripheral to public power but was eventually expressed openly by emerging elites with consolidated control of both elected and appointed political institutions.

As emerging elites consolidated their control, they transformed the local political economy along unequal and exclusionary lines. Working people have experienced ever greater exclusion and poverty, with conditions of life allocated according to ascriptive racial, gender, and immigration-status differences. To resist these conditions, popular-sector and working-class actors have forged alliances across workplaces and communities. By attacking exploitation manifest at work and at home, they have had some success in defending prior gains and resisting elitist designs. To place these processes in their more general context, the following paragraphs explore themes of development, urban politics, and working-class experience as relevant to New Orleans after Katrina.

Dual Development and Segmented Labor Markets

An important part of the New Orleans experience since Katrina has to be understood in the context of rapid changes in local development. After a post–World War II military-industrial boom, the city experienced a secular decline of its manufacturing base, accelerated by the 1980s oil crash and further driven by an elite fragmented among growth-oriented elites and backward-looking factions resistant to change (Whelan 1987; Molotch 1976, 1979, 1988; Logan and Molotch 1987).[1] Out of this late-twentieth-century stagnation a new development model has emerged, with the city emphasizing sectors integrated with global processes of accumulation, including tourism, services, and the temporary speculative boom in construction following disaster (Gotham 2007; Souther 2006).

This section explores relevant aspects of this development trajectory by reflecting on global integration, regional economies, and urban renewal. Based on these reflections, the section describes a framework to understand post-Katrina New Orleans development that rests on the concept of dualism—an economy divided between a high-growth sector articulated to the global economy but with few connections to the rest of the local economy and few benefits for the majority of the population.

Contemporary patterns of global integration are related to transformations begun in the 1970s. These included technological shifts in the emergence of high-speed information and transportation flows, an international regime shift with the breakdown of Bretton Woods monetary arrangements, and a policy shift removing many national-level regulations (Marglin and Schor 1990). These changes brought more people, from more distant regions, into greater contact with one another in the process of capitalist production. Capitalist social relations were applied more intensively to more areas of human life—liberalization—and reached a more extensive number of places and people—globalization—creating a particular kind of liberal, globalized integration (Arrighi 2010).

Liberal globalization allows goods and services to travel increased distances at higher speeds, making it possible to integrate economic activity ever more deeply across the globe. Inputs can now be extracted in one place, transformed in another, assembled in another, and consumed in yet another. Globally integrated production presents opportunities to produce for faraway markets and accumulate by coordinating production across space and over time (Harvey 2007).[2]

Global integration forces shifts in our understanding of regional economics, which rests on the intuition that clusters of activity occurring within close proximity create synergies of increased efficiency and productivity. Where such "poles of development" exist, they can pull neighboring areas forward (Hirschman 1958). But, liberal globalization has lowered the costs to longer-distance integration, and rapidly growing regions can now integrate with regions in faraway countries, leaving close-by poor neighbors behind.

Liberal globalization poses an additional challenge, as the way regional actors fit into the global economy matters for regional development. Regions that house higher-value activities secure advantages in the form of linkages to other activities and opportunities for high standards of living, while other regions are forced to provide raw materials or low-skill labor, obtaining few linkages to other activities or potential to scale up to more lucrative opportunities. To capture higher-value activities, wealthy regions possess advantages in the form of already existing infrastructures, including physical, financial, and human capital. These initial advantages provide a head start to enter those activities that allow them to remain at the forefront of globally integrated production (Garrett 2004).[3]

The changing operation of regional economies takes on additional nuance when considered at the level of cities. Economic geography posits that cities concentrate the inputs to production in close proximity, shrinking the time and distance capital and products must circulate to generate wealth (Harvey 2012). Yet high-speed global integration removes some of the advantages of urban concentration, evident in the loss of industrial dynamism in cities in the northern United States and the shift in production to developing countries and rural areas of developed countries (Chomsky 2008).

To retain their relevance and promote development, northern cities seek to capture the coordinating positions of globally integrated production chains (Reich 1992). The commanding heights of globally integrated activities determine what stages of production are to occur in what places, and coordinate the movement of inputs and outputs from stage to stage in the production process. Such cities act as "nodes" to connect multiple, global processes (Castells 1996) and require high-technology advantages and cosmopolitan networks, sustained especially by an abundance of "knowledge workers," the creative workers with the adaptability and potential to command and connect a variety of different global productive chains (Kaplinsky 2005).[4] Some observers champion this transition, advocating cultural amenities and livable environments to attract the high-skill workers that supply cosmopolitan cities (Florida 2003). Others worry that globally networked classes are increasingly likely to constitute a sheltered, transnational elite whose accumulation bears little connection to the rest of society (Sassen 2001; Harvey 2012).

For New Orleans, the implications of these global, regional, and urban dimensions of economics are captured in the concept of dualism. The original concept of dualism was used by Nobel Prize–winning economist Sir Arthur Lewis in the 1950s to describe patterns of growth in developing countries (W. A. Lewis 1954). In places like his native Saint Lucia, Lewis observed an advanced sector well integrated with international processes of capitalist accumulation, such as plantation enclaves. Enclaves had highly developed infrastructure to connect them to the international economy and operated with high rates of productivity.[5] Yet enclaves had few linkages with other activities on the island, provided only limited employment, and left most people of the island in low-productivity subsistence activities—a dual economy.[6]

Dualism provides a useful guide to New Orleans development. The southern United States, and New Orleans along with it, has long attracted comparisons to colonial and postcolonial economies (Persky 1991). Some trace the lack of regional development to the legacy of slavery and the destruction that occurred during the Civil War (Engerman 1971). Others place the blame on external control of southern economic activity, in which northern ownership of key natural resources, finances, transport, and technology held back southern industrialization (Woodward 1951). Still others blamed the labor-repressive system of agricultural production for the lack of agricultural modernization and weakness of democracy (Moore 1966). Finally, some authors emphasized labor markets truncated from the rest of the country by authoritarian limitations on movement and frozen at a low-level equilibrium through racial division and oppression (G. Wright 1986).

In its high levels of poverty, New Orleans bears the marks of southern underdevelopment, but as a thriving port city it also displays the arc of industrialization and deindustrialization familiar to the "rust belt" (Hirsch 1983). New Orleans was the transportation, commercial, and financial hub of the South in the nineteenth century, and it saw important upscaling into industrial processing of southern and midwestern agricultural goods as well as expansion into chemical and petroleum processing in the early 1900s.

The petroleum boom that began in the twentieth century allowed economic diversification, especially with federal infrastructure investments of the New Deal and World War II defense stimulus to boost industrial and military production. While petroleum buoyed industrial production into the 1950s, activity associated with the port eventually began to decline, as containerization weakened labor needs and made possible expansion in competing regional ports. By the 1960s, creeping deindustrialization had ceded to a rising tourist and services sector, with public investments targeting convention facilities, sports arenas, and the upgrading of the central business district (Passavant 2011).[7] Fluctuating oil prices during the 1970s and 1980s further undercut the remaining industrial core of the city, as did declining port market share and the failure of local elites to coalesce around an alternative development strategy (Baumbach and Borah 1981). By the 1990s the fastest growing sectors were services and tourism, though the wealth generated was concentrated in few hands, and employment, working conditions, and income for the majority of the population remained stagnant (Bobo 1985).

The post-Katrina moment appears to be heralding a new chapter in dualist New Orleans development. Rapid expansion is occurring in sectors adapted to internationally integrated activities, such as tourism, technology, biomedical services, film and creative industries, and food services. Even sectors that might not immediately seem international, such as construction, have been internationalized, as post-hurricane reconstruction turned New Orleans into a platform for international construction companies and immigrant labor.

The inputs used and markets served by these sectors are international; they operate at high levels of productivity and provide opportunities for significant wealth accumulation. Yet, typical of dualist patterns, these leading sectors are disconnected from the rest of the city; provide few linkages or spillovers to stimulate other activities; provide limited employment; do little to raise levels of productivity in other sectors; and offer little in terms of raising the income or consumption of the general population. For liberal observers, the poverty of the majority population of New Orleans is merely an unfortunate side effect of globalized capitalism that privileges workers with human capital, such as high levels of education.[8] More-critical observers reject the notion of inequality and exploitation as unfortunate afterthoughts, considering them core components of a post-Katrina growth strategy, "disaster capitalism" (Klein 2006).

To make further sense of the poverty of working people in the context of dualism, this book applies the concept of segmented labor markets. Piore defined a segmented labor market as comprising a primary market in which wages and conditions are decent, and a secondary market in which they are not. In the secondary market "the jobs tend to be unskilled, generally but not always low paying, and to carry or connote inferior social status; they often involve hard or unpleasant working conditions and considerable insecurity; they seldom offer chances of advancement toward better-paying, more attractive job opportunities; they are usually performed in an un-structured work environment and involve an informal, highly personalis-tic relationship between supervisor and subordinate" (Piore 1980, 17).[9]

To create and preserve a segmented labor market, secondary-market workers must be denied power to improve their condition or mobility into primary markets, raising the importance of race, ethnicity, gender, or other ascriptive characteristics. Such traits mark membership in a group and are used by employers to assign people to different segments of the labor mar-ket. By stripping rights from workers with certain ascriptive characteristics and/or workers in certain occupations, employers can preserve segmented labor markets, producing heightened workplace exploitation in general and of ascriptively defined communities in particular (Omi and Winant 1994). Prejudice based on race, ethnicity, and gender thus reinforces exclusion from labor rights, relegating certain populations to secondary-sector mar-kets, preventing mobility from secondary to primary work, and permitting heightened exploitation (Piore 1976).[10]

In New Orleans, as in the rest of the United States, race plays a central function in segmenting labor markets.[11] Racism rests at the core of politi-cal institutions and economic structures that continually strip non-white people of rights, receiving legal and institutional form for African Ameri-cans in the form of slavery, Jim Crow apartheid, and the contemporary prison-industrial complex (Wacquant 2001).[12]

Other patterns of exploitation based on ascriptive characteristics are also evident in New Orleans labor markets, such as ethnic division or xenophobia.[13] Historically, elaborate schemes have been devised to deny immigrants full citizenship rights, keeping them in vulnerable conditions on guest worker visas, temporary resident visas, or with no visas at all. These distinctions perpetuate low income and exclusion, and as a result, immigrants are largely poor, with over 30 percent earning less than $20,000 in 2001 (Vega, Sribney, and Achara-Abrahams 2003). Further, immigrants concentrate in sectors with the worst workplace violations and character-ized as low-wage by the Department of Labor, such as private household work, agriculture, textiles, food services, and construction (Bruno 2015).[14]

The immigrant population of New Orleans is not new, but its character has changed over time. Much of the working class in the nineteenth century was filled by waves of German, Irish, and then Italian immigrants.[15] These immigrant groups were eventually absorbed into the white population, partly as a result of emphasizing black-white difference in Jim Crow legislation, with African Americans constrained to menial work and excluded from education and other services (Fussell 2007). As a port city and the original home of the United Fruit Company, the city received a twentieth-century wave of Central American immigrants, especially from Honduras, and during the 1970s the city was the recipient of South Vietnamese evacuees located along the Gulf Coast (Zhou and Bankston 1998). Post-Katrina, Mexican and Central American immigrants have been the largest influx, inserted into the low-wage construction and service workforce of the city and tripling the Latino proportion of population from 3 to 9 percent (Fussell 2009). The undocumented status of many of these newest immigrants has exacerbated patterns of exclusion, following national patterns in which undocumented immigrants earn 40 percent less than documented immigrants, are twice as likely to live in poverty, have children who suffer higher risks of poverty and poor health, and are more than twice as likely to lack health insurance (Passel 2006).

The concepts of dualism and segmented labor markets offer a useful lens on poverty in New Orleans, but they do not explain the politics of why these patterns of development are pursued over alternatives. The city could have gone several directions post-Katrina, but internationally integrated sectors displaced rival elite factions and imposed their agenda for segmented labor markets and enclaves of internationally oriented development disconnected from the rest of the population. To understand how this could occur, the next section explores the politics of development in terms of urban political regimes, growth machines, and local political institutions.

Politics of a Globalized Growth Regime

The structural changes described above are partly driven by global economic change, which has positioned globally oriented elites at the fore of previously stagnant and fragmented New Orleans capitalist factions. Rising elites could emerge in part because the disaster of Katrina dislocated existing African American political machines, and paths to power were facilitated by the peculiar fragmentation of New Orleans political institutions. Political science and sociology provide understandings of local politics and institutions that shed light on these processes.

The primary political science approach to urban politics explores urban regimes (C. N. Stone 1989, 2005). As outlined by Clarence Stone (1993), urban regime theory takes the view that governing elites require a social coalition of support to mobilize resources to "get things done." Relatively stable urban regimes are defined by their combinations of social forces, patterns of linkage to governing elites, and agendas for public policy.[16] From pluralists, urban regime theory acknowledges the combinations of social forces represented in the state and borrows from Marxists the indispensable and structural power of capital.[17]

Urban regimes mobilize resources from private actors, and this requires the political effort of bridging private-sector and government interests (Mossberger and Stoker 2001).[18] Variations in the coalitions formed and agendas pursued have been described in four ideal-typical regime types evident in the United States: maintenance (low tax and services); development (expanding growth through valorizing land values);[19] middle-class progressive (addressing environmental, preservation, and other quality-of-life issues);[20] and lower-class opportunity expansion (extending employment and justice to excluded groups).[21]

To these categories of regime should be added Adolph Reed Jr.'s conceptualization of black urban regimes. Such regimes incorporated African Americans, especially preestablished economic and political elites and professional middle classes. Some benefits reached working-class African Americans, but the progressive potential of black urban regimes was constrained by three factors relevant to the case of New Orleans (1999, 79–115).[22] The first constraint was a changed economic base, as industrial activity had already begun to abandon traditional urban centers by the time black urban regimes took power, and many cities were forced into a growth imperative focused on expanding an "advanced corporate services component not likely to create much of a direct employment benefit for city residents" (1999, 91).

The second constraint on black urban regimes was limited fiscal space. Fiscal constraint was exacerbated on one side of the ledger by the burden of increased service obligations that were the legacy of post–World War II developmentalism as well as increased popular demands. On the other side of the ledger, black urban regimes faced tax losses associated with white flight and reductions in economic activity, as well as reduced federal transfers associated with the post-Reagan efforts to shrink the state, especially in its welfare and local functions (Reed 1999, 93–95).

The final constraint was political, as the social coalitions supporting black urban regimes often produced cycling coalitions that systematically excluded working-class demands. While African American working classes pressured for redistribution, such demands had to be layered atop existing efforts to extend benefits to other ethnic and white working classes, leading to conflicts within working-class communities. Further, African American elites were primarily interested in capturing some of the benefits of pro-growth policies, a strategy of development that only reinforced popular exclusion and created closer affinity between black elites and their white elite counterparts than African American working classes.[23] As a result, only in rare occasions could African American working classes actually participate in black urban regimes.

To core constituencies among African American voters, black urban regimes represented the fulfillment of the civil rights struggle and the delivery of certain benefits, such as curbing the worst of police brutality and adopting racially redistributive public contracting and employment practices. Still, the "benefits clustered disproportionately among middle- and upper-strata blacks" (Reed 1999, 102). In examining the way African American elites disserved black popular classes, Preston Smith describes what he terms "racial democracy": "Racial democracy accepted class inequality in housing for several reasons. It considered class stratification normal; it accepted class inequality temporarily while the ideology focused on racial disparities; or it held that the best way to attack class segregation was through opposing racial inequality. Whatever the rationale, acceptance of class stratification within the ideology of racial democracy did not serve the housing needs of the black popular classes well" (P. H. Smith 2012, xiii). These limitations appear repeatedly when considering the trajectory of black-led regimes in New Orleans.

There has been important work applying the regimes framework to New Orleans, tracing the evolution from maintenance to progressive to development regimes from the 1960s to 1990s (Whelan, Young, and Lauria 1994). Still, even within these shifts, the main characteristic of New Orleans has historically been the relative lack of dominance of any particular sector of business elites, who remain internally factionalized and forced to accommodate competing land valorization, preservationist, and popular demands (Whelan 1987).[24] The indecisiveness produced by this factionalization was revealed in the disastrous response to Hurricane Katrina, evidence of the absence of any coherent regime. The political establishment proved itself to be a "non-regime," unable to mobilize the resources it needed to protect itself from disaster or respond to disaster when it struck (P. Burns and Thomas 2006).

While work on urban regimes has been dominant within political science, the discipline of sociology has articulated a narrower view of local-level social coalitions and governmental agendas focused on growth. The traditional growth agenda seeks to boost property values, turning city institutions into instruments of growth—"growth machines" (Molotch 1976, 1988; Logan and Molotch 1987; Logan, Whaley, and Crowder 1997; Gendron and Domhoff 2009).[25] Growth machines are guided by propertied elites—real estate investors, property owners, and developers—whose accumulation is that of a rentier class, dependent on enhancing the value of property they control. Typical sectors dependent on increased property values are those who can speculate and capture rents from property, such as elites operating in utilities, construction, and finance (Harding 1995).[26]

Propertied elites act as "place entrepreneurs," using public power to add market value to land, for example, by bringing unused land into use or intensifying the use of existing land (Logan and Molotch 1987).[27] The growth imperative pressures for a constant intensification of use, as if on a "treadmill," running to stay in place, as place entrepreneurs must accommodate themselves to evolving demands for investment opportunities (Gould, Pellow, and Schnaiberg 2004). "Place entrepreneurs expend considerable effort in keeping up with the changing locational needs of corporate capital. . . . The most important activity of a local growth coalition is to provide the right conditions for outside investment" (Domhoff 2009, 44).[28]

The emergence of growth coalitions oriented toward globally integrated activities produces a specific set of requirements. These take the form of "material support to flows of information and interactions" (Castells 1996, 147), such that cities can act as hubs or nodal points at which various networks intersect in what Castells labels "the space of flows" (1989, 347; 1996). "Global cities" are those with the potential to operate at the peak of global value chains, housing internationally influential firms, politically powerful international institutions, and centers of cultural innovation and influence (Sassen 1991). One implication is a requirement of ever greater resources for infrastructure, tax incentives, and subsidy to satisfy increasingly mobile capital (Molotch 1988).[29]

In low-tax regions like New Orleans, without much in the way of local public finance, such resources are often drawn from higher levels of government, leveraged through congressional delegations, partisan affinities, and other mechanisms.[30] For example, in the post-Katrina reconstruction effort, the higher-level support provided for canals, levees, and other flood control and mitigation efforts was channeled through entities such as the Army Corps of Engineers and handed out in contracts to global firms such as Halliburton and Odebrecht (Youngman 2011; Gotham 2007).[31]

In New Orleans, the character of the globally oriented growth machine was marked by dual development, in which sectors and actors adapted to global accumulation could flourish, while most of the economy and much of the population was left behind, often on the basis of racialized, gendered, and ethnic segmentation. Globally oriented elites also built their dual development model atop the residue of the black urban regimes that had existed before. This produced a few particularities in the social and political practice of the dual development regime. At its heart, obviously, were those factions of local capital adapted to global accumulation, though in a city like New Orleans their function is more that of a subservient ally to global interests than drivers of accumulation themselves (Cobb 1994). Their function is to advance a policy framework with a host of incentives, giveaways, and deregulations and otherwise act as intermediaries to accelerate the entrance of external actors to local economic activities. The legacy of black urban regimes was a narrow population of black bourgeoisie, and they are invited to participate in the dual development regime, even occupying official and elected office, but only if they accept and advance development projects that abandon most of the city. To induce the collaboration of legatees of black urban regimes and to create something they can offer their working-class co-ethnics, dual development is fully compatible with anti-racist legislation and actions, but only as far as these efforts make local social relations palatable to external actors and do not interfere with practices of segmentation and exploitation in labor and other markets.

While the imperatives of globalized growth regimes are clear, the ability of globally oriented elites to impose their preferences depends critically on their ability to navigate local political institutions. Institutions can be both formal, with written rules and legal architecture, and informal, in terms of the norms and customs that bound behavior (Hall and Taylor 1996). Institutions are the "rules of the game" for political actors, defining who can participate, what policy options exist, and what choices are more or less attractive in any given moment (Steinmo 2008, 123).

The institutional incentives that privileged the emergence of globally oriented elites in New Orleans were provided by an unusually fragmented local state. For a variety of reasons, public authority in New Orleans had been fragmented into a bevy of boards, commissions, public-benefit corporations, and other quasi-public entities. These entities are summarized here with the term "satellites," meaning they are closely related to and connected to, but not entirely of, city government. Such entities are not totally unusual, as across the United States such entities have proliferated, with the U.S. Census Bureau noting a more than threefold increase since 1950.[32]

Interpretations of local institutional fragmentation vary. On the positive side are those public choice economists who laud the efficiency potential of matching services specifically to constituent preferences (Tiebout 1956),

Weberian public administration theorists who praise technocratic rationality as a counter to politicization (Weber [1922] 1968), pluralist arguments that praise the opening provided by fragmented authority to allow contestation among multiple interest groups (Dahl 1961), and state capacity arguments that emphasize the ability to mobilize revenues (Bollens 1957) or provide needed services (Porter 1992).[33] On the negative side are those public choice economists who worry about the use of satellites to evade limits on deficits or debt (N. Burns 1994), Wilsonian public administration theorists who critique the confused lines of accountability that allow corruption and cronyism (Cook 2007),[34] incrementalist critiques that satellites accumulate haphazardly over time (Wildavksy 1964), sociological growth coalition and power structure arguments that emphasize the potential for limited participation and capture by elite interests (Domhoff 2009), and urban regimes arguments that explore the variety of class, race, ethnic, and partisan coalitions expressed in satellite institutions (C. N. Stone 1989).

The accumulation over time of such institutions left New Orleans with a peculiarly fragmented public sector. This fragmentation can be blamed in part for the slow and incomplete pace at which the local regime changed over time and the operation of the non-regime when Katrina struck. Although political and economic elites would have liked to mobilize resources and get things done—fragmented actors and institutions acted as obstacles to coordinating the activities of the local state.

For at least two reasons, fragmented public authority proved convenient to globally oriented elites. While such elites were blocked from direct control of the state by the electoral dominance of black urban regimes, the limited accountability of fragmented institutions made them available for capture. Globally oriented elites focused on those parts of the local state that were important to them, such as boards and commissions active in tourism and services, and special taxing jurisdictions where they could target benefits to themselves. This partial capture of the state may have been insufficient to fully launch a globalized-growth machine, but it provided institutional hosts in which they could cultivate their membership and wait for an opportunity to extend control. Katrina provided that opportunity, and globally oriented elites have quickly gone to work coordinating their previously fragmented institutional hosts with their current electoral emergence.

Contexts of Class Formation

While dual development, segmented labor markets, and fragmented authority create social relations that exacerbate poverty, working classes and popular sectors find ways to resist. To understand resistance and the ways it responds to intersectional racial, ethnic, and gendered oppressions, this project applies the concept of class formation. Class is not easy to pin down, as resistance is difficult and actors within the popular sector shape themselves into classes only in the process of struggle. Class is therefore a contextually specific, dynamic, and ongoing process, and struggle is all too often unsuccessful.

For Marx and Engels, class formation was the evolution of a class "in itself" to a class "for itself" (Marx and Engels [1847] 2012, 137). As capitalism gathers workers in ever increasing numbers and ever worsening immiseration, "the mass is thus already a class as against capital, but not yet for itself. In the struggle . . . this mass becomes united, and continues itself as a class for itself" (Marx 1976, 109). In the case of the industrial working class, Marx notes that the first response was a Luddite attack on machines: "It took both time and experience before the workers learned to distinguish between machinery and its employment by capital, and therefore to transfer their attacks from the material instruments of production to the form of society which utilizes those instruments" (Marx [1894] 1993, 555).[35] Hensman appreciates the process of learning in class formation as a fundamentally human act of agency: "Workers as human beings capable of making mistakes and learning from experience seems much more realistic than conceptions that see them either as born revolutionaries or as incapable of achieving a consciousness of their common interests" (2011, 16–17). For Lenin, agency in shaping class consciousness was exercised by a vanguard: "This struggle must be organized, according to 'all the rules of the art,' by people who are professionally engaged in revolutionary activity" ([1902] 1969, 87). Chief among the vanguard, for Gramsci, were those "organic intellectuals" drawn from working classes who could interpret and elaborate class consciousness (1971).

The centrality of struggle, learning, and agency contextualizes class formation, which takes shape according to contingent circumstances. The nature of class in any given context depends on dynamic processes, as working classes must overcome collective action problems, repression from dominant classes and the state,[36] and challenges to consciousness with "class content and class-pertinent effects" (E. O. Wright 1997, 195). The dynamics of class formation appear in the contradictory and stuttering evolution of class struggle, as people draw on inherited repertoires of resistance, indigenous resources such as social networks, and evolving identities.

For Aronowitz, the contextually specific character of class formation "sunders" the presumed distinction between identity-based struggle in communities, the ambit of social movements, and resistance to material forms of exploitation in the workplace: "Genuine social movements are struggles over class formation when they pose new questions concerning the conduct of institutional and everyday life" (2004, 52).[37]

The connection between identity-based and class-based struggle requires attention to the way such intersections evolve over time. "It is not only a repeat of an age-old racial divide, but also a statement of a relatively new public chasm that has been growing for years," a particular version of neoliberalism characterized by "demonization and privatization of public services, including schools, the military, prisons, and even policing; by the growing use of prison as our primary resolution for social contradictions; by the degradation and even debasement of the public sphere and all those who would seek to democratically occupy it; by an almost complete abandonment of the welfare state; by a nearly religious reverence for marketized solutions to public problems" (Hill 2016, 29).[38]

Although the attack on communities represented by dual development manifests in struggles over everyday life, Gibson-Graham also sees "multiple axes of economic diversity . . . an emancipatory project of repoliticizing the economy" (2003, 126). Struggles over identity and local control can be steps toward broader articulations of working-class struggle, and this is itself a contingent part of class formation, as opponents will attempt to limit such movements to efforts to diversify dominant classes without attacking capitalism and exploitation (Reed 2013).

In describing the "making of the English working class," E. P. Thompson weaves together workplace and identity struggles that occurred among the urban mass of Irish and English workers expelled from the countryside and absorbed in industrializing cities. Their class identity drew on rural traditions, generations of urban survival, and an accretion of strategies, tactics, mobilizations, and counter-mobilizations that reflected both ethnic and economic imperatives—"the making of the working class is a fact of political and cultural, as much as of economic, history" (1966, 194).[39]

Thompson outlines his understanding of the contingent and historically rooted nature of class formation in the preface to his book:

> By class I understand an historical phenomenon, unifying a number of disparate and seemingly unconnected events, both in the raw material of experience and in consciousness. I emphasize that it is an *historical* phenomenon. I do not see class as a 'structure,' nor even as a 'category,' but as something which in fact happens (and can be shown to have happened) in human, historical relationships. . . . The relationship must always be embodied in real people and in a real context. Moreover, we cannot have two distinct classes, each with an independent being, and

then bring them into relationship with each other. . . . [C]lass happens when some men, as a result of common experiences (inherited or shared), feel and articulate the identity of their interests as between themselves, and as against other men whose interests are different from (and usually opposed to) theirs. . . . Class-consciousness is the way in which these experiences are handled in cultural terms: embodied in traditions, value-systems, ideas, and institutional forms. . . . Consciousness of class arises in the same way in different times and places, but never *just* the same way. (1966, 9)

In understanding class struggle in New Orleans, it is important to recognize the inchoate character of class formation. Following Erik Olin Wright, class formation is "any form of collectively constituted social relations which facilitate solidaristic action in pursuit of class interests" and class formation is "organized forms of antagonistic class practices" (1997, 191–92). Forms of resistance currently appear as multiple and varied, in part because class struggle in New Orleans addresses intersecting dimensions of poverty by "respecting difference and otherness" (Gibson-Graham 2003).

This expressly intersectional approach to class remains incipient, though what brings varied struggles together is the shared opposition to a globally oriented elite agenda of dual development and labor markets segmented according to ascriptive characteristics of race, ethnicity, and gender. At stake in these identity and workplace struggles is ultimately the same thing—the extraction and control of surplus from working people and popular sections that occurs in both workplaces and communities.

Extraction from Workplaces and Communities

The globalized growth regime imposed by elites includes economic and non-economic preconditions that extend extraction from workplace to community (Jessop 1983). Exploitation at work seeps into communities, and communities themselves become sources of capital for use in workplaces. Three strategies of extraction help make sense of the linkage: expanded reproduction, social reproduction, and accumulation by dispossession.

Expanded reproduction refers to efforts to increase the relative surplus and rate of turnover in productive investment, "reproducing" the original capital as it returns to owners in "expanded" form. Increasing the relative surplus in any given process includes driving down wages, cutting back on benefits, and skimping on other costs of production, such as health and safety (Bernhardt et al. 2001). Efforts to increase the rate of profit also accelerate the rate of turnover by which productive processes make use of capital and return it to investors, including extending the workday, speeding up production, and adding more previously accumulated capital in the form of technology.

To increase the amount of relative surplus and rate of turnover, racial, ethnic, gender, and other ascriptive divisions among working people play a role. Such divisions provide ready categories of segmentation, blocking mechanisms of mobility from one category of work to another, and play into divisions among workers, complicating efforts to unite and build worker power. By stimulating ascriptive divisions, efforts to expand reproduction bleed into communities, often literally, in racist, misogynist, and nativist segregation and violence.

Expanded reproduction bleeds further into communities during moments of crisis and overproduction. In the 1970s, post–World War II recovery in Europe and Japan and incipient industrialization in developing countries flooded international markets with manufactured products, producing crises of stagnation and inflation in developed countries (Marglin and Shor 1990). The decline forced urban areas to compete to attract new activities, exemplified by the concentration on tourism and services in New Orleans. Efforts to attract such activities with tax incentives have been typical (Harvey 2007), and while data for New Orleans are not available, Louisiana offered the third-highest absolute value of subsidy among all states in film ($191 million in 2011) and in oil, gas, and mining ($449 million in 2013). The total subsidy amounted to almost $1.8 billion per year on incentive programs, equal to $394 per person and 21 percent of the state budget, even as Louisiana was the third-poorest state in the country (Story, Fehr, and Watkins 2016).

Paying for tax giveaways affects communities by pressuring processes of social reproduction. In communities, society "reproduces" itself through the consumption of goods such as health, education, and housing. As a poor city in the Deep South, New Orleans never had a particular abundance of such goods, but the disappearance of such public support was accelerated by tax incentives and a political agenda antagonistic to the public sector. These cuts to the public sector force communities into the open market to satisfy their basic needs, opening particularly attractive sources of profit to capital. Basic needs are mostly consumed in direct exchanges and face little of the global competition that could control their prices. People have little choice but to buy them—they cannot survive or live a full life without them.

Already-low taxes and competition to offer generous giveaways to globally integrated activities erode the public services that sustain social reproduction. As service quality declines, elites pressure further to shift them to private control, transforming public services into public-private partnerships and private activities. The private sector can then absorb those few government resources that remain, and in the absence of government regulation they can raise prices and absorb what little wealth exists in communities. As Marx and Engels observed, "No sooner is the exploitation of the laborer by the manufacturer so far at an end that he receives his wages in cash, than he is set upon by the other portions of the bourgeoisie, the landlord, the shopkeeper, the pawnbroker, etc." ([1847] 2012, 18).[40]

When social reproduction is abandoned, neglected, or stripped from government, it becomes an opportunity for elites to accumulate surplus and removes public life from public control. "By injecting moneymaking into the relationship between a citizen and the basic services of life—water, roads, electricity, and education—privatization distorts the social contract" (Hill 2016, 177). Efforts to turn social reproduction into an opportunity for accumulation do not just impoverish and immiserate; they fundamentally alter the relationship between community and the state.

One example of the opportunity for accumulation available in New Orleans social reproduction appears in housing. Housing is a necessary expense, representing a captured market, and public housing often occupies prime real estate in U.S. urban centers. After years of neglect and underinvestment, such housing represents an easy target for rezoning and privatization, and federal and state programs incentivized the transformation of public housing into mixed-income neighborhoods (Arena 2012).

A final strategy that links extraction in the workplace to that occurring in communities appears in efforts to appropriate goods produced in communal and non-market processes. Harvey calls this "accumulation by dispossession,"[41] in which urban elites appropriate public assets, communal land, and those goods and services that operate outside market processes.

In cities like New Orleans, accumulation by dispossession often takes cultural form in the dispossession of the unique community cultures and practices of working classes and popular sectors. Elites appropriate popular cultures to "brand" cities with "marks of distinction . . . some special quality resource, commodity, or location," as a way to turn non-market resources and activities into opportunities for profit (Harvey 2012, 91).[42] In New Orleans, tourism elites attempt to appropriate community-generated identities surrounding jazz, food, and architecture by packaging and selling them as tourist attractions (Sakakeeny 2013).[43]

Accumulation by dispossession extends also to efforts to turn antipoverty programs into opportunities for accumulation. Such strategies are given labels such as corporate social responsibility, triple bottom line, and social entrepreneurship. To take the social entrepreneurship example, it directs the entrepreneur toward the public good—"social entrepreneurs are one species of the genus entrepreneur. They are entrepreneurs with a social mission" (Dees 1998).[44] This can include those who innovate in the social sector, for example, by applying business principles to improve the provision of basic services like health and education, or those firms whose activities generate both profits for their owners and benefits to society (Seelos and Mair 2005, 244). Social enterprises are certainly to be preferred to firms with no social mission, but social enterprises are compatible with elite projects of dual development precisely because they leave control in the hands of elites. Elites therefore prefer social enterprise to unions, cooperatives, or autonomous community organizations, which seek to build working-class and popular power and shift social relations by removing the ability of elites to decide how to organize productive and community life (Parkinson and Howorth 2008, 291).

A related strategy of co-opting working-class and popular power operates through the funding and support provided by elite actors. Unlike unions, which can fund-raise through membership dues and salary deductions, advocacy organizations from worker centers to community activists have become increasingly dependent on support from foundations and payment for facilitating government services (Fine 2006). Dependence on such funds compromises the potential for radical action, for fear of losing future funding streams, and privileges organizations staffed and led by individuals comfortable circulating in cosmopolitan circles (Arena 2012).

Joined-up Workplace and Community Struggle

In the context of social relations that extract from workplace and community, effective opposition emerges in those episodes in which resistance also bridges workplace and community. Joined-up struggle draws on the context-specific ways in which extraction occurs, forming class rooted in cultural, historical, and dynamic struggles that include class and identity struggles.

Efforts to join such struggles are difficult, but unions and movements and other actors have found strategies to work in tandem. One example is efforts by unions, which have traditionally focused on workplace issues of expanded reproduction, taking up community issues of social reproduction and accumulation by dispossession. "Unions have developed a practice of forming project-specific labor-community coalitions to extract community benefit agreements and organizing rights in neighborhoods" (MacDonald 2014, 255). Such agreements force negotiation over the ways in which infrastructure, housing, and other public projects will be implemented, though there is a fine balance between allying with communities and "negotiated gentrification" in which coalitions gain short-term access to jobs, wages, and benefits on public projects but have limited ability to block the privatization of public assets or marketization of basic needs (2014, 256). By consistently taking up community concerns with the cost of basic needs and the privatization of public assets, unions can confront strategies to extend surplus extraction into communities.

At the same time, traditional community-based organizations such as neighborhood and identity-based movements also innovate by defining their demands in terms that bridge to workplaces. For example, worker centers have specialized in sectors where unions have had difficulty organizing, among vulnerable populations such as undocumented immigrants and women, and in sectors relatively unprotected by labor legislation, such as farmworkers, taxi drivers, domestic servants, and restaurant workers (Fine 2006). To reach these sectors, worker centers attend to issues such as access to services, discrimination in housing, freedom from police harassment, and in the case of immigrants, protection from deportation.[45] In the process, they build movements that also oppose strategies of capital in the workplace, demanding better wages, working conditions, and benefits.

For both workplace and community-based movements, the challenge has been to build those bridges. Identity-based groups organized and in many cases secured access to local power, but this often reached only elites within each ethnic group. As Reed explains:

> [Identity] politics is not an alternative to class politics; it is a class politics, the politics of the left-wing of neoliberalism. It is the expression and active agency of a political order and moral economy in which capitalist market forces are treated as unassailable nature. An integral element of that moral economy is displacement of the critique of the invidious outcomes produced by capitalist class power onto equally naturalized categories of ascriptive identity that sort us into groups supposedly defined by what we essentially are rather than what we do. As I have argued, following Walter Michaels and others, within that moral economy a society in which 1% of the population controlled 90% of the resources could be just, provided that roughly 12% of the 1% were black, 12% were Latino, 50% were women, and whatever the appropriate proportions were LGBT people. (Reed 2015)

As an alternative, joined-up struggle in communities and workplaces suggest a specific form of class formation and may even present certain advantages. First, labor struggles are more likely to succeed when they have support from popular actors organized outside the workplace, as attacks on communities are often more deeply felt and more readily available within social memories and practices. Second, community struggles are more likely to succeed when they can enlist workers who possess the organizational and material resources to sustain struggle and whose leverage against capital comes precisely from their ability to shut down production (Piven and Cloward 1978). There really is no alternative: surplus extraction occurs in the workplace and in the community; resistance must therefore bridge both places.

In New Orleans, past successes in workplace struggle addressed identity-based forms of community exclusion. New Orleans riverfront workers at the turn of the twentieth century gained a degree of control when black and white workers collaborated to "counter the dominant trend of black subordination, exclusion, and segregation in the age of Jim Crow" (Arneson 1994, ix). This effort was possible because of powerful black unions and a pro-labor Democratic political machine, operating through "a biracial network of institutionalized solidarity," the Cotton Men's Executive Council (1880–94) and the Dock and Cotton Council (1901–23).[46] Such efforts were successful because they bridged workplace and community struggle to establish common rules, wages, and job categorizations, overcoming a racially segmented labor market (Arneson 1994).[47]

While the councils addressed racial segmentation as part of their workplace struggle, other New Orleans movements built cross-class coalitions to address racist segregation laws operating in communities. In 1890 the Citizens Committee of New Orleans, a group of prominent African Americans, mostly resident in the Tremé neighborhood, staged an infraction of racist segregation laws by placing fair-skinned Homer Plessy on a whites-only train car at the busy Press Street wharf during the height of commuter business hours. The case resulted in the 1896 U.S. Supreme Court ruling in *Plessy v. Ferguson*, which validated the doctrine of separate but equal, but despite this early setback, it evolved into the successful strategy of using the Fourteenth Amendment to address racist Jim Crow regulations. These finally bore fruit in the NAACP 1954 *Brown v. Board of Education* case.[48]

Globally integrated dual development and segmented labor markets bridge workplace and community extraction in ways different from the Jim Crow and exclusionary practices of a century ago. Still, in some ways contemporary bridges are even more clear, as "contemporary forms of oppression are not propelled by the need to subjugate black labor to the interests of Southern planters and industrialists, but as a means of managing a growing class of Americans who are not exclusively black but have been made obsolete by hyper-industrialization, the large-scale introduction of automation and cybernetic command, just-in-time production, and other strategies of flexible accumulation in US farms and factories" (Cedric Johnson 2016).

Ever more clear connections between the social exclusion of racism in communities and exploitation of labor in workplaces require struggles that bridge community and workplace. Elite agendas play up ethnic, gender, and racial distinctions in efforts to keep working people and popular sectors divided, but resistance is strongest when it identifies common interests, common organizations, and common alternatives to elite-led development.

Commoning

While still weak and inchoate, New Orleans movements of resistance occasionally lay out their alternatives to elite development strategies. Their demands take shape through and advance class struggle, and they continue to evolve. In their clearest and most successful moments, joined-up workplace and community struggle articulates an alternative to dual development that focuses on collective and non-commodified production and consumption.

David Harvey describes this as "commoning," an alternative to the capitalist laws of value determination. Commoning is an "anti-wealth politics" and "construction of alternative social relations," with a "material but also a spiritual and moral" shift. The spiritual and moral shift includes ecological sustainability; race, gender, and ethnic justice; and "the abolition of the dominant class relation that underpins and mandates the perpetual expansion of surplus value production and relation" (2012, 126–28).

While elite strategies of accumulation extract from workplace and community, popular and working-class resistance seeks to reclaim and extend those areas of life considered "both collective and non-commodified — off-limits to the logic of market exchange and market valuations" (Harvey 2012, 73). This includes defending, reclaiming, and establishing public goods and communal resources protected from a market logic of extracting surplus. Instead, such goods and resources obey a community-defined logic, providing for basic needs and affirming community rights to define the terms of social relations. A lower-class project seeks also to rearrange the social relations of workplaces. Such a project seeks to build worker power, rooted in communities, to define the nature of social relations in the workplace. In particular, production for the purpose of extracting surplus, useful only for reproduction of capital to be accumulated and reinvested, is replaced by production for use, in which the reason for economic activity is to serve human needs, rather than accumulate wealth.

To exemplify the alternative logic of commoning, Harvey draws especially on the Paris Commune of 1871: "I take it as symbolic that the first two acts of the Paris commune were to abolish night work in the bakeries (a labor question) and to impose a moratorium on rents (an urban question)" (2012, 120). As in nineteenth-century Paris, contemporary struggle includes workers and other categories of the marginalized facing extraction and oppression in the workplace and in their communities.

These working-class and popular principles are the polar opposite of the poverty meted out by global growth regimes. In the workplace, joined-up workplace and community development includes improvements in working conditions, wages, and benefits, with salaries set at livable levels and reasonable expectations of progression up a salary scale over a career. Careers follow predictable and extended trajectories, with a lifetime of work that includes progressive increases in training, promotion, and seniority. Decency in work also includes safety and health, as well as freedom from abuse and discrimination. Further, workers and communities struggle for popular control over the production process, including representation and a voice in major decisions through workplace organization as in a union and neighborhood and community regulation of activities. Working-class and popular control of production turns production away from a singular focus on surplus extraction and toward a more holistic view of the livelihoods made possible both in the act of production and in the consumption of goods produced.

Decency at work is rounded out by an active community life not subjected to the rules of the market. This includes non-commodified access to basic needs like education, housing, and health. Further, an active community life includes recreation, public spaces for organization and debate, and the infrastructure to form networks, bonds, and relationships. In particular, an active community is free from the ascriptive oppressions used by elites to segment labor markets and maintain divisions and oppositions within popular sectors.

Decency at work and an active community life are important not only as things to be consumed but also because they enable citizenship and political engagement. Engagement begins with a basic minimum of human capital, things like income, education, health, and organizational skills.[49] To enter relationships with other members of the community, people also require shared ideas, communication, and networks to simplify interaction, bonds that hold them together and accumulate as social capital, a concept traced to sociologist James Coleman (1988).[50] Such bonds are especially important to oppose segmented labor markets, as working people have to work doubly hard to overcome imposed divisions rooted in ascriptive characteristics.[51]

This chapter has argued that the struggles of working people and popular sectors can be understood as a process of class formation that bridges workplace and community. In those rare instances and narrow sectors in which workers can engage in community-based resistance that bridges ascriptive divisions, they have a chance at workplace dignity and an active and engaged civic life. Such joined-up workplace and community development is an alternative to the more common and dominant pattern of elite-led dual development, in which globally oriented elites impose a segmented labor market characterized by exploitative working conditions and a divided community life.

Dual development in New Orleans has been imposed by a particular faction of capital who consolidated their control over the local institutions that shape development policy. Globally oriented elite control has become possible as a result of the displacement of Katrina, which accelerated the decline of African American political elites and calmed divisions among local capitalist factions. With political control of key institutions, emerging elites atop sectors such as tourism, services, and construction have been able to advance their designs for local and regional development.

The agenda of emerging elites is a dual development model, turning New Orleans into a platform and nodal point within transnational production processes. Transnational accumulation offers opportunities for rapid growth, but internationally integrated sectors are poorly connected to other parts of the local economy and offer few benefits to working and poor people.

CHAPTER TWO

The Rise of a Globally Oriented Elite in a Fragmented City

Shifts in the global economy mobilize new factions among local elites, and these factions seek the policies and institutions that can propel their accumulation. They do not always get what they want, however, as they must navigate existing institutions and compete with rival elite factions and popular sectors in pursuit of power and policy. In New Orleans after Katrina, emerging elites with a globally integrated development agenda faced fragmented structures of public authority, characterized by a mix of elected and appointed, on-budget and off-budget quasi-governmental entities. This web of authority can be characterized as a "satellite" government, in which a host of boards, commissions, public-benefit corporations, and other entities exercise public authority in combination, and occasionally in competition, with formal legislative and executive powers.[1]

The satellite fragmentation of local authority interacts with and contributes to well-known characteristics of New Orleans public life. Over decades, New Orleans governance was known for stalemate and stagnation, in which the fragmentation of public power offered multiple veto points to rival political actors seeking to block public action (Whelan 1987). New Orleans has also been known for the gradual political incorporation of racial and ethnic minorities to whom fragmentation offered multiple avenues of access to public power (Germany 2007). In the post-Katrina era, fragmentation has further contributed to the shift to a globally oriented development regime, offering a set of institutional hosts where rising elites could capture portions of public policy in preparation for the change in governance that would come after Katrina.

This chapter takes a political and institutional look at the city's tourism and services development model. Following political science theories of urban regimes, it explores governance patterns as a combination of social, institutional, and policy elements that "mobilize resources to get things done" (C. N. Stone 1993, 5). Three dimensions important to the study of urban regimes are the social coalitions that support the government, state capacity to mobilize and deploy resources, and agendas for public policy. Qualitative shifts in regimes can be perceived over time as social coalitions, governance practices, and changes in public goals. Further, some periods are marked by regime weakness that appears in excessive conflict among social actors, weak state capacity, and/or indecision or incoherence in setting public goals.

To make sense of the post-Katrina political and institutional reality, the institutions of satellite governance offer a useful and original source of data. Changing regimes leave their imprint in the institutions of the local state by creating new institutions to manage areas of public policy. Once inaugurated, such institutions often outlive the regime that put them into place, leaving a residue as evidence of historical periods and fragmenting public administration. Already in 1934, New Orleans reformer Harold Stone, chief executive of the Bureau of Government Research, likened the forty-three independent boards and commissions of his day to "a piled up dish of spaghetti. . . . With so many boards commissions, and agencies all tumbled together like toys in a child's playpen, it is a wonder anything is accomplished" (1934, 309).

As of 2010 almost 250 satellite entities had accumulated. They were disrupted but not washed away by Katrina, and they set the context for the contemporary emergence of a globally oriented elite. The rise to prominence of this elite, the ways they reoriented the bureaucracy and capacity of the local state, and their dual development goals in public policy appear in their actions through satellite government entities and their graduation to elected public authority.

This chapter contains three sections. The first describes the regimes that characterized New Orleans government since the late 1800s, focusing on social coalitions, state capacities, and goals of public power, using satellite entities created in each period to illustrate the operation of political actors and institutions. The second section describes the evolution of a particularly emblematic commission, the Audubon Commission, which has evolved over time in response to various New Orleans regime characteristics. The third section explores emblematic subsets of satellites: membership-only entities such as security districts and entities oriented toward the promotion of a tourism and services economy. These satellites shed light on the nature of the social coalition articulated by globally oriented elites, the ways they reorganize state capacity, and the public purposes they pursue. Finally, the chapter finds evidence that popular sectors recognize the fragmented nature of New Orleans governance and seek to create their own entities to demand input into the direction of city government. Chapter 3 uses quantitative techniques to explore some of the characteristics of satellite governance.

Institutional Legacies of Shifting Urban Regimes

In Louisiana, the end of Reconstruction was violently accelerated in 1874 by the Battle of Liberty Place, a three-day putsch led by the White League paramilitary of Confederate veterans backed by local merchant, finance, and planter classes opposed to Republican government.[2] In the aftermath, New Orleans politics came to be dominated by the Old Regulars, an immigrant-incorporating machine similar to machines existing in other cities of the late 1800s, exchanging access to jobs and services for support from ethnic populations, including Irish, Italian, and German immigrants. The Old Regulars balanced their ethnic support base with the interests of local businessmen, co-opting opposition with a generous distribution of public contracts. African American populations had achieved some success both as a legacy of prior French dominion and postwar reconstruction, but they were viciously re-subjugated by Jim Crow legislation.

While the Old Regulars were turned out occasionally by reformers, they won almost every election from 1876 to 1946, armed with an electoral machine that solidified as they expanded public infrastructure and development focused on the port of New Orleans. They often feuded with state governments in Baton Rouge eager to tame an independent source of power in New Orleans, but eventually they were absorbed and allied to the populist Huey Long machine once he consolidated power at the state level in the 1930s (Boulard 1998). Figure 2 displays the mayors of New Orleans with their primary political association.

Satellite government began to take shape in the first sequence of pre-1900 governments. The city sought to recapture the pace of development that had made it among the most populous and commercially active in the nation prior to the Civil War, and government took on increased responsibility for public works. One of the main challenges was taming the Mississippi River and the uninhabitable swampland around the city, and Mayor John Shakespeare (1880–82 and 1888–92) initiated the Levee Board in 1890. The Levee Board undertook major infrastructure projects, controlling semi-annual river floods and reclaiming land for developers eager to construct living areas and industrial possibilities around the port. While non-Regular Shakespeare had created the Levee Board according to professional criteria, the Old Regulars reclaimed power and made use of the

Edward Pilsbury	1876–78	Regular Democratic Organization
Isaac W. Patton	1878–80	Regular Democratic Organization
Joseph A. Shakespeare	1880–82	
William J. Behan	1882–84	
J. Valsin Guillotte	1884–88	Regular Democratic Organization
Joseph A. Shakespeare	1888–92	
John Fitzpatrick	1892–96	Regular Democratic Organization
Walter C. Flower	1896–1900	Citizens League
Paul Capdevielle	1900–1904	Regular Democratic Organization
Martin Behrman	1904–20	Regular Democratic Organization
Andrew J. McShane	1920–25	Regular Democratic Organization
Martin Behrman	1925–26	Regular Democratic Organization
Arthur J. O'Keefe	1926–29	Regular Democratic Organization
T. Semmes Walmsley	1929–36	Regular Democratic Organization
A. Miles Pratt	1936	Regular Democratic Organization
Fred A. Earhart	1936	Regular Democratic Organization
Jesse S. Cave	1936	Regular Democratic Organization
Robert S. Maestri	1936–46	Regular Democratic Organization
deLesseps Story "Chep" Morrison	1946–61	Crescent City Democrat Association
Victor H. Schiro	1961–70	Crescent City Democrat Association
Maurice "Moon" Landrieu	1970–78	Crescent City Democrat Association
Ernest Nathan "Dutch" Morial	1978–86	Louisiana Independent Federation of Electors
Sidney Barthelemy	1986–94	Community Organization for Urban Politics
Marc Morial	1994–2002	
C. Ray Nagin	2002–10	
Mitch Landrieu	2010–	

FIGURE 2. Mayors of New Orleans.

large construction contracts and employment to gain electoral patronage.[3] "If you were willing to work for them, they could provide work for you: the city and sewerage board alone was worth more than four thousand jobs; there were jobs in the police and fire departments, jobs on public-financed construction projects, jobs hauling garbage, jobs working in city hall. Only through the Old Regulars could New Orleanians gain access to these jobs" (Boulard 1998, 40).

While the Old Regulars could capture the Levee Board and its patronage, another quasi-governmental entity was initiated explicitly to constrain
machine politics. The Board of Liquidation of City Debt was established
during Shakespeare's first two-year term (1880–82) and was made a "body
corporate" separate and distinct from the city of New Orleans in his second term. The Board of Liquidation served to protect the financial and
commercial elite of the city from the financial risk of ballooning city debt.[4]
The Board of Liq, as it is known, separates and excludes general obligation bonds from the operating budget and receives all ad valorem taxes
levied by the city for the purpose of repaying its debts. Only after the
Board of Liquidation has made all bond payments does the city receive its
remaining property tax receipts. The members of the board were typically
businessmen and leaders of major banks in the city, and until a change in
the charter in the 1990s the board was self-perpetuating, with members
appointed for life terms (Kendall 1922). With the power to disapprove all
bond sales, the Board of Liquidation provided the commercial and financial elite a veto against some of the fiscal indiscipline and indebtedness of
the Old Regular regime, as well as an easy source of rentier accumulation
in the form of city debt.[5]

By 1904, one of the most durable of the Old Regulars, Martin Behrman,
had risen to the top of the organization. He held the mayor office for four
terms, until 1920, returning in 1925 for a last, two-year term. Berhman's
seventeen years made him the longest-serving mayor in the city's history,
and his years in power could be considered the peak of the Old Regular
regime in terms of electoral dominance secured through the combination
of public works, corruption, and patronage distributed to secure the votes
of immigrants and ethnic populations.[6]

Toward the latter half of the 1920s, the Old Regular machine entered a
bitter feud with Huey Long's growing statewide populist machine, culminating in Old Regular support for efforts to impeach Long in 1929. After
a brief interlude, the Long machine and the Old Regular machine entered
open conflict once again, resolved only when the Old Regulars acquiesced
to the imposition of a Long candidate, Robert S. Maestri, as head of the
Old Regulars and mayor of the city from 1936 to 1946. Maestri's reign
coincided with an increased flow of resources from the state and federal
government, especially in the context of New Deal efforts to jump-start
the economy.[7]

In 1946, Maestri's machine was displaced by deLesseps Story "Chep"
Morrison's (1946–61) Crescent City Democratic Association (CCDA),
backed by the city's civic and business class and championing reform.
Morrison governed through what has been labeled a "privatist" regime of

upper- and middle-class white supporters, presenting himself as a moderate segregationist. He passed reforms to wrest control of the city from the state government, enacting a new charter that included a strong mayor format and the formalization of a number of regulatory and planning-oriented entities targeted on economic growth and professionalization of the public service.[8]

Morrison's successor, Victor H. Schiro (1961–70), governed during a time of increasing national unrest around civil rights, and his vacillation in the face of federal orders of desegregation offered one indicator of the increasingly stalemated government of the 1960s (Fairclough 1995).[9] His government was the last of the segregationist mayors before his CCDA successor, Maurice "Moon" Landrieu (1970–78), integrated City Hall as the last white mayor before a series of governments led by African Americans.[10]

The period of rule by the CCDA (1946–78) saw a rapid increase in the number of satellite entities, starting with the 1954 passage of a Home Rule Charter. Three types of entities are useful indicators of political dynamics during the period—rational, developmental, and privatizing. The first type of entity sought to rationalize the local state by introducing professional and legal standards for the operation of public decision making. These entities recalled the spirit of turn-of-the-century Progressives and targeted the corruption of Maestri and the Old Regular period. A good example was the City Civil Service Commission, an entity that Governor Earl Long had eliminated statewide when he reclaimed the governorship in 1948 after eight years of reformist government (Kurtz and Peoples 1991, 114–16). The New Orleans Civil Service Commission initiated in 1954 established merit-based exams and professional requirements for bureaucratic offices. It sought to remove what were termed "deadhead" employees, those appointed by the Old Regulars, who drew a salary (and provided campaign contributions) but did not actually perform work.[11]

The second type of entity embraced the planning and development objectives of the Morrison and Schiro governments, including efforts to revitalize the port and associated industrial activities as well as enhance the tourism sector. One example was the City Planning Commission, established in 1954, with a mission described in the charter to "prepare, adopt, amend, and recommend to the Council a twenty year Master Plan for the physical development of the City" (New Orleans City Council 1954). This mission of long-range planning was in line with trends in public administration sparked by the New Deal expansion in state activity and post–World War II approaches to Keynesian demand management.[12]

As racial tensions mounted and federal desegregation orders emerged during the 1960s, a third type of entity accommodated the reality of white flight—making public resources available for private accumulation. "The city lost around 250,000 whites in the 1960s and another 150,000 in the 1970s, with the black population only increasing by 60,000 over the same period" (S. E. Thompson 2009, 214).[13] At the same time whites left the city, taking their tax bases with them, white elites sought to privatize public assets. This accomplished two things: it protected white privilege from growing African American political influence in the context of civil rights legislation, and in the context of 1970s economic stagnation, it renewed opportunities for accumulation.

A useful example of privatizing public assets is the Audubon Commission and its associated private or semi-profit arms, the Audubon Nature Institute and the Audubon Foundation. Over time the city zoo had fallen into disrepair, and reforms reorganized the governance structure in the 1970s with two institutional innovations. The first was the creation of the private Audubon Nature Institute, to manage and operate the zoo and park, and the second was the Audubon Foundation, to pursue related financial and fiscal operations. The city pumped public resources into the entities with a 1972 voter-approved referendum to issue bonds backed by tax revenues, and the infusion of funds immediately triggered an expansion in Audubon holdings. The Audubon Nature Institute established the Aquarium and Riverfront Park, the Species Survival Center, the Louisiana Nature Center, and the Audubon Insectarium.

According to the financial statements of the Institute, its board is related to the Audubon Commission through the interaction of their boards of directors and their contractual management agreement, by which the entities "often engage in operations through one organization to the benefit of the other" (Audubon Institute 2008, 5–10). The accounts of the two entities are available from the State Legislative Auditor office and offer a few clues to their collaboration. For example, the Audubon Commission averaged an operating loss of $11.6 million per year, though it was subsidized by an average annual grant from the Audubon Institute of $4.5 million and dedicated tax revenues from the city of $7.7 million. Meanwhile, the Institute had an average annual gain of $1 million. Both entities also counted substantial assets, with net 2007 assets at the Institute of $41 million and $95.6 million at the commission.

In 1978 the city elected its first African American mayor, starting a string of what Adolph Reed Jr. has labeled black urban regimes— "black-led and black-dominated administrations" (1999). The first was Ernest Nathan "Dutch" Morial (1978–86), who won with a majority of the African American vote and a minority of the white vote (B. Liu and Vanderleeuw 2007).[14] He successfully introduced minority hiring quotas for city contracts, increased the number of African Americans in both City Hall and on the police force, and directed public funds to projects to incorporate African Americans, drawing especially on federal programs such as the Office of Economic Opportunity Community Action and the Model Cities Experience (Karnig and Welch 1980, 50–78).

Yet, Morial had to also focus on the growth agenda, presiding over an expansion in downtown office construction and the attraction of corporate headquarters for firms targeting the booming oil and gas exploration and refining operations along the Gulf Coast (Exxon, Chevron, Gulf Oil, Amoco, Mobil, Murphy Oil, Texaco, Shell, among others). The resources, jobs, and contracts generated during the period allowed Morial to build his electoral organization, Louisiana Independent Federation of Electors (LIFE), and compete with existing African American political brokers known by their own acronyms—BOLD, COUP, and SOUL.[15] Still, just as the theory of black urban regimes predicted, Morial and subsequent governments faced fiscal and structural constraints as white flight eroded the New Orleans revenue base (Bankston and Caldas 2002), the 1982 and 1986 oil price crashes further accelerated long-term deindustrialization, and the cutbacks of Reagan's New Federalism withdrew federal funding (Bullard 1989).[16]

In the deepening fiscal and structural crisis of the city, the second African American mayor, Sidney Barthelemy (1986–94), turned even more aggressively toward tourism and service interests, moving away from the declining oil and manufacturing sectors.[17] He presided over the legalization of a land-based casino at the foot of Canal Street, a new aquarium, new downtown malls, a new sports arena, the conversion of a downtown department store into apartments, and an expansion in the convention center, attracting mega-events such as the Republican National Convention of 1988 and the NCAA Final Four basketball championship. While his governments foreshadowed the shift to a dual development strategy rooted in tourism and services, his terms in office were also marked by elite factionalism, institutional fragmentation, and inertia that prevented the imposition of a coherent development strategy.

Marc Morial, son of Dutch, was the last of the true black urban regime mayors, governing during the more expansionary 1990s (1994–2002). Among his major achievements was taming an out-of-control police department, as he worked with the FBI and named a forceful police chief to address issues of corruption and racially targeted abuse, coinciding also with a decline in violent crime rates in the city. Like previous mayors he also emphasized African American hiring within the public sector and contracting.

Yet, Morial was constrained to fit his efforts at African American inclusion within a growth agenda that offered little to working-class African Americans. John Arena (2012) describes in detail how this played out in terms of public housing. Morial embraced the Federal Hope VI program to convert low-income housing into mixed-use developments. To achieve this end, he managed a coalition of African American and white developers, local nonprofits, and local and federal oversight entities, even as he sidelined or co-opted what had been autonomous and historical organizations of working-class public-housing residents (Arena 2012, 106–12). Morial's redevelopment efforts prompted a construction boom, for example, bringing $40 million from the federal government to redevelop the St. Thomas housing complex into the privately run River Gardens and subsequently remaking the neighborhood by offering Tax Increment Financing (TIF) and property-tax-backed Payment in Lieu of Taxes (PILOT) funding to bring in a Walmart.[18] Paradoxically, the flip side of the construction boom was a drastic reduction in available public housing, falling from a peak of fourteen thousand in the 1980s to six thousand units by the end of the 1990s. The homes being built and the remaking of the downtown were oriented to housing middle-class residents and globally oriented businesses, leaving behind the working-class and African American population of the city (BondGraham 2010).

Two types of satellite entity were typical of the period of African American–led governments in New Orleans: African American incorporating entities and entities to ring-fence public power. The entities incorporating African Americans were frequently motivated by federal programs, targeting African American and inner-city development in housing, education, health, safety, nutrition, recreation, transportation, anti-poverty, and urban development, and creating a flow of resources to the local level (Brown and Erie 1981).[19] These programs created an architecture of local government and nonprofit efforts into which African Americans could fit, what Kent Germany labels the "soft state . . . a loose set of short-term political and bureaucratic arrangements that linked together federal bureaucracies, neighborhood groups, nonprofit organizations, semipublic political organizations, social agencies, and, primarily after 1970, local government to distribute (occasionally in an ad hoc manner) upward of $100 million in federal funding (over $512 million in 2006 dollars) in predominantly black neighborhoods" (2007, 15).[20]

In New Orleans, the soft state created opportunities for a portion of the African American population, especially an African American middle class and professional elite (Bullard 1989), and frequently took the form of satellite entities such as Total Community Action. Total Community

Action (TCA) is a private, nonprofit organization initially authorized by the Economic Opportunity Act of 1964, though it was at first constrained by Mayor Schiro and local politicians who opposed its mission as too "liberal" (TCA 2001, 25–26). Under the 1970s and 1980s black-led regimes, TCA expanded significantly, incorporating into its governing board leaders of associations from majority African American neighborhoods and addressing areas including employment, education, health, development, housing, and leadership. Mayors Dutch Morial and Sidney Barthelemy were associated with TCA early in their careers, and by 2001 it counted seventeen African Americans who had emerged from its programs to hold city and statewide office (TCA 2001, 48). TCA continues to channel federal and foundation funds to neighborhood and developmental organizations, including the Lower Ninth Ward Neighborhood Council, People's Methodist Community Center, Central City Economic Opportunity Corporation, and the Gentilly Development Association (TCA 2001, 55). According to its 2011 submission to the Louisiana Legislative Auditor, TCA had total revenues of over $39 million.

The second type of entity emerging during the period of black-led regimes can be categorized as ring-fencing. Entities that take this form include specialized subdistricts that mobilize revenues for a service or good but preserve control, oversight, and benefits only for those deemed to be eligible. Entities with ring-fencing characteristics have appeared at various intervals in urban history, including periods of resource constraint, when revenues fell or spending limits starved local governments of resources (ACIR 1964). In the context of black-led urban regimes, ring-fencing offers white members of the community the additional possibility of creating a club good[21] outside the control of city government and targeted on the basis of neighborhood, membership, or some other criterion that preserves racial privilege.

Good examples of such ring-fencing are districts for security or neighborhood improvement. Such districts levy a special tax or other contribution on those who own property inside a geographical area and typically use the revenue for extra security.[22] Such districts began forming in 1997 and numbered twenty-five in 2012.[23] Average revenues were $200,000 per district and their total revenue raised was $5.1 million, with one tony district raising almost $1 million in 2011 and sitting on assets worth slightly more, the Garden District Security District.[24] Within their boundaries, most of these special districts provide additional security by contracting with off-duty police officers (or on-duty officers earning overtime, in some cases) using official vehicles, uniforms, and equipment.[25] According to the Office of the Inspector General, "security districts had a whiter and wealthier population than New Orleans as a whole. . . . With the exception of a portion of the Mid-City security district, low income areas were not included in security districts" (OIG 2013, 17).

In addition to creating a club good targeted to wealthier and whiter districts, these entities had eroding impacts on the New Orleans Police Department (NOPD). According to a 2011 report by the U.S. Department of Justice, "Virtually every officer works a Detail, wants to work a Detail, or at some point will have to rely on an officer who works a Detail. The effects of Details thus permeate the entire Department. It is widely acknowledged that NOPD's Detail system is corrupting; as stated by one close observer of the Department, the paid Detail system may be the 'aorta of corruption' within NOPD" (Department of Justice Civil Rights Division 2011, 17).

In the context of black-led regimes, African American incorporating entities and ring-fencing entities serve fairly obvious cross-purposes. African American incorporating entities provided avenues of access to a long-excluded community, opening especially to middle-class, professional, and political elite segments of the African American community. Ring-fencing entities created club goods enjoyed by wealthy whites excluded from executive elected authority but able to capture elements of control over services reserved for themselves.

The end of black-led urban regimes began paradoxically under an African American mayor, C. Ray Nagin, whose period in government foreshadowed the shift to a cosmopolitan agenda of connecting to global patterns of accumulation. Nagin was originally a Republican, had corporate experience as a sports executive, and was vice president and general manager of local cable monopoly Cox Television. Against Morial's former police chief, Nagin won with overwhelming white support (87 percent), having been reputedly drafted to stand as a candidate by a cabal of uptown white businessmen looking for an African American candidate to back (B. Liu 2006). Nagin's first term (2002–6) began with aggressive pursuit of small-scale corruption, such as a kickback scheme within the automobile inspection and taxicab licensing bureaucracies,[26] and he rapidly entered open disputes with members of the African American establishment, using the official city website to endorse a Republican candidate for governor.[27] Nagin's failed attempt to privatize the sewerage and water system controlled by the Sewerage and Water Board demonstrated both his own commitment to a private-sector agenda and the ongoing difficulty of pushing through any coherent development program in the context of fragmented local government and fractious relations among local political and economic elites (Associated Press 2004).

Katrina shifted the terms of political conflict in the city. While Nagin's incompetence had soured his relationship with globally oriented elites, he was able to win reelection against a white challenger[28] by pivoting his rhetoric to secure a majority of the African American vote, famously declaring post-Katrina New Orleans to forever be a "Chocolate City."[29] Despite his reelection support in the African American community, he remained intent on advancing a pro-business agenda and became increasingly exposed in his own corrupt designs on public resources.

Nagin's second term (2006–10) was marked by uncoordinated attempts to respond to Katrina, halfhearted attempts to encourage internationally oriented capital to engage in New Orleans, and the appearance of ongoing stalemate and incompetence in public administration. His weakness can be traced to two sources: his racial polarization of the 2006 election had terminated his legitimacy within the white elite community, and the 2008 financial crisis temporarily constrained the interest of international capital in risky ventures like transforming the New Orleans economy.

Still, New Orleans was partially able to weather the crisis as a result of capital targeted to reconstruction, which the next mayor could corral and direct toward a globally oriented tourism and services development model. The son of Moon Landrieu, Mitch, won the 2010 mayoral election with African American support that recollected his father's integration of City Hall. He joined this base to the newly dominant globally oriented white tourism and services elite. Landrieu could claim a globally oriented track record as a result of his performance as lieutenant governor of Louisiana (2004–10), a relatively powerless position that he used to burnish his record as a promoter of tourism. His office issued the 2005 report, *Louisiana: Where Culture Means Business*, describing a tourism development strategy: "Louisiana's cultural economy encompasses a rich ecosystem of informal, nonprofit, and commercial organizations that address virtually every aspect of cultural expression and development. But while there is an abundance of organizations and activities, Louisiana's cultural constituency tends to be fragmented, undercapitalized, and operating in isolation from one another. In a sector characterized by 'planktons and whales,' there is plenty of plankton but too few whales" (Mt. Auburn Associates 2005, 82).

Landrieu entered office following the stop-start Katrina recovery of Nagin's second term and the boiling scandals at the NOPD, in the local justice system, and in Nagin's executive. To consolidate control over New Orleans authority, Landrieu quickly announced a fiscal shortfall of $67 million and added another $11 million some months later, spurring furloughs, hiring freezes, and redoubled efforts to attract federal funding. Part of this effort was an attempt to rebrand the city as focused on "results," including a "Budgeting for Outcomes" strategy. This countered both the narrative that New Orleans was a carnavalesque city of sin (Parent 2006)[30] and the perception that government was fragmented among competing constituencies: "You can't hide behind race any more. You can't hide behind class structure any more. You can't hide behind family. You need to produce," he proclaimed.[31]

Landrieu's efforts to turn New Orleans into a globally oriented city focused on tourism and services handily won him reelection in 2014. Among other rebranding projects, he has targeted recreation (such as a new riverfront park), an expanded private biomedical district to replace discarded Charity Hospital, and infrastructure to link New Orleans to global markets, including an expanded airport.[32] While the City Council has returned to an African American majority, they generally represent those factions of African American elites accommodated to a globally oriented development strategy.

In terms of his relationship with satellite governance entities, the mayor's approach to satellites matches his rebranding effort. His assistant called the author and his collaborator for advice on which entities could be dissolved to streamline authority, and the administration created its own website with links to all satellites under the executive branch, including information on board composition, term length, and legal authority enacting the entity.[33]

Landrieu has not shied away from adding entities that match his services and tourism dual development project. Emblematic of these efforts was the New Orleans Recreation Development Commission (NORDC), modeled after the Audubon Nature Institute. The NORDC was approved by a referendum advanced by the mayor five months after taking office, altering the city charter to create a new commission that would manage public parks and recreation, moving all previous recreation department employees out of civil service protection, earmarking a new property tax millage, and closely integrating the NORDC with a privately managed foundation that would raise additional funds. As in the case of the Audubon Commission, Nature Institute, and Foundation, the amendment made a public asset available for private accumulation, once again in the sector most important to a globally connected tourism and services elite.

This chapter has outlined the sequence of urban regimes in terms of their social coalitions, agendas for public policy, and state capacity to mobilize and deploy resources. To illustrate these regimes as well as to trace the accretion of institutional innovations, the paragraphs have highlighted the satellite entities that can be consider emblematic of each period. Figure 3

Political Period	Example Entity	Character	Year
Old Regular 1876–1946	Dock Board, Port of New Orleans Board of Commissions	Ethnic incorporating	1896
Old Regular 1876–1946	Board of Liquidation of City Debt	Machine constraining	1880
Crescent City Democrat Association 1946–78	Civil Service Commission	Rational	1954
Crescent City Democrat Association 1946–78	City Planning Commission	Developmental	1954
Crescent City Democrat Association 1946–78	Audubon Nature Institute, Audubon Foundation	Privatizing	1972
Black Urban Regime 1978–2002	Total Community Action	African American incorporating	1964
Black Urban Regime 1978–2002	Garden District Security District	Ring-Fencing	1998
Dual Development 2010–	New Orleans Recreational District Commission	Dual development	2010

FIGURE 3. Typical satellite entities by period and character. Source: Author compilation from www.nolasatellitegovernment/tulane.edu.

displays example entities along with the period in which they were initiated and the character of the agenda they advance.

Evolution of a Commission

While the previous section traced the history of the city by flagging indicative satellite entities to characterize urban regimes, the current section dedicates some attention to a useful case, the Audubon Commission. The Audubon Commission is useful because it is considered by many observers to be a model of efficient and effective management of a city resource, and it has also evolved over a century in ways that reflect multiple moments of New Orleans governance.

The story of the Audubon Commission begins in a sequence of subterfuge, corruption, and mismanagement dating back to 1871. Two speculators purchased the Foucher Plantation for twenty-seven notes of $27,000 each. Three months later, they promptly sold a portion of the property to the City Park Commission, "a profitable but shady scheme" having lobbied the state legislature by offering legislators prime building lots along St. Charles Avenue, securing $800,000 for the river side of the park, $150,000 for the lake side, and selling the remaining portions to Tulane University and the Jesuits for Loyola University (Christovich et al. 1995, 40–43). To raise funds for the purchase, the city mortgaged the downtown City Park, initiated a special park tax, and ultimately had to disband the City Park Commission and refinance the loan when it came overdue. Despite the debacle of the purchase and loan, in 1884 the city supported the Cotton Exposition with free use of the park, an exposition pavilion, and $100,000. The Cotton Exposition ended with "a dismal record of attendance and lack of financial profit. Promoter Edmund Burke fled the country before the discovery of funds missing from the state's coffers, perhaps diverted to the strapped exhibition account" (Christovich et al. 1995, 40–43).

The modern-day Audubon Park Commission was created in 1914, when Act 191 authorized the city to raise $100,000 for Audubon Park Bonds to beautify the park. The members of the board of the Audubon Park Commission took advantage of the location and beauty of the area to create other activities under separate management. For example, in 1927 board members secured agreement to lease the natatorium and swimming pools of the park, as well as athletic fields, on which they would be able to operate amusement, concessions, and merchandise.

The park, like other boards and commissions, was subject to political tugs-of-war between the city and the state. In 1954, as the CCDA machine confronted the Earl Long state administration, the city adopted a new charter to consolidate control over entities considered part of municipal authority.

The current flagship of the park, the zoo, came about as a result of insurance payments for losses in a 1916 storm, private donations during the 1920s, and the aid of the New Deal during the 1930s. Even with this outlay, the zoo eventually deteriorated into a run-down place with poorly kept animals, dubbed in 1958 a "zoological Ghetto" (Cangelosi and Schlesinger 2000, 54). It was only after New Orleans voters approved a millage tax and bond issues in 1972 that the Audubon Zoological Society, later transformed into the Audubon Institute, came to manage and operate the zoo and park. Now the Institute also manages the Aquarium and Riverfront Park, the Species Survival Center, the Louisiana Nature Center, and the Audubon Insectarium. As mentioned before, the interrelated boards of the Audubon Commission, Nature Institute, and Foundation collaborate in the management of a multimillion-dollar enterprise using public credit and tax contributions to sustain profits and promote expansion.

The evolution of the Audubon Commission reflects periods of governance in New Orleans. The current format, established in 1972, responds to the impending emergence of African American power and the stagnation of the New Orleans economy. It represents efforts to make public assets available to private development, specifically for tourism. While the coherent shift to a services and tourism development model was stalemated during the period of black urban regimes, the Audubon Commission, Nature Institute, and Foundation provided a convenient and lucrative place of refuge for white uptown elites, including Director Ron Forman, who receives an annual salary of approximately $700,000 and is a perennial Republican hopeful for mayor. With the contemporary model of a decidedly globally oriented services and tourism development, he has championed further privatization of public assets, vocally supporting the reform of the New Orleans Recreation Department and Commission and the creation of a private NORDC Foundation to parallel Audubon.

This chapter explores the trajectory of regimes in New Orleans. Each regime period is characterized by the social coalitions that support the government, state capacity to mobilize and deploy resources, and agendas for public policy. In some periods, fragmentation within social coalitions, limited capacity, and/or an incoherent agenda for public policy constrain government and prevent the consolidation of any regime, leaving government unable to get things done. For some observers, this was the situation in the years prior to Hurricane Katrina, exhibited in the inability of local elites or government authorities to prevent or respond to the disaster.

The evolving regimes of New Orleans governance left their residue in accumulated institutions, described here in terms of satellite entities closely connected to government and exercising a degree of public authority. Over time these institutional legacies built up, both telling the story of changing historical priorities and complicating local government.

When Katrina struck, new dynamics unfolded and operated through satellite governance. Globally oriented elites had already captured portions of power by occupying satellites of interest to their tourism and services development strategy. They consolidated their power as the hurricane upset existing balances of power among rival economic and political projects. The current period has been characterized by the dominance of the dual development agenda, with devastating impacts on working people and popular sectors. The next chapter will explore in more detail how satellite government distorts local public policy and privileges globally oriented elites.

CHAPTER THREE

Satellite Governance, Public Finance, and Networks of Power

The previous chapter explored the nature of satellite governance through the comparative historical and qualitative analysis of urban regimes. The current chapter makes use of the data on satellite entities to conduct quantitative analyses of public finance and networks of power. Three observations are relevant. First, the fragmented character of satellite government complicates public finance in ways that make monitoring difficult and weaken state capacity. Second, the accumulated layers of satellites show a certain structure in terms of what kinds of satellites tend to be associated with one another. Third, coordination through satellites gives globally oriented elites an opportunity to capture resources and shape public policy.

The data for the analyses below can be found in an online, searchable database.[1] The database was built with the help of Professor David Marcello, longtime activist for transparency in New Orleans government, serving in both the Marc and Dutch Morial administrations, running the Public Law program at Tulane University, and head of Landrieu's transition team on housing. With the help of student assistants, the database was maintained through 2011, and there are efforts to renew the database to continue serving the public interest. In the database, satellite entities include the diverse array of boards, commissions, public trusts, public-benefit corporations, security and development districts, and other entities, some of which were described in the previous chapter in terms of the period of urban regime politics in which they were initiated. In focusing on satellites, the database excludes core agencies and departments of city government, and also does not include entities that are essentially subcontractors for the city.

For an entity to be considered a satellite, it must satisfy one or more of the following characteristics: (1) created by local or state law; (2) expend significant public funds, acquired either through revenue-raising powers of their own or via appropriations or grants received from or on behalf of city government; (3) dependent on government agents or appointees for some members of their boards or administrations; (4) is regulated by public rules for their operations, staffing, budgeting, or oversight. A full list of satellites appears in the appendix.

The next section explores public finance of New Orleans to get a sense of how New Orleans is different from other cities. The comparison suggests that there is something unusual about the city in terms of revenues and expenditures and that part of what makes it unusual is the distortion created by the accumulation of satellite entities. Subsequent sections look more directly at the inner workings of satellites, with a particular focus on the networks formed by members of their boards.

Satellites and Public Finance

This section explores the political economy implications of local fiscal capacity. In specific terms, public finance is the mobilization and deployment of resources by governing authorities, focused here on taxes, general revenues, expenditures, and assets. More generally, public finance can be treated as a reflection of past social struggles and contemporary relations of power, written in the numbers of the budget. The extraordinarily rich information available in the public finances of a city like New Orleans falls into the category of fiscal sociology, that domain of social science that reads in fiscal data "the spirit of a people, its cultural level, its social structure, [and] the deeds its policy may prepare" (Schumpeter 1918, 7).

To explore the public finances of New Orleans, this section makes use of publicly available, though difficult to obtain, data on the finances of New Orleans as compared to other cities. Comparative data are drawn from fiscal year 2005, which ended in July 2005, before Hurricane Katrina. The regression results indicate that New Orleans is a city that does not have complete democratic control of the funds mobilized for public action. While the city appears to mobilize similar amounts of revenue through tax as other cities, it has far lower total revenue and spends far less than other cities. A closer look at the finance of satellites offers an explanation—significant resources and assets are controlled by unelected and difficult-to-monitor entities, some of which are entirely off-budget.

The analysis begins by collecting data from across cities on likely determinants of urban public finance, such as population, income, and area. According to 2005 estimates from the U.S. Bureau of the Census of places with more than 100,000 residents, New Orleans had a population of

454,000, a per capita income of $21,998, a poverty rate of 24.5 percent, and a geographic area of approximately 180 square miles. This compares with a national average population of 283,000, per capita income of $24,569, a poverty rate of 15.5 percent, and a geographic area of 91 square miles. Compared to national averages, New Orleans is slightly larger than the average for population and area, slightly lower on per capita income, and higher on poverty.

In terms of public finance, total revenues for New Orleans were approximately $947 million, tax revenues were $403 million, and expenditures were $853 million, compared to national averages of $530 million, $215 million, and $541 million. Table 2 presents the descriptive statistics for these variables.

To get a more complete sense of how New Orleans public finance compares to the rest, revenues, taxes, and expenditures were regressed on population, income per capita, poverty, and area for the almost 150 places with data from the U.S. Bureau of the Census. Each independent variable can be considered a reasonable predictor of public finance, though with slightly different implications for outcomes. More populous cities can be expected to require more public expenditures in terms of schools, hospitals, and other public services. Also, wealthier cities can be expected to generate more tax revenues and therefore have more funds to spend. Cities with more poverty might also be expected to spend more, as there is more need, though one would not expect their tax revenues to be as high. Finally, a larger geographic extension has ambiguous impacts on public finance, as there is more area to cover with infrastructure, though larger areas may also be more rural, in which case investment in urban infrastructure tends to be less intensive.[2]

TABLE 2. Population, Area, Wealth, Poverty, and Public Finance

	New Orleans	National Mean	Standard Deviation
Population	484,674	283,476	4.19E5
Area	180.6	91.30	165.35
Income Per Capita	21,998	24,569	6687
Pct below Poverty Line	24.46	15.56	6.84
Revenues (in thousands)	946,695	529,818	9.96E5
Taxes (in thousands)	403,252	214,806	4.13E5
Expenditures (in thousands)	852,828	540,849	4.20E5

Sources: for first four lines, U.S. Census Bureau website, www.census.gov; for last three lines, New Orleans Annual Budget, http://www.nola.gov/mayor/budget.

Table 3 displays the regression coefficients for the different variables. As expected, needier cities, as indicated by greater poverty, have larger public sectors. For every 1 percent increase in poverty, revenues increased by $37,000, tax revenues increased by over $13,000, and expenditures increased by $37,000. For every 100-person increase in population, revenues increased by $178, taxes increased by $70, and expenditures increased by $191. For every $100 increase in per capita income, revenues increased by approximately $4,000, taxes increased by almost $1,800, and spending increased by almost $4,000. Perhaps because of the opposing impacts of geographic size, its impact, though negative, was without statistical significance.

The most important finding of this simple comparison was that New Orleans taxes not too far below what is to be expected but has far fewer revenues and even lower expenditures. Taxes were only $7 million less than predicted by the model, but revenues were approximately $100 million lower and expenditures were almost $250 million lower than expected. New Orleans appears to tax its citizens the same but undertake less public action than other cities.

A reasonable explanation is the proliferation of satellite entities, many of which are off-budget, difficult to monitor, and undertake significant fiscal action in the form of revenues, expenditures, and accumulation of assets. To explore these entities, data were drawn from 2007 and 2008, gathering information from city budget documents, Louisiana Legislative Auditor

TABLE 3. Determinants of Public Finance

Variable	Tax Revenues	Total Revenues	Expenditures
Population	.704 (.055)***	1.78 (.122)***	1.91 (.13)***
Area	−26.00 (138.74)	−69.32 (306.55)	−10.76 (316.28)
Poverty	13,837 (3,883)***	37,363 (8,582)***	37,044 (8,853)***
Wealth	17.92 (3.86)***	41.07 (8.53)***	39.74 (8.81)***
R^2	.62	.68	.69
N	146	146	146
New Orleans predicted	410,968	1,057,775	1,097,012
New Orleans actual	403,252	946,695	852,828
% Difference	−1.8	−10.5	−22.3

Source: Author's statistical analysis.
***Coefficient statistically significant at the 1 percent level.

reports, and accounting documents collected directly from some entities. City budget totals include revenues and outlays by some boards, commissions, and public-benefit corporations, as they are considered component units of city government, and therefore government accounting practices require them to be included in the city's comprehensive financial report. Not all entities are so considered, however, and they vary in the degree to which their accounts appear in the public record. Some provide comprehensive financial reports to the Legislative Auditor's Office, others keep accounts according to government accounting standards but do not report them anywhere, and still others do not keep accounts in any easily comparable fashion.[3]

Even though Tables 4, 5, and 6 cannot be considered complete, they communicate the divergence between reported public accounts and the full details of public money. The columns of Table 4 display the revenues of the city of New Orleans and the official and semi-official entities associated with it.[4] Within revenues, the table starts with the reported on-budget revenues going to the city's General Fund. This can be considered the minimal version of city government, financed mostly with taxes, licenses and permits, charges for services, and fines. The second column includes on-budget revenues from other funds, including funds financed with state, federal, and other transfers, as well as debt, capital projects, and other financing sources. This can be considered the full calculation of on-budget revenue directly controlled by the city. The third column is an initial attempt to calculate the revenues of the boards, commissions, public-benefit corporations, and other entities that are considered component units of the city or state-authorized entities for accounting purposes, and therefore must submit their accounts in a formalized way either to the city or to the State Legislative Auditor. Together, these three columns offer an indication

TABLE 4. Public Revenues (thousands)

	General Fund	Official Funds	Component Units	Noncomponent Public Entities	
				Public Money	Non-Public Money
2007	389,356	395,703	393,876	174,028	1,462,358
2008	401,145	275,539	295,302	185,185	1,244,384

Source: Author calculations from City of New Orleans, *Annual Budget*, various years; City of New Orleans, *Comprehensive Annual Financial Reports*, various years; Component Units and Unincorporated Public Entities, *Comprehensive Annual Financial Reports*, various years; and Unincorporated Units, *Financial Reports*, various years.

of the revenues that can be considered on-budget, reported by the city and its component units. Finally, the last columns of the table include a sum of additional funds gathered in the public interest that are not incorporated into the city accounts because they are undertaken by off-budget quasi-fiscal units whose accounts had to be collected piecemeal where possible. In terms of satellites, some fall into the column of component units, while others are noncomponent units of local government.

As is evident from Table 4, far more public money is mobilized than that which appears in the General Fund or even in relatively easily over-seen forms. In 2007 revenues to the General Fund were $389 million, while another $396 million came through other official funds, and $394 million was raised by component units. Noncomponent units were actually the largest single category of revenues, even as 174 million of their dollars came from the city budget or from taxes the city collected on their behalf.

Table 5 looks at expenditures. Once again, the first column shows just those funds financed locally, while the second adds other official outlays and the third counts funds spent by local government component units. What is striking is that the total amount spent by noncomponent units, the amount that is difficult to monitor and oversee, is more than what is spent through on-budget activities or those reported in the annual financial report.

Finally, Table 6 presents data on net assets of the city. These are the product of prior-year assets inherited, the accumulation of current and capital assets, as well as liabilities. While the budget represents the dynamic flow of city accounts in terms of changes from year to year, net assets indicate the overall financial position in terms of the stock of wealth held by public and satellite entities in the city. Table 6 once again presents what can be considered the on-budget assets of the city, including results of General Fund and capital transactions by the city was well as its component

TABLE 5. Public Expenditures (in thousands)

	General Fund	Official Funds	Component Units	Noncomponent Public Entities
2007	425,915	273,333	337,118	1,354,670
2008	462,473	368,751	350,372	1,490,384

Source: Author calculations from City of New Orleans, *Annual Budget*, various years; City of New Orleans, *Comprehensive Annual Financial Reports*, various years; Component Units and Unincorporated Public Entities, *Comprehensive Annual Financial Reports*, various years; and Unincorporated Units, *Financial Reports*, various years.

TABLE 6. Public Assets (in thousands)

	Primary Government	Pensions	Component Units	Noncomponent Public Entities
2007	71,529	646,671	1,743,098	6,249,975
2008	-11,362	427,342	1,710,687	6,056,949

Source: Author calculations from City of New Orleans, *Annual Budget*, various years and City of New Orleans, *Comprehensive Annual Financial Reports*, various years.

units. The size of the assets held by noncomponent public entities dwarfs those held by more easily monitored on-budget entities and those reported in city financial reports.

The point of this section has been to demonstrate the sheer amount of revenue, expenditure, and wealth that is managed outside the traditional oversight channels of city budget process and state audits. This fragmentation and dispersal of public power weakens the local state in fiscal terms and can be understood as part of the general weakness and ineffectiveness that led some to characterize New Orleans governance as a non-regime before Katrina.

While the local state may have been weakened by the fragmentation of multiple difficult-to-monitor entities, the same fragmentation may strengthen the power of political and economic elites to capture power and direct public policy toward their ends. To explore the way elite interests work through satellites, the next section explores the networks that structure the interaction of satellites.

Networks of Satellite Governance

One way to explore the networks that join satellites is by considering their leadership. In most cases this focuses on members of boards, some of whom are elected, as in the case of the Orleans Parish School Board, while others are appointed, as in the case of charter school operators. In some cases appointments are made by elected officials, such as the mayor or members of the City Council, and in some cases elected officials automatically serve on boards. To explore the relationships among satellites, the current analysis focuses on common membership among the leadership of entities. Common members of their boards seem a reasonable indicator that a common set of interests are being represented and that there is some overlap across satellites. Common members of boards is also a fairly conservative way to measure overlap, which could operate through more distant connections such as a husband serving on one board and a wife on another, or common general counsel or administrative staff. For now, the conservative approach to measuring relationships among satellites seems reasonable.

To map the networks among satellites, data on board membership were used to create an adjacency matrix in which each vertex, or node, in the network is a satellite entity. The links, or edges, between satellites are provided by common board members. The stata network commands (nwcommands) function offers options to plot connections and calculate descriptive statistics based on common board membership. There were 210 satellites and 133 links among them, or to use the terminology of network analysis, there were 210 "nodes" and 133 "edges." Of the 2,151 names of board members, 1,611 were unique.

To make it available to ongoing research and manipulation, the data have been preserved online in several locations and formats. Organized as a civic tool for the people of New Orleans, the database exists in a format that can be sorted according to a number of criteria, including board member, entity, function, and category.[5] Also, the following figures and the adjacency matrices that produced them are preserved at the University of Denver Center for Statistics and Data Visualization.[6] One advantage of storing this information online is that some functions that are unavailable in the static form of a book are available in the more interactive form of a web page. For example, users can view the figures below and scroll closer to focus on specific entities or clusters that may not be as visible from the birds's-eye presented on the pages of a book, including such details as the names of different nodes. In the following discussion, the names of individual nodes will be discussed, and readers can view their relationship to other entities online.

When analyzing a network, among the most interesting descriptive statistics are measures of centrality, and the simplest is degree centralization.[7] Degree centralization measures the number of links possessed by each node, in which the ties are board members and vertices are organizations, and the degree centralization is a standardized sum of the centrality indices of each vertex.[8] Network clustering measures the degree to which vertices cluster together as an average of the clustering coefficient of each vertex (Corten 2011).[9] Both degree centrality and clustering vary from zero to one, with higher scores indicating a more tightly linked and interrelated network. An additional criterion for describing networks is the potential for some nodes to serve "bonding" and "bridging" functions. More central nodes, with many links, can be said to "bond" multiple entities. Similarly, when an entity links one cluster of entities to another, it can be said to "bridge" them. In Figures 5–9, a bridging node will be indicated by a dark circle with a light arrow inside, and a bonding node will appear as a light circle with a dark arrow inside.

An initial plot of the satellites (Figure 4) looks like the jumble one would expect in attempting to map the layers of entities built up over time. Nodes have been coded according to the historical and functional categories outlined in the previous chapter. For the purpose of clarifying contemporary political and developmental dynamics, the categories coded include African American incorporating (star), ring-fencing (square), privatizing (diamond), and dual development (circle) entities. Bonding nodes tend to be

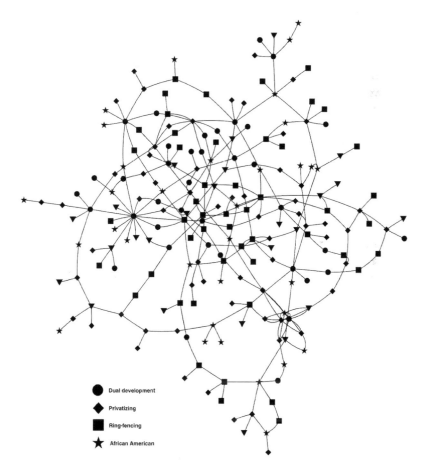

FIGURE 4. Network of satellite entities. Source: Author compilation from www.nolasatellitegovernment/tulane.edu.

more centrally located in the figure and have higher measures of centralization. Nodes that share few edges indicate entities that share few board
members with any other entity, and they tend to be located toward the
outer limits of the figure.[10] Descriptive statistics for the overall network
indicate an average clustering coefficient of .064 and degree centralization
of .24. These fairly low measures of clustering and centralization suggest
that there may be more structure organizing the subnetworks than the
entire universe of satellites.

While the jumble of nodes and edges is difficult to read when presented
in its entirety, a few areas of the figure are suggestive. For example, toward
the center left of the figure, a circle-marked node shares edges with twelve
other nodes. As it happens, the circle-marked node is the New Orleans
Multicultural Tourism Network, and among the nodes with which it shares
board members are the Vieux Carre Commission and the East New Orleans
Neighborhood Advisory Commission. Just below and to the right of that
cluster is a cluster of entities bonded by the square-marked French Quarter–
Marigny Historic Area Management District. This entity shares edges with
six other entities, including the Biosciences District and the New Orleans
Public Library Foundation. Interestingly, perhaps, the entity that serves as
the bridge between the two clusters bonded by the Multicultural Tourism
Network and the French Quarter–Marigny Historic Area Management District is the Louisiana Biomedical Research and Development Park Commission, another circle-marked entity.

To explore the degree to which the categories of entities meaningfully
structure the network, a separate analysis was conducted on adjacency
matrices including only satellites in the same category. To begin, African
American incorporating entities were selected, including federally motivated welfare state entities, such as Total Community Action, and entities
that tend to incorporate members of the African American professional
and political elite, such as judicial bodies. Also included were entities traditionally important to incorporate ethnic populations because they control
large numbers of employees and relationships with small and medium-size
contractors, such as the Sewerage and Water Board. In Figure 5 these entities were marked by stars, and a total of thirty-four entities were coded
as African American incorporating. They had a degree centrality measure
of .38, higher than the overall network. In fact, a visual plot of the African
American incorporating entities suggests that the network is itself divided
into subnetworks, with one grouping in the center including mostly the
elected boards, such as judges, sheriff, and school board, where the electoral functions of African American political machines could still operate.
While vote-mobilization machines may no longer dominate tightly fought

citywide elections to offices such as mayor, offices such as judges and school board are often held in off-election years or months, attracting lower rates of participation in which the limited remaining mobilization capacity of African American machines may still be relevant.

The other network loosely holds together the rest of the African American incorporating entities. The most interesting observation to make about this subnetwork is the role played by certain bonding entities that would

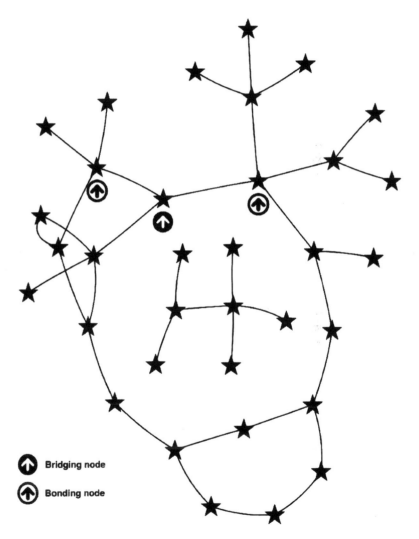

FIGURE 5. African American incorporating entities. Source: Author compilation from www.nolasatellitegovernment/tulane.edu.

appear to cluster several others. For example, the Orleans Parish Civil District Court Judges, the Workforce Investment Board, the New Orleans Council on Aging, and the New Orleans Redevelopment Authority share edges with four other entities. Between the clusters bonded by these entities, other nodes act as bridges. For example, the Human Relations Advisory Committee serves as a bridge between the Orleans Parish Civil District Court Judges and the New Orleans Redevelopment Authority, and both of these clusters are bridged to the New Orleans Council on Aging by Total Community Action.

Once the African American incorporating entities are extracted, it is also possible to explore each of the other categories, starting with ring-fencing entities. Entities such as security districts and other geographically

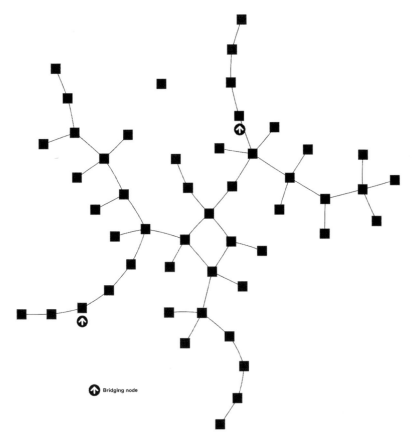

FIGURE 6. Ring-fencing entities. Source: Author compilation from www.nolasatellitegovernment/tulane.edu.

delimited entities were considered ring-fencing for their function of creating club goods for those who live within their jurisdiction without offering the same public goods to the rest of the city. In total there are fifty-three entities in this category displayed in Figure 6, with the largest number accounted for by security districts and neighborhood development districts. The ring-fencing satellites appear structured in three directions, with slightly more overlap toward the left and two more strings moving up to the right and straight down. Overall, the degree centrality of this group is .23, lower than the figures above, and consistent with the notion that these are geographically circumscribed entities in which members are less likely to overlap. There are fewer bonding entities that link to many others, though a few entities share edges with four others (such as the Hurstville Security and Neighborhood Improvement District, New Orleans City Park Improvement Association, Garden District Security District, and Friends of Lafitte Corridor). What is more striking about this figure is the apparently large number of bridging nodes, indicated by the long strings of entities that would appear to bridge from one to the next to the next, as in the string of four nodes extending upward indicated by the dark circle and light arrow on the upper right or the string of five nodes extending down and to the left indicated by the other dark circle and light arrow.

The next category of interest was entities with privatizing functions, those that set aside public resources for private accumulation, such as charter schools. In total there are sixty-four entities in the category, displayed in Figure 7. The figure has a degree centralization of .26, slightly higher than the ring-fencing category but lower than the overall network. The privatizing entities show their own internal structure, with a much greater degree of concentration at the center indicated by the thick web of overlapping connections among entities. The cluster of entities toward the center shows shared edges among multiple nodes, suggesting a large number of bonding entities. A few of the entities are farther away from the concentration in the center, such as certain charter schools like the James M. Singleton Charter School in the bottom left quadrant, and indicated as a bonding node by a light circle and dark arrow. This school is associated with the former councilman James Singleton and the Central City YMCA, perhaps suggesting it ought to have been included in the African American incorporating entities.

Other entities, such as the Industrial Development Board and the Dock Board, appear toward the lower right quadrant of the figure and are less connected to the central concentration. One implication is that a contemporary association with privatization has not overwhelmed its original functions, as the Dock Board was initiated during the machine politics Old

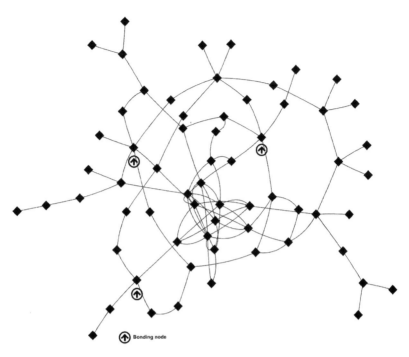

Bonding node

FIGURE 7. Privatizing entities. Source: Author compilation from
www.nolasatellitegovernment/tulane.edu.

Regular period and the Industrial Development Board during the developmental period of the Crescent City Democrats.

Dual development entities were those that operated in the tourism and services sector, such as the New Orleans Tourism Marketing Corporation. In total, the category includes thirty-four satellites, and its network appears in Figure 8. Indicated by the light circle and dark arrow, a central grouping is bonded by the New Orleans Museum of Art, which shares edges with eleven other entities. Among the entities bonded with the Museum of Art, a few also appear to bridge to other clusters, such as the New Orleans Business Alliance, bridging to the Louisiana Stadium and Exposition District and New Orleans Aviation Board. Similarly, the New Orleans Medical Complex bridges to a cluster bonded by the Arts Council of New Orleans and another bonded by the Greater New Orleans Sports Foundation Executive Council, toward the lower right. The New Orleans Chamber of Commerce bonds four entities toward the upper right quadrant, including the Biosciences District of New Orleans and the Algiers Economic Development Foundation. Among the entities located farther from the center are satellites such as the Public Belt Railroad, created during the early-twentieth-century Old Regular regime, and the Southeast Regional Airport, created during the post–World War II developmental regime, suggesting that they may preserve some of their original connection with the periods in which they were initiated. Overall, the category has a degree centralization of .75, the highest of any category, suggesting that this category has the most linkages among its boards.

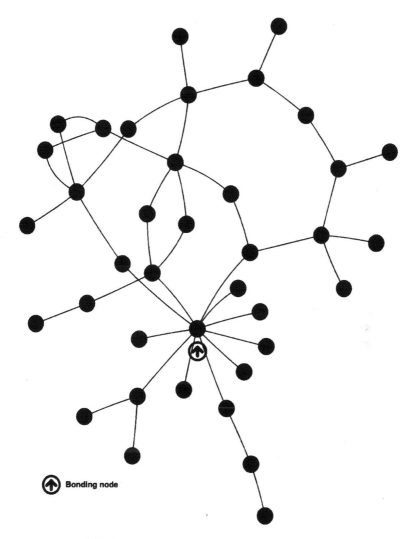

FIGURE 8. Dual development entities. Source: Author compilation from www.nolasatellitegovernment/tulane.edu.

Finally, it is worthwhile to view together the subsets of entities categorized as dual development, privatizing, and ring-fencing. The total number of satellites included in this subset was 153, and they have a degree
centralization of .31, slightly higher than the degree centralization of the
overall network and slightly lower than the African American incorporating satellites. Clustering is slightly higher than the overall measure, at
.092. One pattern that appears to operate is a concentration of entities to
the middle-left of Figure 9, bonded by the square symbol, which is the
ring-fencing entity Fairgrounds Citizens Advisory Committee, sharing edges
with thirteen other entities. Somewhat below, another ring-fencing entity
with a square symbol is the Piazza D'Italia Development Corporation,
bonding eight other entities. Between the two squares, two entities appear

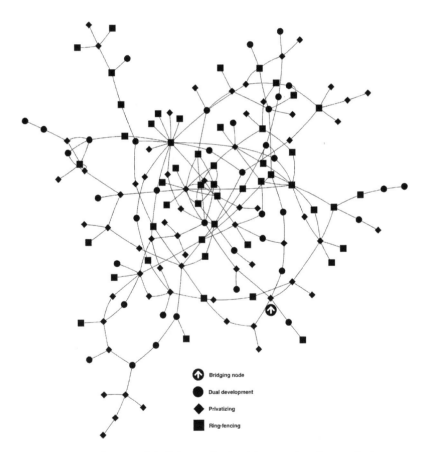

FIGURE 9. Ring-fencing, globalizing, and privatizing together. Source: Author
compilation from www.nolasatellitegovernment/tulane.edu.

to bridge the clusters, a diamond-marked privatizing entity, Board of Liquidation of City Debt, and a circle-marked dual development entity, New Orleans Medical Complex. This sequence, square-circle-diamond, is interesting to consider. To measure this sequencing pattern, the concept of transitivity is scored from zero to one, as in the case of clustering and degree centralization. The ring-fencing, privatizing, and dual development entities score a transitivity index of .57, suggesting a fairly high rate of connection from one entity to the next. One way to interpret this pattern is that ring-fencing entities begin with a base in a geographic area and then serve to link privatizing entities that make public assets available for private accumulation. Further links to dual development entities work to promote development consistent with the tourism and services dual development strategy. To take one example, in the bottom right a dark circle with a light arrow indicates the Audubon Area Security District (ring-fencing), which bonds further to the Audubon Nature Institute Foundation (privatizing) and the New Orleans Recreational Development Foundation (dual development). Together, these entities can be understood to share members of their boards who work in coordination to promote tourist development by turning public assets over to private accumulation while providing club goods to members.

Popular Response

At the current moment, the fragmented character of satellite government in New Orleans privileges globally oriented elites who coordinate ring-fencing, privatizing, and dual development entities for the purpose of promoting an exclusionary tourism and services development model. The legacy of prior regimes also leaves room for an African American professional and political class to retain a degree of access to public power. Working classes and marginalized communities of racial and ethnic minorities recognize that they too must build power to contest state authority. In the fragmented structure of New Orleans authority, this has meant forming their own satellite entities, as emerged in confrontations over the expansion of the New Orleans airport.

The New Orleans airport is governed by the City of New Orleans and the New Orleans Aviation Board, and it announced a major expansion to include investments of approximately $826 million between 2014 and 2018, employing more than twelve thousand people in construction. In light of the significant resources and impact and the lack of transparency of the bidding and selection process, community members took steps to place the selection process under greater scrutiny and impose community-based criteria into the process, such as "fair employment" with adequate wages and a dispute resolution mechanism, and "full employment" with targeted community hiring.[11]

The community effort was spearheaded by Stand with Dignity, an organization of public-housing residents and working people, mostly African Americans (Community Evaluation Commission 2014a).[12] They initiated their efforts when the Aviation Board initial review awarded the contract to a bidder associated with a subcontractor with a record of racism in their work rebuilding public housing. "What happened was that one of the bidders had included a contractor that is known to be racist. We had experience with them on the C. J. Peete project. Back then, they called themselves the Sturdy Group, and they had a racist supervisor. He told an African American woman helper on a site, 'If that N-word B-word wants water, I'll spit in her mouth'" (Interview, August 2014). After this and other irregularities appeared, the bid process had to be redone, opening an opportunity for community input through the creation of an unofficial Community Evaluation Commission (CEC).[13] While the bidders declined to submit their bids directly to the CEC, one bidder wrote a letter acknowledging the community effort, the activities of the community mobilization attracted ongoing press attention, there were changes in the composition and commitments of the bidders, and the bidder that had originally won the contract was replaced.

The CEC included workers, community organizers, pastors, and former public officials. They included a time line for bids to be submitted and evaluated in parallel with the cycle of the Aviation Board, and scored the bids according to community criteria. CEC activities pressured the Aviation Board to take their observations into account, both in selecting a contractor and in the terms of the agreement with the winning bidder.

Commissioner Janell Perry noted the lack of accountability in traditional satellite entities with limited oversight: "They go back on those agreements, say they will do one thing and then do another. So, in the Aviation Board, we set up a parallel process. We were excluded from the Aviation Board, so we set up our own system to evaluate bids." Commission co-chair and Stand with Dignity member Roy Brumfield added: "We decided we could do the same thing as the aviation board, but our RFP [Request for Proposals] includes community concerns. . . . Two bidders enter a competition, one of them wins, but the community always loses. We need the chance to make our own decisions" (Interview, August 2014). Said Commissioner Ernest Jones, "When public money is being spent, it should benefit the public. This is going to be an historic, long process" (Community Evaluation Commission 2014b, 73).

Commissioner Roy Brumfield noted the need for community representativeness in entities with powers like the Aviation Board: "Without people like us it will be impossible for the city to solve the problems faced by people like us." Former councilman and Community Evaluation Commission co-chair Oliver Thomas observed the need for working-class voice: "This community is making history today. We're at the front end of a movement in America. Working class families are going to have to be noticed." "I'm here for the 52% of black men in New Orleans who are unemployed," said Commissioner Reginald Junior (Community Evaluation Commission, 2014b, 73–74).[14]

Among the priorities articulated by the CEC, training for local workers and public-housing residents to enter decent work and move onto long-term careers figured highly.[15] They based this priority on their experience with public-housing redevelopment, where many residents of public housing were excluded from the construction jobs to rebuild their homes. Said Oliver Thomas, "Our first struggle was with HANO to make sure that as they rebuilt public housing they would do it by hiring locally and paying a living wage. We learned that we could put pressure on and get results. Now, as we focus on the airport, we know that we are having an impact. They are paying attention to us. They originally promised $100,000 for training local workers, but now they are promising $2 million" (Interview, August 2014).

Where they were successful, the members of the CEC attributed their success to the bridges built across workplace and community. As Oliver Thomas observed, "What brings me to this commission is the chance to stand with working people. . . . Through this process we have a chance to build a working class, a working class that gets decent work. For that to happen though, we have to be intentional. That means we have to understand the relationship between violent crime in our neighborhoods, African American women who can only work service jobs, and low money for our workers. There is public money out there to build livable wages for a working class, and it is time for us to take control. . . . It's time for politics to be about working people demanding respect in an era of disaster capitalism" (Interview, August 2014).

Other commissioners also recognized the role of changing workplace social relations in order to change communities. "Getting a good union job changed my life. Every time I talk to young people doing the bad things I used to do, they always say they would do differently if they could get a good job," said Commissioner Chased Smith (Community Evaluation Commission 2014b, 74).

Still, even in their moments of success, the limits to workplace and community struggle within satellite frameworks was evident. In the context of difficult-to-monitor and poorly accountable entities, community efforts were frequently rebuffed by actors within the executive or nonprofits eager to assist in the service and tourism dual development model. Stand with Dignity organizer Colette Tippy observed: "When we announced who were the commissioners, we saw where people stood. Barbara Major (of Citizens United for Economic Equity) dropped out, so did the Tulane University Cowen Institute and Catholic Charities. We learned the difference between those who have courage and those who stand on the wrong side of history." Another Stand with Dignity organizer, Toya Lewis, noted: "We met with Amy Quirk, the city economic advisor, and she said she would never turn down a business that wanted to invest. . . . She said she would accept all business and not put any limits on them. But, it's impossible to say there will be benefit for the community without having community involvement. . . . If they want to stop us, now we just tell them, give us what we want. Otherwise, we will arm ourselves for struggle by organizing the community, the people who are most affected. . . . The day will come when the community is involved and can't be ignored" (Interview, August 2014).

Even Oliver Thomas had been an inconsistent champion of working-class and popular demands. As a member of City Council and board member of the Downtown Development District, he had articulated African American elite desires for incorporation in growth strategies, voting to replace the St. Thomas public-housing complex, failing to champion efforts to raise the city minimum wage, and attacking poor residents of public housing after Katrina: "We don't need soap opera watchers now. We're going to target the people who are going to work" (Oliver Thomas quoted in Reed 2016, 15). His City Council term was ended with a conviction for corruption in 2007, and perhaps he viewed joining the CEC as a chance at redemption. Still, his ambiguous positioning over time demonstrates the difficulty of finding members of the African American political elite open to working-class and popular-sector priorities.

This chapter continues the analysis from the previous chapter to argue that there is an explanation for and an outcome of the fragmented character of New Orleans government. To begin, fragmentation weakens state capacity, as it directs resources through a bevy of boards and commissions. It also complicates democratic oversight, as many entities consist of appointed and difficult-to-monitor boards.

In addition, satellites are organized according to two logics, perhaps competing. The first logic is that of African American incorporating, in which boards appear linked in support of a common cause of incorporating

African American professionals and preserving some of the power of African American political elites. The second logic is a combination of ring-fencing, privatizing, and dual development functions. Tourism and services elites appear to ally with geographically circumscribed actors to capture public power for private accumulation and deliver club goods to members.

In response, working classes and popular sectors attempt to build alternative models of governance. They work across workplaces and communities to advance an alternative set of objectives within public policy. In place of dual development, working classes and popular sectors demand development strategies that privilege decent livelihoods and dignity for marginalized groups. While such resistance has achieved important victories, as in the case of the airport bid, there are important limitations. Efforts to ally with actors in the local state and in the corporate sector were rebuffed once the conflict with the dual development agenda became clear. In other cases, establishment actors were willing to collaborate, but their ambiguous history of sometimes opposing and sometimes supporting popular struggle made them extremely unreliable allies.

The politics of competing development paradigms are evident both in control of political office and in the reorganization of key economic activities. With their base in difficult-to-monitor satellite government entities, globally oriented elites interacted closely with elected political leaders to shape the outcomes of elections and executive power. With control of local political offices came power over development policy, which they used to reorganize key economic sectors. The next chapter focuses on the political dynamics of winning elections and governing, while subsequent chapters explore original data on construction, tourism and services, and manufacturing.

CHAPTER FOUR

The Post-Katrina Political Transition

This book emphasizes the politics of elite emergence since Hurricane Katrina. That emergence has solidified the power of globally oriented elites and their political representatives, and they have been forced to adapt their dual development project only moderately to placate rivals. The main condition for rival access has been acceptance of the dual development project, a condition that both elite and popular actors have all too often accepted. In exchange, the main accommodation has been to soften the worst excesses of ascriptive segmentation, introducing some diversity into local elite factions able to enjoy the fruits of a dual development project. Yet even in its best moments, such accommodation has extended minimal benefits to working classes or popular sectors.

To trace the politics of globally oriented elite emergence, the chapter avoids traditional horse-race-style descriptions of the advance or retreat of one individual or faction. Instead, the chapter identifies moments and episodes of confrontation as useful examples of shifting political and institutional balances among competing economic, social, and political projects. The first section highlights elections, which are particularly useful moments to negotiate and clarify political leadership and definition of development priorities. The second section includes institutional and organizational changes to satellite institutions, attempting to lock in rising elite preferences, burnish the city's global orientation, and turn public resources over to the private sector. The final section describes disputes over a particular policy issue as a useful example of the dynamics of competition and accommodation among rival political elite factions as well as some of the space opened to working classes and popular sectors in the interstices of elite conflict. While moments of division among elites offer openings to insert alternative preferences into politics, working classes and popular sectors have yet to articulate a coherent political project capable of competing with the dual development project advanced by globally oriented elites.

Transition in Electoral Politics

The first sign that emerging elites would be drawn directly into politics came shortly after Hurricane Katrina when the 2006 election returned Mayor Ray Nagin to power. As a former Republican and local business leader, Nagin had been supported by a majority of white residents in the 2002 election. He won in 2006 with a majority of the black vote and vote from low-income neighborhoods. The shifting dimensions of support suggested a new set of cleavages orienting local politics.

A number of factors made the result surprising. Turnout was low, more than 10 percent less than the previous election, and many people traced the low turnout to the many people displaced from the city and unable to return, even with a significant effort to allow people to vote absentee from distant locations. Most of those displaced were low income and African American. While African Americans were still a majority, their share of the electorate fell from 63 percent in 2002 to 57 percent in 2006. Affluent white neighborhoods such as the French Quarter and Garden District showed greater turnout than in 2002, and turnout fell significantly in poor African American neighborhoods. For example, it fell almost 40 percent in the Lower Ninth Ward (Logan 2006b, 6).

Incompetence in his first term and disastrous ineffectiveness during the hurricane had lost Nagin the support of his original base among white elites, who signaled their support for other candidates. Nagin, however, outmaneuvered them all, announcing in a Martin Luther King Jr. Day speech, "This city will be chocolate at the end of the day." The comment repelled his 2002 base—"uptown saw 'chocolate city' as the end of Nagin" (Rivlin 2015, 248)—and indicated the potential for him to exploit the cleavage between white elites and a majority of "black and low to middle income residents" (Logan 2006b, 2).

Having abandoned Nagin, the globally oriented elite split. Some backed Mitch Landrieu, who received 29 percent of the vote to Nagin's 38 percent. As lieutenant governor Landrieu had advocated state tourism efforts, so he could lay some claim to lead the dual development project; however, as son of integrationist mayor Moon Landrieu and part of the Democratic machine that had elected his sister Mary Landrieu as U.S. senator, globally oriented elites remained unconvinced by his leadership. At least some of them found a more explicit representative of their project in Republican

Ron Forman, director of the Audubon Institute and one of the principal architects of the tourism and services agenda in the city. Candidate spending indicates a fairly even split in financial support, with Forman spending almost $2.2 million and Landrieu almost $1.9 million. Both candidates far outspent Nagin, and Forman quickly threw his support to Landrieu in the May 20 runoff with Nagin (Brox 2009, 8). Still, the white elite remained fragmented, with the fourth-place finisher, Republican Robert Courhig, supporting Nagin.

What pushed Nagin over the edge was a united front from the African American and poor majority. According to Diarra Osei Robertson, chair of the Department of History and Government at Bowie State University, "The political context of Katrina created a nonphysical conflictual environment between blacks and whites over the future of New Orleans, and in such an environment racial symbolism can be very powerful. Nagin deserves credit for skillfully manipulating the context, but the true victors (at least symbolically) were the black voters of New Orleans" (2008, 49). Nagin won with 52 percent of the vote to Landrieu's 48 percent, and surveys indicated that support for Nagin became "increasingly racially polarized throughout the campaign" as the stakes of the election became more clear (Lay 2009, 656).

While the split in white elites opened an opportunity, Nagin was a poor vehicle to maintain a mobilized African American majority. Most recognized that he had performed indecisively during the hurricane; he was a weak representative for African American interests and an even worse representative of poor and working-class New Orleanians. Nagin could not sustain their support, and by 2007 white politicians had taken a majority of the City Council, with the deciding election won handily by Jacqueline B. Clarkson "for an at-large Council seat decided largely along racial lines," in a vote with less than half the level of turnout of May 2006 (Nossiter 2007).[1] Clarkson joined the other white at-large council member, Arnie Fielkow, who won a November 2006 election after serving as attorney for the New Orleans Saints football team, CEO of local electricity company Entergy, and advocate for tourism, services, and charter schools. White candidates won state legislative seats long held by African Americans, and a white candidate won the election for state court judge, a seat traditionally held by African Americans. In 2008, amid a corruption scandal, Republican Anh Cao displaced African American William Jefferson for the U.S. Congress seat representing New Orleans.

Some took this series of events to signal a marked political realignment in which cleavages between white and black residents had disappeared. A statement issued by Bill Clinton pollster James Carville and conducted by Tulane University in 2009 argued that "there is much more that unites New Orleans voters than divides them, and they are desperate to move forward together" (Carville 2009, 1). The statement was followed by survey results showing minimal differences between black and white voters on the major issues facing the city—crime, education, corruption, and economic growth.

Backed by this cross-racial coalition, Mitch Landrieu won the 2010 election handily. A 2010 University of New Orleans survey of quality of life showed high levels of support across groups, with 78 percent of whites and 72 percent of African Americans approving of winning candidate Mitch Landrieu (Sims 2010, 4). After winning the 2010 elections in a landslide, Landrieu was returned to office in 2014 by a similar margin, winning 66 percent in 2010 and 64 percent in 2014. He attempted to paint the victories as an indicator of consensus across black and white populations in favor of his reforms: "The results tonight confirm what we hoped was true four years ago, that people of this great city are ready to move forward" (C. Robertson 2014).

Sharper observers noted that something else was afoot. "Advances made by African American elected officials and the African American political structure over the last 30 years . . . right now are in neutral or being lost. . . . Symbolically what it shows is that we have a realignment politically" (Joyner 2007). A growing racial gap appeared in approval for the City Council, at 71 percent of whites and 49 percent of African Americans (Sims 2010, 5). By 2012, approval of the mayor had also started to diverge between whites and African Americans, with 84 percent of whites approving of Landrieu, compared to only 58 percent of African Americans. Still, even to those worried about the decline of traditional African American political elites, the terms of realignment remained obscured.

Read closely, however, the post-2010 environment begins to reveal signs of a different kind of realignment. What defines the post-Katrina environment is a deepening cleavage between those benefiting from the dual development model and those left behind.[2] Even as Landrieu remained popular overall, working-class and popular-sector opposition began to materialize. One 2010 mayoral candidate, housing advocate James Perry, attempted to mobilize this division. In addressing the tourism economy, he said, "New Orleans has a system that is almost designed to be oppressive. If we paid people a living wage, then we could really transform our city" (Flaherty 2010a).[3]

Intersecting class and race distinctions emerged further in public-opinion data. "The decline in approval for the mayor appears to be due to two factors; jobs and crime. . . . Four years ago, 32 percent of African Americans felt positive about employment opportunities. Today, only 10 percent feel that way," and positive attitudes about jobs coming to the parish fell among African Americans from 29 percent to 18 percent (Chervenak and Mihoc 2012, 12). Table 7 displays some of the data. For poorer residents, 25.8 percent of those with incomes below $10,000 disapproved or strongly disapproved of the mayor, as did 18.6 percent of those with incomes up to $25,000 and 21.2 percent of those with incomes up to $40,000. Among respondents with incomes over $100,000, disapproval sat at only 12.6 percent. For the City Council, the same three low-income categories showed 31.6, 33.7, and 35.1 percent disapproval, versus a disapproval rating among wealthy respondents of only 15.0 percent. In short, disapproval was twice as high among poor residents as it was among rich residents.[4] Rather than an undifferentiated-white and undifferentiated-black cleavage, the emergence of globally oriented elites draws attention to intragroup distinctions based on class in which elite factions among African Americans and elite factions among whites increasingly shared the dual development project. Landrieu's support from and collaboration with perennial Republican mayoral candidate and Audubon director Ron Foreman only confirmed the alignment of elite interests.

The articulation of a dual development political base was evident as far back as 2006, as shown in the bottom three rows of Table 7. Landrieu polled higher in rich white neighborhoods than poor ones, 22.9 percent versus 11.4 percent. He also polled relatively better than Nagin in rich white neighborhoods, with a 13.9 percent advantage, versus a 5.2 percent advantage in poor white neighborhoods. Further, Landrieu almost tied Nagin in rich black neighborhoods, losing by only 3.5 percent, while losing by much larger margins, 14.6 percent, in poor black neighborhoods (Logan 2006b, 21).

A further indication of interracial consensus around the dual development program was the result of the 2014 elections, when the City Council returned to an African American majority. Rather than suggesting a resurgence of traditional black political power, the elections signaled the successful incorporation and distribution of some benefits to middle- and upper-class African Americans. Former councilman Oliver Thomas observed that "when companies across the nation see that many African Americans on the Council, they are then forced to do business with us. They are forced to hire attorneys and lobbyists and people who look and think like us to advance their issues" (Harrison 2014).

Critics note that such symbolic inclusion absorbs African American elites willing to acquiesce and participate in a dual development project but that this weakens working-class and popular-sector alternatives. "Post-Katrina

TABLE 7. Intersecting Race and Class Cleavages over Dual Development (%)

2012 Approval	<$10K	$10–25K	$26–40K	$41–60K	$61–80K	$81–100K	>$100K
				Mitch Landrieu			
Strongly Approve/Approve	67.3	74.3	70.3	61.1	76.3	71.4	79.7
Disapprove/Strongly Disapprove	25.8	18.6	21.2	31.2	20.9	28.6	12.6
				City Council			
Strongly Approve/Approve	49.1	53.0	50.0	46.8	65.3	62.8	68.8
Disapprove/Strongly Disapprove	31.6	33.7	35.1	33.8	39.5	22.8	15.0

2006 Neighborhood Vote	White < $20K	White > $60K	Black < $20K	Black >$60K
Nagin	6.2	9.0	29.8	9.6
Landrieu	11.4	22.9	15.2	6.1
Landrieu Margin by Race/Class	5.2	13.9	-14.6	-3.5

Source: Adapted by the author from http://www.uno.edu/cola/political-science/documents/2013-Job-Approval-Ratings-for-Mayor-Landrieu-and-Orleans-City-Council.pdf: 2, and Logan (2006, 21).

New Orleans thus illustrates strikingly how what we think of as black politics is embedded in a political common sense that is not merely compatible with urban neoliberalism but is a dynamic element in its institutional and organizational, as well as ideological, reproduction" (Reed 2016, 10). Even Oliver Thomas acknowledged that political diversification targeting elites held only symbolic benefits for working-class or popular sectors, noting that "the people on the Council don't identify with the people, but a Black majority [on City Council] presents the opportunity for the people to identify with them" (Harrison 2014).

Electoral trajectories after Katrina suggest a new cleavage between those who benefit from dual development and those who do not, with globally oriented elites and their representatives fairly solidly in control. Room opened for African American elites, as indicated by their majority on the City Council, but their role is limited to supporting, legitimating, and participating in the dual development project. In the absence of a clear political vehicle for opposition rooted in working classes and popular sectors, those left behind gain symbolic representation but have not mounted an independent political program or secured many benefits. James Perry was prescient in his observation on the intersection of race and class within the politics of dual development: "There are folks who are really focused on the interests of the wealthy and upper-income African American community, and then there are folks like me who are focused on low-income communities and focused on really answering the question of why people are poor and transforming our community" (Flaherty 2010a).

Transition in Satellite Entities

Electoral trajectories are not the only indicator of the political transition tracing the rise of globally oriented elites, especially in a city characterized by an elaborate network of satellite entities. This section describes the consolidation of a dual development project in the entities parallel to formal electoral power described above. The poorly monitored and less accountable satellite entities described in chapter 3 interact closely with organized interest groups, especially those drawing particularly from globally oriented elites.

To advance the dual development agenda, elites pursued a selective reduction and extension of satellite government architecture. With respect to extension, it was necessary to create a host of civic and official entities to coordinate accumulation through sectors privileged by global integration. With respect to reduction, it was important to eliminate entities that besmirched the pro-business environment or provided resources and patronage to elite factions outside the much narrower coalition of globally oriented elites.

Some of the entities set up by the city and tourism and other globally oriented interests long predated Katrina.[5] In the 1980s, the heads of fifty New Orleans businesses established the Business Council of New Orleans (BCNO; now known as the Business Council of New Orleans and the River Region), seeking to address corporate tax issues they believed to affect the business climate and otherwise influence public policy on everything from schools to housing to development. Among the entities they established were also Metrovision, Greater New Orleans Inc., and the Committee for a Better New Orleans. They worked with a single-minded focus on transforming the economy of the city toward services, tourism, and entertainment, backing 1990s efforts including the state's only land-based casino and $140 million of public money for sports facilities, including a basketball arena next to the Superdome (they did not secure a basketball team to fill it until 2001), a minor league baseball stadium, and a training facility for the Saints professional football team. Despite this marshaling of resources and the slow accretion of private and public entities, "the consensus, even among people who belonged to these organizations, was that New Orleans's economic development profile lagged far behind that of the rest of the country. Economic development was haphazard and uncoordinated, and when it did occur, it proceeded in stops and starts" (P. Burns and Thomas 2015, 30).

After Katrina, the business community coalesced more forcefully and sought to influence a wider variety of public-policy issues through satellite entities. Their first targets were some of the sources of patronage that supported previously dominant black urban regimes. To advance their attack, globally oriented elites created a new organization, Citizens for 1 Greater New Orleans, and allied with like-minded organizations that favored a new development agenda and governing coalition.[6] Among the sources of patronage they sought to consolidate and regulate were the levee boards (reduced from ten to two), property tax assessors (reduced from seven to one), city courts (reduced from three to one), clerks and sheriffs (eliminated half). They also pushed to implement and strengthen an Office of the Inspector General, enacted in the 1995 revision to the city's home rule charter but yet to be implemented.

To change the state constitution, many of these changes required action from the governor and the legislature as well as majority support from voters. Consolidation of the levee boards received overwhelming support, though the vote to reduce the number of assessors began to expose differences in support from African American as opposed to white voters. When the issue of consolidating the courts made its way to the legislature, African American legislators forced a delay until 2014 (P. Burns and Thomas 2015, 30–38).

Other dual development efforts aimed to build up the architecture of entities that could facilitate accumulation by globally oriented elites. Many of the new entities were privatizing, making public assets available for accumulation, and among the most emblematic was the creation of the New Orleans Recreational District (NORD). Enacted in 2010 through a publicly approved referendum, the NORD Commission followed the model of the Audubon Commission, channeling public funds from the general budget and receiving its own dedicated tax millage. The dedicated 1.5 mills were estimated to produce $4.4 million in 2015, essentially doubling the recreational budget of the city (Bureau of Government Research 2015, 21).

Operating alongside the NORD Commission but outside the regulations governing government entities, the city created the NORD Foundation, a 501(c)(3) nonprofit organization. As a nonprofit, it could receive tax-deductible contributions from the local corporate sector, and donors were offered the power to "restrict their gift to a specific playground or program, or give funds to support NORDC's priority needs, such as athletic equipment and outfitting new recreation centers."[7] The board of the NORD Foundation includes one ex officio chair from the NORD Commission; the rest are drawn from corporate leaders from sectors such as finance, energy, construction, tourism, and oil and gas.

To privilege the interests of such corporate leaders in broader development strategy, globally oriented elites and their political allies also sought to extend the network of satellites with explicit coordination functions. While Nagin had initially supported a "public-private partnership to recruit and retain businesses" in his second term, he suspended the creation of the organization, which "would have to await new mayoral leadership" (P. Burns and Thomas 2015, 50). In August 2010, shortly after taking office, Mayor Landrieu announced the creation of the New Orleans Business Alliance (NOBA), "to take most of the economic development function away from the city," as explained by NOBA vice chairperson and charter school advocate Leslie Jacobs. The NOBA board included the "CEOs or owners of the New Orleans Saints, Royal Engineers, Whitney Bank, Bayou Equity Mortgage, and Entergy New Orleans," and the city dedicated $1.5 million from its general fund. Corporate donations added another $500,000 (Gotham and Greenberg 2014, 198).

While the African American political establishment bristled at first at the elimination of key sources of patronage, they quickly found themselves invited into positions of power in newly created satellites. As Adolf Reed

Jr. noted, "The histrionics that captivated so much of the black commen-
tariat when Mitch Landrieu was elected mayor of New Orleans in 2010 . . .
were naïve; those who fretted about loss of 'black political power' misun-
derstood the extent to which the governing classes in those cities that have
had black-led governments are by now integrated racially. . . . The notion
that a deep racial divide separates black and white governing elites rests
on a presumption that explicitly racial subordination remains the dominant ideological framework for the maintenance of class power. It does
not" (Reed 2016, 15–16). In a deepened architecture of satellites to manage the dual development project, white and African American elites found
an institutional accommodation by bringing African American elites into
the boards of entities meant to coordinate dual development, just as they
regained electoral relevance by accommodating dual development with
their African American majority on the City Council..

After Katrina, globally oriented elites worked to rearrange the institutions of satellite governance to more effectively implement their dual
development program. In a number of cases this involved consolidating,
eliminating, and regulating satellites that created an impression of inefficiency or otherwise besmirched the perception of New Orleans's business
environment. In other cases, reform involved reorganizing satellites or creating new ones to channel the assets and power of the local state into the
hands of local private actors operating in strategic sectors like tourism, construction, and services. The BCNO expressed its general satisfaction with
the alignment of local political elites around a dual development agenda:
"The Mayor and the City Council have been appropriately supportive of
key economic engines, including tourism, the hospitality industry, and the
biomedical corridor, though we urge work toward policies that drive economic development in destination healthcare and research commercializa-
tion" (P. Burns and Thomas 2015, 53).

Intra-elite Conflict, Accommodation, and Opportunities for Resistance

Even as steady accretion of the elite political project can be detected within
electoral and satellite institutions, there were ongoing conflicts among rival
factions. Such moments of friction within the globally oriented elite coalition provide two insights. First, elite factional conflict suggests that rival
factions are still working out how and under what conditions they will
accommodate themselves within the dual development project. The minimum requirement is that they accept the dual development strategy, but
there is great room for rival factions to jockey for control of resources
and authority within that strategy. A second insight is that moments of

intra-elite squabbling can provide openings for working-class and popular-sector actors to access power. Unfortunately, such access is partial, and moments of opening tend to be brief. As a result, while small victories are possible, they have not yet built into a coherent political alternative. One episode that displays these patterns was the rivalry between the mayor and the sheriff, focused particularly over control of the city jail, Orleans Parish Prison, from Landrieu's election until at least the federal consent decree in 2013, and forward.

While the mayor is clearly the preeminent citywide elected official, the sheriff's office enjoys significant autonomy and independent sources of revenue, and the sheriff is also elected in an election district coterminous with city boundaries. Confrontations between Sheriff Marlon Gusman and Mayor Mitch Landrieu expose some of the frictions within the dual development class project. The fact that Landrieu is white and Gusman is a black member of the Creole elite foregrounded some of the racial undercurrents of elite factionalism even as it displayed the fluidity of white and black elite claims to leadership and forced them to find common ground within the dual development project.

Part of the sheriff's autonomy comes in the form of the legal architecture provided by the Law Enforcement Taxing District, a satellite with a jurisdiction also coterminous with the boundaries of the city. The Law Enforcement Taxing District has the power to raise taxes and issue bonds, an annual budget of approximately $70 million, a workforce that grew to as many as twelve hundred, and a sheriff who is the lone board member. Among the major assets of the sheriff's office is the city jail, Orleans Parish Prison (OPP). After suffering major damage during Katrina, the jail attracted inflows of $145 million in FEMA funding and an additional $100 million potentially available to add facilities (Rainey 2015). In addition, OPP captures external funding by housing state and federal prisoners, producing an estimated $11.1 million in 2011, with the jail holding more state prisoners than any other parish facility in Louisiana. An additional $22 million in outlays was obligated when the city agreed to a federal consent decree in 2013.

With its bases of legal authority and fiscal resources, the jail attracted competing claims for control. The competing claims produced fluid and sometimes contradictory positioning, even as they affirmed the alignment of leading black and white elite-class factions in conflict with the interests of working classes and popular sectors. For a number of reasons, the sheriff consistently argued for a larger facility: even though Louisiana has the highest per capita incarceration rate in the world, New Orleans already jailed its residents at five times the national average on the eve of Hurricane

Katrina; the jail had grown to become the eighth-largest penal institution in the United States in total number of inmates; it was the single largest local jail as a proportion of the total population local in the United States; and it houses a prison population that is over 90 percent black (Johnson, Laisne, and Wool 2015).[8] Still, black political elites, represented by church leaders, tended to line up behind the sheriff as one of the few remaining African American citywide elected authorities.

In favor of a smaller jail, the mayor allied with the majority-white City Council to pass resolutions limiting jail size. They rejected the sheriff's request for a jail close to 5,000 beds (down from an average of 6,500 before Katrina) and instead authorized rebuilding to a size of 1,438 beds. This 2011 law was followed by occasional and frequent eruptions of conflict between the mayor and the sheriff, and four years later Landrieu had his Safety and Permits office issue a stop-work order when Gusman attempted to build a third wing at the prison to hold an additional 750 beds for sick and mentally ill inmates (Rainey 2015).

Landrieu and the City Council attempted to portray themselves as aligned with prisoner rights advocates; Gusman attempted to portray himself as aligned with African American communities fighting their loss of political access. In fact, these confrontations reflected neither the substance of debates about the jail nor alignment with popular sectors. Rather, they expressed struggle for primacy within the dual development project. Evidence of a shared elite project appeared when the mayor and the sheriff worked together when it came time to use the jail to make new revenues available for development. To take advantage of FEMA money to rebuild the jail and to generate new resources to fund the 2013 consent decree, the mayor and the sheriff campaigned publicly for new revenues and greater freedom to shift resources between FEMA and General Fund accounts, backing a referendum advocating for $8 million in new revenues that could be dedicated to dual development priorities. As Landrieu's chief administrative officer noted, "If I have to cut $8 million out of the budget, that's 80 percent of the Recreation Department's budget" (Naomi Martin 2014a).

Episodes of conflict demonstrate some of the jockeying for position within the dual development project. Yet, rival white and black elites fought not over the substance of dual development but rather how to divide authority within the project, sharing in efforts to channel greater resources to the city and to the tourism and services economy. Still, episodes of conflict also opened opportunities for working-class and popular-sector advocates to insert their demands into policy debates and link prison reform struggles to broader social issues.

The jail had a long history of abuse and inhumane conditions, operating under the longest federal consent decree in history, lasting from 1969 to 2004.[9] Most of this period was under the supervision of Sheriff Charles Foti, who served from 1974 to 2004 and increased the jail from 800 beds to 8,500. Part of this growth was driven by tough-on-crime and war-on-drugs minimum sentencing and jail for nonviolent offenders, and Foti played along in efforts to maximize payments as a recipient site for state and federal prisoners. On the eve of Katrina, OPP was the largest jail in the state, larger even than the notorious state Angola prison (Gerharz and Hong 2006).

The overflow of inmates from state and federal courts, some of whom were jailed for violent crimes, presented particular complications. Because OPP is a county jail, many inmates are held on attachments—minor violations for warrants for failure to appear in court, traffic and municipal charges, and non-felony state offenses. The mix of those held for violent crimes and those who could be issued citations or held in mental health facilities overran the capacities of poorly trained and equipped officers. In 2013, a hearing on conditions at the jail was upended by "a video depicting drug use, gunplay and beer drinking by inmates inside the Orleans Parish jail complex, and one video showing an inmate hanging out on Bourbon Street."[10]

Extreme conditions, such as those during Katrina, proved completely overwhelming. Prisoners were not evacuated, and juvenile prisoners housed with adults had to compete for scarce food and water. Some prisoners were locked in first-floor cells as water and sewage rose around them. Even before Katrina, the record of inhumane treatment was astonishing. The prison was among the top five nationally in substantiated reports of sexual violence, and in 2001 a prisoner jailed on traffic charges died of dehydration after being held in restraints for forty-two hours. There were numerous cases of prisoners dying of treatable conditions such as bacterial pneumonia and meningitis, officers were reported to have engaged in mock executions, and two officers were indicted for beating to death an inmate jailed for public drunkenness.[11] A video showed sixty-four-year-old retired African American schoolteacher Robert Davis "having his head repeatedly slammed into a brick wall by police until he collapsed into a pool of his own blood," and another showed a group of six officers fatally shooting a mentally ill man who was holding a three-inch knife (Gerharz and Hong 2006). A 2009 Department of Justice report found "conditions at the OPP violate the constitutional rights of inmates . . . a pattern and practice of unnecessary and inappropriate use of force by OPP correctional officers including several examples where OPP officers openly engaged in abusive and retaliatory conduct, which resulted in serious injuries to prisoners. In some instances, the investigation found, the officers' conduct was so flagrant it clearly constituted calculated abuse" (as quoted in Flaherty 2010b).

The dreadful conditions at the jail provoked action from prisoner advocates, who formed the OPP Reform Coalition in 2004.[12] They were supported by other activist organizations, including New Orleans: Safe Streets/Strong Communities, Voice of the Ex-Offender, and New Orleans Worker Center for Racial Justice. In 2006, activist Shana Sassoon remarked: "OPP has long been a shameful centerpiece of New Orleans' broken criminal justice system with its history of human and civil rights abuses, fatal disease, and institutional violence. It's no coincidence that OPP has also emerged as a centerpiece of political power in New Orleans" (Gerharz and Hong 2006).

As discussion of post-Katrina rebuilding and expansion accelerated in 2009, the OPP Reform Coalition published a full-page ad in the local newspaper listing the things that money spent on OPP could buy. The ad was supported by a host of local celebrities and the cast and crew of the HBO show *Treme*, each paying $22.39, equal to the amount charged per inmate per day. In response to their pressure, and to put pressure on the sheriff's office, the mayor formed a working group, including members of the OPP Reform Coalition and the Public Defender Office. The working group commissioned an expert analysis of the appropriate size for the jail and an outline of plans for reform. Ultimately, prisoner advocates prevailed in the form of the City Council legislation limiting the jail to 1,438 beds (Eggler 2011a).

Almost immediately after this victory, room opened for prisoner advocates once again, as the MacArthur Justice Center filed a federal lawsuit on behalf of prisoners for mistreatment. Popular pressure and the federal lawsuit prompted a Justice Department investigation and a new federal consent decree signed in 2013, including an independent jail compliance director who would take over effective operational control of the jail, which eventually occurred in June 2016.[13] When the mayor and sheriff sought voter approval to shift $8 million in FEMA funding, prison reform advocates organized in opposition, clarifying the cleavage that united elite African American and white interests against the working-class and popular sectors left out of the dual development project (Naomi Martin 2014a).

Journalist Jordan Flaherty had earlier framed debates over the jail in stark terms: "Ultimately, this struggle over the size of the jail is also about the city's incarceration priorities. If the city builds a larger jail, it will have to keep filling it with tens of thousands of people" (Flaherty

2010b). Moments of elite division also opened room for popular-sector advocates to link prison reform to broader social struggles. Orleans Parish Prison Reform Coalition advocate and local activist Rosana Cruz noted that "the police operated with full impunity. . . . The abuse was widespread, though most rampant in Black communities. I also heard about immigrants, young people, service industry workers, the LGBTQ community of every race, but there were strong community organizations, some led by public housing residents, standing up and organizing and that legacy informs these post-Katrina reforms" (Mock 2015).

The confrontation and accommodation over the jail exposed the dynamics of fitting rival elites within the dual development political project. Zero-sum conflict over resources and authority triggered competition among local elites and opened room for popular sectors to insert themselves into public debates. While such episodes produced important victories for popular sectors, they also displayed the ability of rival elite factions to negotiate the terms of their accommodation within a shared project and to close ranks around a dual development agenda.

As globally oriented elites consolidated their leadership among factions of capital after Katrina, they increasingly sought to navigate themselves into positions of political authority. This process took time, as appropriate political vehicles who could win elections had to be found and rival aspirants for electoral leadership had to be disciplined within the requirements of dual development at the same time they articulated a viable political coalition. Where direct conservative white elite representation was easily defeated by an inconsistent African American candidate who zigzagged across issues (Nagin), a moderate white Democrat with a clear development agenda could secure popular support while articulating the interests of black and white upper classes (Landrieu).

In addition, the dual development project required reworking the complex array of satellite institutions. Entities that represented patronage, corruption, or other threats to the external image of the city had to be eliminated. At the same time, new institutional architectures were necessary to lock in the dual development project, shift public resources and assets to the private sector, and coordinate local and external business interests while providing channels of access into the local state.

Divisions and rivalries among local elites created openings for working-class and popular actors to insert themselves into policy-making spaces. Such opportunities scored important victories, especially in some of the most outrageously oppressive institutions, such as local criminal justice. Still, it was telling that despite important and courageous victories, working

classes and popular sectors were unable to shift the general public commitment to dual development or present a durable working-class and popular-
sector political project to compete with the electoral and institutional
framework erected by globally oriented elites. In fact, rival elites appealed
to working classes and popular sectors when it was convenient, only later
to subordinate them within their dual development project. Reed makes a
similar observation with respect to struggles over housing: "That it was
not possible to generate significant black popular or working-class support for demands to preserve and restore decommodified public housing
for poor people in New Orleans . . . is a testament to the reality that what
we understand as black politics is thoroughly embedded within the neoliberal regime and its ways of seeing" (2016, 9).

CHAPTER FIVE

Globalized Construction and Ethnic Segmentation

Construction is central to urban growth regimes, and this is nowhere truer than in New Orleans after Katrina. The 2005 hurricane damaged approximately 515,000 homes in Louisiana and destroyed 200,000 homes in New Orleans, as well as 850 public schools, not to mention the system of levees and canals (Plyer 2008; Louisiana Restaurant Association 2006). Reconstruction buoyed the regional building sector, and investment was further multiplied by billions in local, state, and federal dollars to repair damaged infrastructure, construct new hurricane defenses, and undertake a major overhaul of public buildings, including schools, hospitals, and housing. The massive amounts directed toward post-Katrina building attracted both local and international firms, consolidating the construction sector as a new source of transnationally oriented accumulation.

Employers took advantage of the hurricane aftermath to segment their workforce, using race and immigration status as a convenient way to allocate workers and working conditions. A few good jobs were reserved for native-born white workers, and everyone else performed the many bad jobs characterized by workplace violations and poverty wages. Interestingly, over time such conditions were extended to all workers, including the native-born white workers who had previously enjoyed moderately better treatment.

This chapter will explore the construction sector in New Orleans after Katrina, making use of an original survey of construction workers conducted in 2006 and 2009. Based on the results of these surveys and individual worker stories, one gets the impression that transnational elite control over the construction sector has consolidated exaggerated profits and exploitative labor markets. Still, this need not be the final story, and there are important points of resistance. Workers are organizing, even and especially the most vulnerable undocumented immigrant workers. They are forging alliances with organized labor, finding common cause with African American working classes and popular sectors, and joining with progressive middle-class community groups to offer an alternative vision of development.

Transnational Growth Regimes and a Deregulated Construction Boom

Massive infusions of capital in the years after Katrina turned construction into an irresistible source of accumulation. Funds were absorbed by various actors, from small local contractors to massive international conglomerates. Of particular note within the sector were two kinds of action taken by local, regional, and national governments. First, they undertook all manner of intervention to maintain capital inflows, including direct investment funded by taxes, grants, and loans. Second, official actors gave power to employers to determine how to allocate those funds within the process, with particular impact on the amount distributed in wages and spent to maintain decent working conditions.

Funds were stimulated by Katrina, but the construction boom did not start there. Like the rest of the country, the city rode the housing bubble of the 1990s and early 2000s, reversing trends of previous decades in which the number of households stagnated. Between 1960 and 2000, central, historic areas of New Orleans had lost about thirty-five thousand homes while farther-flung, suburban areas gained about the same number (Plyer, Ortiz, and Horwitz 2011).[1] New housing activity in the early 2000s targeted the central business district just outside of downtown, where historic and underutilized warehouses were turned into a neighborhood of art galleries, loft apartments, and trendy restaurant and shopping sites (Plyer, Ortiz, and Horwitz 2011). Local government encouraged the boom with its own investments, issuing a record $260 million bond issue in 2004 to renovate parks and recreation facilities, improve streets, and renovate public libraries and other public facilities. The city dedicated a further $14 million to public-housing redevelopment and another $20 million to projects along the Lakefront and Canal Street, the street bordering the French Quarter.

Recovery efforts after Katrina massively accelerated this boom. Federal funding totaled $120 billion, within which the Army Corps of Engineers accounted for $14.5 billion to repair damaged flood protections and establish new ones. Projects included the longest surge barrier in the United States, a swinging barrier that could be closed to obstruct the inflow of Gulf of Mexico flows into Lake Bourne and then Lake Ponchartrain to the north of New Orleans. To block the outflow of water from Lake Ponchartrain into the industrial canal that had flooded the Lower Ninth Ward, the corps installed a new floodgate, and spent more than $1 billion to close the Mississippi River–Gulf Outlet, a canal they dug but never filled once it fell into disuse (Ahlers, Plyer, and Weil 2008).

The influx of capital may seem sui generis, but it fits with broader understandings of booms and busts in disaster-prone areas.[2] Such areas follow cycles of disaster-recovery-disaster, in which disaster provokes investments in safety improvements, engineering areas that were previously considered unfit into usability. As subsequent generations occupy newly usable areas, they lose or are not provided knowledge of the danger of their location, making subsequent disaster more likely. When the inevitable disaster strikes, the cycle starts anew (Kirby 1990).

The amount of money dedicated to infrastructure reconstruction attracted large-scale firms and multinational corporations. Only they had the access and capacity to secure large bids, as well as operations big enough to absorb the funds. For example, based on their expertise in the management of levees, one Dutch firm was awarded an "Indefinite Delivery Indefinite Quantity" contract of $150 million (Arcadis, N.V. 2004).[3] Halliburton subsidiary KBR received $160 million for the long-term rebuild of naval facilities and infrastructure.[4]

In total, $71 billion in federal assistance funded three thousand individual infrastructure projects and repaired one hundred thousand homes. The Federal Emergency Management Agency (FEMA) provided $5.3 billion in temporary assistance, $283 million for street and bridge repairs, $524 million after Hurricane Rita, and $842 million for safety-net programs such as food stamps, welfare, and unemployment. More than $1.15 billion was spent clearing debris, and $9 billion was spent through federal insurance Road Home program and $13.2 billion through the National Flood Insurance program. The U.S. Department of Transportation spent $208 million on streets and $770 million to repair the twin spans that cross Lake Pontchartrain and connect New Orleans to the rest of Louisiana. Canal Street streetcars received $17.9 million and the Superdome received repairs worth $137.5 million. Although Charity Hospital was discarded, $1 billion was made available for the new University Medical Center and $49.8 million to turn Methodist Hospital into New Orleans East Hospital. Homeowners and small businesses received $6.3 billion in loans from the U.S. Small Business Administration, and the school system received $1.8 billion in repairs. The single largest item was the $14.5 billion upgrade to the levee system (Adelson 2015).

While international firms garnered the largest contracts, less competitive local businesspeople were able to capture smaller-scale and shorter-duration infrastructure projects, such as locally based Boh Brothers Construction Company, which received a $30.9 million contract for the Interstate 10 highway repair immediately after the hurricane. In addition to receiving the smaller contracts unattractive to international capital, local elites took on the role of intermediating and partnering with external actors. Immediately after the hurricane, the mayor authorized a local commission, the Bring New Orleans Back Commission, to include notable local business-people and their allies in planning post-hurricane redevelopment.[5] The plan included $14.5 billion in spending on infrastructure, and local businesses and nonprofits took on the role of smoothing entrance for national firms (Mikell 2007).[6]

In particular, local elites sought to legitimize and participate in the redevelopment of health, housing, and education facilities. This included the shuttering of Charity Hospital, the only major hospital serving low-income residents, with nearly 75 percent of its users African American, 85 percent with incomes below $20,000, and one of the busiest emergency departments in the country (Rudowitz, Rowland, and Shartzer 2006, 394–95). The redevelopment plan sought to turn the Charity Hospital neighborhood into "the anchor for an entire medical and biotechnology industrial district in Downtown and Mid City New Orleans" (quoted in BondGraham 2011, 298), with spending totaling more than $1.2 billion, a mission to promote biotech research, and no longer committed to services for the poor.[7]

With respect to education, the city fired seven thousand public school teachers and staff and turned 80 percent of students over to charter schools. While the mass firing was ruled illegal in 2012, it was too late to change the makeover of public education.[8] Spending on demolition, reconstruction, and building included $750 million in a first phase, $380 million in open contracts for state-funded schools as of December 2012, $417 million in open contracts for locally funded schools, and total federal funding of approximately $2 billion (Smith, White, and Dobard 2012; Cowen Institute 2012).

While large-scale projects required alliances with external capital, local real estate developers were themselves equipped to capitalize on the need for smaller-scale residential housing repair and building.[9] The amounts for individual or small-scale residential projects were smaller, though they collectively accounted for a significant boost to the local economy—approximately 45 billion federal dollars, $6.5 billion in charitable funds, and $25 billion in private insurance claims, along with $8.7 billion in state Road Home grants distributed to 127,947 pre-Katrina homeowners (Plyer, Ortiz, and Horwitz 2011).[10]

With respect to public housing, local developers and nonprofit allies collaborated with national foundations to promote the conversion of relatively undamaged public housing. While a disruptive protest movement attempted to oppose demolition, they were unable to resist the inflow of funds. Local foundations gathered national funds and distributed them to nonprofits, dividing the opposition movement and advancing planned redevelopment by the private sector (Arena 2012).[11] The City Council eventually approved the demolition of forty-five hundred units of low-income housing, replacing them with two thousand units of mixed-income housing, only fifteen hundred of which would be for low-income residents, opening the gates to Federal Housing and Urban Development spending of $597 million.[12]

The changes to health, housing, and education took public infrastructure and made it available to private building firms in the name of redevelopment. For large projects, the sums were large enough to attract international developers, while local capital acted as facilitator, intermediator, and partner and took responsibility alone for smaller, residential projects.

Incoming funds greatly boosted construction activity, increasing the number of people employed in the sector. While hospitality, professional services, health care, and education had grown in the twenty-five years prior to the storm, their growth stopped after 2005, and they joined sectors such as retail, transportation, manufacturing, and warehousing in relative decline.[13] Construction replaced them as the main sector of employment, growing by 158 percent in the years after Katrina (A. Liu, Fellowes, and Mabanta 2006).

As construction work expanded, employers worked to secure control of the workplace by removing federal, state, and local regulations. The federal government suspended affirmative action requirements in contracting and temporarily halted Davis-Bacon Act prevailing wage requirements, I-9 employment verification requirements, and Occupational Safety and Health Administration requirements.[14] Lobbyists from the Louisiana Association of General Contractors successfully advanced legislation to remove Project Labor Agreement requirements from public infrastructure projects (Jindal 2011), and local government declined to enforce regulations that might protect residents from fly-by-night home contractors who stole from both homeowners and workers, with more than nine thousand homeowners reporting theft by contractors (Sisco 2009). Nor was there oversight on public projects, such as school reconstruction. In response to nonpayment of overtime wages and other violations on school construction worksites, Schools Superintendent Paul Pastorek responded: "Does anyone expect me to do anything about this? It's not the Recovery School

District's responsibility. . . . I hope it doesn't slow them down too much, because I'd like them to finish the work out there" (Charpentier 2007).

With respect to housing, the racial and class impact of the dual development approach was expressed perhaps too honestly by local developer Pres Cabacoff in a 2014 interview:

> The city got a lot from Katrina and BP. About $100 billion came through here after Katrina. That's juice that no other city really got. . . . I tried to influence the federal government to increase the tax incentive for affordable housing so it wasn't just for people making 60 percent of median income but 120 percent. That worked. . . . So when you did use subsidies you'd not only be dealing with the very poor but the working and middle classes. . . . And it's true when a neighborhood comes back many people who found it to be an affordable place are priced out. . . . But the cold truth is, if you're going to revitalize a neighborhood that's in bad shape or where market rate won't go—because the amount of crime, the amount of poverty or the amount of minorities, or whatever keeps market rate uncomfortable moving there—one of the realities is that when the market rate come in, those people move to another neighborhood. It's a pain in the ass, but they move. . . . In terms of race, black people in this town have less money. When neighborhoods revitalize, I think it chases all the poor out, and in our city the poor are almost all black, so it's more a coincidence. And there is probably some racism involved in that. That's the downside of neighborhood improvement. (Moskowitz 2015)

Segmentation of Work by National Origin

The destruction of the hurricane and the massive influx of capital increased demand for labor, filled at least in part by an inflow of immigrants, many from Latin America. The city gained 4,101 Latinos from 2000 to 2010, and the metro area gained 36,761, with the Latino population rising by 63 percent to 2011, much faster than the national growth rate of 47 percent. According to the 2010 census, Latinos account for 5.2 percent of the New Orleans population, up from 3.1 percent in 2000 (Plyer, Ortiz, and Horwitz 2011). Some migrated from other parts of the United States, and others came straight from Latin America, often attracted by labor recruiters who falsely promised work and legal status (SPLC 2013).

The economic condition of these immigrants mirrored national trends. Immigrants are generally poor, with more than 30 percent earning less than $20,000 in 2001, and more than half with fewer than six years of education

(Vega, Sribney, and Achara-Abrahams 2003). Even those who are well educated or trained for other professions often work in jobs requiring limited formal training or certification. They often perform low-wage work subject to the worst violations, in sectors such as private household work, agriculture, textile, food services, and construction (Bruno 2015).[15] Those without documentation are especially vulnerable—they earn 40 percent less than immigrants with documents; they are twice as likely to live in poverty; their children suffer higher risks of poverty and poor health; and they are more than twice as unlikely to have health insurance (Passel 2006).

Many in New Orleans recognized the importance of the rapid-response immigrant workforce that was willing to enter the difficult and dangerous conditions of post-hurricane cleanup and recovery, yet few recognized the mistreatment these workers experienced, both on the job and in the community. Nativist justifications hid some of this mistreatment behind anecdotal tales of foreigners stealing jobs, utilizing public services, or disrupting political and social life. In New Orleans an additional wrinkle was added by the specific context of racial divisions. Immigrant populations were inserted into racial and labor market divisions previously divided along white and black lines (Bonilla-Silva 1997; Stoll, Melendez, and Valenzuela 2002; Pastor and Marcelli 2003; Borjas 1998). More than one hundred thousand African Americans were expelled from the city as a result of Katrina and its aftermath, and their percentage of the population fell from 67 percent to 59 percent.[16]

Activists recognized that an exploitative secondary sector previously filled with African American workers was incorporating immigrant workers. In construction, the secondary sector is identifiable in several ways. First, construction contracts are themselves bifurcated into a primary sector of lucrative, large-scale contracts for public infrastructure and major corporate projects, absorbed by international firms and factions of local capital that can facilitate access. Construction and reconstruction of individual homes is left to local contractors and smaller developers, with narrower margins. Second, within these smaller home-construction jobs, certain activities are defined as primary, usually requiring formal training or certification, such as electrician, carpenter, and plumber, while others are characterized as secondary, such as laborer, painter, and landscaper. These jobs were previously performed by unorganized African Americans, who have now been joined by immigrants, with no improvement in working conditions.

The distinction between the primary and secondary sectors is ultimately a constructed one. Employers press for control over the workplace and seek an abundant supply of workers willing to take insecure and low-wage work or unable to find an alternative. In post-Katrina New Orleans, national origin has become a convenient basis to segment between primary and secondary activities.

New Orleans construction also redefined previously existing good jobs to turn them into secondary-sector jobs. Jobs previously associated with high levels of training and remuneration, such as roofing, have been turned into secondary-sector-type jobs, with inadequate working conditions and low wages. Further, workers who previously enjoyed at least some access to primary-sector conditions, including white native-born workers, now find themselves experiencing patterns of abuse previously reserved to African American and Latino workers.

Surveying New Orleans Construction Workers

To tell the story of segmentation in the construction sector, this project takes advantage of an original survey conducted among construction workers across two rounds, in 2006 and 2009.[17] Participation was strictly voluntary, with informed consent, anonymity, and no financial compensation. Interviewers applied a structured questionnaire with 129 questions in either Spanish or English, depending on the preference of respondents. Questions were largely kept constant across years except for questions added to reflect changing circumstances in New Orleans and among immigrant workers, such as abuse by government authorities, victimization by criminals, and worker organization and resistance (Fussell 2011).

The samples aimed at a representative number of respondents, with 212 respondents in 2006 and 150 respondents in 2009. To identify interview sites, the survey randomly selected a proportionate number of addresses from each census tract in the city based on a comprehensive database of addresses. Surveyors were fluent in Spanish, trained in the application of the survey, and traveled in groups of two or more.[18] In total, 296 addresses were selected, a sample size large enough to account for the possibility that no interview would be possible at some of the sites.[19] Once the survey team arrived at a designated sample point, they were instructed to identify the closest construction site within a ten-block radius, and a worker was chosen at random from each site.[20] Of 296 addresses selected in 2006, 84 produced no worker responses, a rate of 72 percent, slightly higher than the rate for 2009, at 59 percent.[21] Areas in which fewer interviews were possible were Lake View, Gentilly, and New Orleans East.

Despite the best efforts of researchers to eliminate bias and preserve reliability, there are limitations. Generalizations should for now be limited to the greater metropolitan area of New Orleans, though they suggest an agenda for ongoing research into their applicability to the national context. Also, the survey addressed sensitive subjects such as discrimination, trauma, immigration status, labor abuse, and abuse by state authorities, and it is possible that respondents did not always answer truthfully. To minimize error, surveyors stressed anonymity in the consent form, never asking or recording names, and repeated promises of anonymity before sensitive questions.[22]

The data confirmed a stable, and perhaps increasing, Latino and undocumented immigrant population. For 2009 the sample consisted of 17.6 percent Caucasians, 17.6 percent African Americans, 1.4 percent other ethnicities, and a majority of 62.8 percent foreign-born Latinos. This was a higher concentration of Latino workers in the residential construction sector than in 2006, when native Caucasians were 28.0 percent of the sample, African Americans were 24.6 percent, and Latinos were 44.6 percent. The proportion of Latinos from different countries was relatively similar over time, with slightly more Hondurans and Salvadorans in 2009, and fewer Mexicans. Of the 127 workers who responded to a self-reported question on documented status, 44.1 percent reported undocumented status in 2009, an increase from 2006, when 25.5 percent of the 208 respondents were undocumented.

At least in part, it would appear that the Latino population has been expanded by new arrivals. Among foreign-born Latinos, 77.5 percent arrived after Hurricane Katrina, with 47.2 percent arriving after 2006. In comparison, only 8.0 percent of African Americans and 32.0 percent of Caucasians were post-Katrina arrivals.[23] The characteristics of undocumented workers and the rest of the population did not appear to change from 2006. On average, undocumented workers were more than ten years younger than documented and native workers, 30.05 versus 40.76 years old, and undocumented workers reported fewer years of education, with 52.7 percent of undocumented workers reporting no education or only primary education compared to only 5.8 percent of other workers. Furthermore, only 1.8 percent of undocumented workers had some form of postsecondary education, as compared to 39.1 percent of other workers. These figures were comparable to 2006, when undocumented workers differed in most descriptive characteristics related to age, country of origin, and education. Chi-squared tests of differences between undocumented and other workers showed statistical significance in both 2006 and 2009 at $p < .001$, and there were no statistically significant differences within groups across years.

With respect to working and living conditions, the paragraphs that follow indicate a set of disturbing trends. First, some of the results attest

TABLE 8. Difficult Living and Working Conditions for All (%)

	2006			2009		
	Undoc.	Other	Difference	Undoc.	Other	Difference
Have health insurance or Medicare	9.4	59.4	50.0***	10.7	50.7	40.0***
Have medicine when needed	37.7	83.8	46.1***	46.4	80.3	33.9***
Sought treatment when needed	7.7	25.2	17.5***	16.0	41.4	25.4***
Harmful substances/Chemicals	20.8	32.5	11.7	30.4	44.9	14.5**
Dangerous conditions	41.5	41.3	0.2	53.6	56.3	2.7
Received general training	39.6	48.6	9.0	54.7	68.6	13.9***
Injury resulting in illness/injury	11.5	12.4	0.9	37.0	39.1	2.1
Physical abuse at work	1.9	0.0	1.9	11.1	10.4	0.7
Receive extra pay when working > 40 hours						
Yes	30.2	28.2	2.0	37.5	34.8	2.7
Sometimes	5.7	2.4	3.3	5.4	10.1	4.7
No	64.2	69.4	4.8	57.1	55.1	2.0

Source: Author-administered survey and statistical calculations.
**Difference in group proportions significant at $p < .05$.
***Difference in group proportions significant at $p < .01$.

to the fact that workers in construction in New Orleans live precarious lives with limited income, unpleasant work, and difficult living situations. These conditions were present in 2006, and they remained all too evident in 2009.[24] Table 8 presents the difficult conditions facing everyone in construction work.

These conditions had not changed much more than five years after Hurricane Katrina. Only 9.4 percent of undocumented workers had health care in 2006, and only 10.7 percent in 2009. Other workers fared better, but far below what might be acceptable, with access to health insurance at 59.4 percent in 2006 and 50.7 percent in 2009. Only one-third of undocumented workers, 37.7 percent, had access to medicine when they needed it in 2006, and this problem persisted into 2009, when 46.4 percent reported lacking access to medicine when they needed it. Once again, while other workers did slightly better, they did not do well, with 83.8 percent with access to medicine when they needed it in 2006 and 80.3 percent had access to medicine in 2009. Access to treatment was even lower, with only 7.7 percent of undocumented workers seeking treatment for a reported medical problem in 2006 and only 16 percent seeking treatment in 2009. Among other workers, only one-quarter sought treatment for their medical problems in 2006 and 41.4 percent in 2009.

The health challenges faced by undocumented and other workers are even worse in the context of the dangerous work inherent in reconstruction of residences after a storm, conditions that remained difficult and even deteriorated over time. In 2006, 20.8 percent of undocumented workers reported exposure to harmful chemicals or substances, compared to 32.5 percent exposure among other workers, rising to 30.4 and 44.9 percent in 2009. Similarly, 41.5 percent of undocumented and 41.3 percent of other workers reported dangerous conditions in 2006, and these numbers rose to 53.6 and 56.3 percent in 2009. Neither undocumented nor other workers were consistently trained, with only 54.7 percent of undocumented workers and 68.6 percent of other workers receiving training in 2009, up from 39.6 percent and 48.6 percent in 2006. Perhaps as a result, both undocumented and other workers reported similar rates of illness or incidents resulting in injury on the job. In 2009, 37 percent of the undocumented workers and 39.1 percent of other workers reported an injury on the job. This is a statistically significant increase ($p < .00$) from 2006, when only 11.5 percent of undocumented workers and 12.4 percent of other workers reported injuries on the job.

In addition, workplace violations would appear to affect both undocumented and other workers, as 11.1 percent of undocumented workers reported physical abuse at work in 2009, a level nearly matched by other workers at 10.4 percent. Further, despite the difficult and dangerous work they undertook, neither undocumented nor other workers were consistently paid overtime for work beyond forty hours in a week. In both 2006 and 2009, other workers actually reported slightly higher rates of overtime nonpayment than undocumented workers some or all of the time, at 71.8 percent in 2006 and 65.2 percent in 2009, compared with 69.9 percent and 65.2 percent for undocumented workers during those years. These living and working environments had predictable impacts on worker health. Both undocumented and other workers reported relatively high rates and similar rank ordering of health issues, though watery eyes and skin rashes were more prevalent among undocumented workers in 2009.

While these figures portray the general difficulty of life as a construction worker in New Orleans, other indicators suggest that distress is meted out particularly on the undocumented. Table 9 shows the results from the survey in which conditions for undocumented workers differed from those for other workers, including statistically significant differences in proportions across groups at $p < .05$.

Worse conditions for the undocumented are evident in looking at within-year comparisons with other workers. In 2009, for example, 54.1 percent of all workers had a spouse or long-term partner, but undocumented workers were much more likely to be separated from their families. Among undocumented workers with a long-term partner, 37.5 percent report that their partner is in New Orleans, compared to 81.1 percent of other workers. Likewise, only 15.8 percent of undocumented workers with children have their children in New Orleans, compared to 64 percent of other workers. Instead of living with their families, undocumented workers were much more likely to live with a larger number of roommates, 4.43, as compared to 2.77 in the households of other workers.[25]

These conditions were matched by other types of vulnerability, such as the inability of undocumented workers to accumulate assets as a reserve for slow times. In 2009, roughly half of the undocumented workers report having access to a vehicle, compared to 84.5 percent of other workers. Also, though home ownership was relatively low among all construction workers, at 28.1 percent, in 2009 no undocumented workers owned their own home, while 49.3 percent of other workers owned their residence. When we explored the 2009 data by race, it became evident that only 8.7 percent of foreign-born Latinos overall owned their own homes, compared with 64 percent of Caucasians and 58.3 percent of African Americans.

Vulnerability in living circumstances was exacerbated by dangerous and risky work. In 2009 only 35.3 percent of undocumented workers reported not being informed about the risk of mold; 43.6 percent were informed

TABLE 9. Worse Conditions for the Undocumented (%)

	2006			2009		
	Undocumented	Other	Difference	Undocumented	Other	Difference
Own their residence	58.5	59.4	0.9	0.0	49.3	49.3
Have partner or spouse	29.0	61.8	32.8***	57.1	52.1	5.0
Partner in New Orleans	69.2	68.4	0.8	37.5	81.1	43.6***
Have children	43.4	20.0	23.4**	67.9	72.9	5.0
Children in New Orleans	37.7	67.1	29.4***	15.8	64.0	48.2***
Informed of risk related to mold	35.8	64.9	34.1***	35.3	65.7	30.4***
Informed of risk related to asbestos	19.2	58.7	39.5***	43.6	62.0	18.4**
Informed of risk of unsafe building	7.7	1.6	5.1**	29.6	65.7	36.1***
Deportation threats for complaints	$10.88	$16.35	5.47***	21.8	3.6	18.2***
Overall wages (hourly)	$10.45	$17.61	7.16***	$11.16	$17.30	6.14***
Skilled worker wage (hourly)				$12.56	$19.64	7.08**
Monthly salary				$1,536	$3,381	1,845***

Source: Author-administered survey and statistical calculations.
**Difference in group proportions significant at $p < .05$.
***Difference in group proportions significant at $p < .01$.

about the risk of asbestos; and 29.6 percent were informed about the risk of unsafe buildings. This is significantly less preparation than other workers ($p < .05$), though even they also did not receive adequate warnings about risks. For example, only 38.0 percent of documented workers were not informed about the risk of asbestos in 2009. None of these indicators had improved since 2006, with no statistically significant change in the proportions of workers suffering these conditions of dangerous and risky work.

Another example of the enhanced vulnerability of undocumented workers was the rate at which employers threatened to deport them if they complained. The rate was predictably higher for undocumented workers, though the rate of threat was non-zero for other workers, and it worsened over time for both groups. Among undocumented workers, threats of deportation affected 7.7 percent in 2006 and 21.8 percent in 2009. Notably, threats of deportation were not absent among documented workers — 1.6 percent in 2006 and 3.6 percent in 2009 — confirming the "deportation threat dynamic" in which employers threaten all Latinos with deportation, regardless of their immigration status (Fussell 2011).

One of the starkest workplace differences was evident in wages and income, which were significantly less for undocumented workers in both 2006 and 2009. On average, wages were $10.88 per hour for undocumented workers in 2006 compared to $16.35 among documented workers, with the difference spreading to $11.16 and $17.30 in 2009.[26] Differences in wages were highly statistically significant, and this difference remained even when we controlled for the type of work. For skilled workers in jobs such as electrical, plumbing, and carpentry, there was a statistically significant $7.08 wage gap for undocumented workers.[27]

To determine the overall financial situation of the workers, questions were asked that addressed both wages and average amount of work. When coupled with the fact that undocumented workers report working fewer hours per week (41.20 hours compared to 49.37), the mean monthly salary for undocumented workers was $1,536.20, less than half the documented worker salary of $3,380.70.[28]

The last pattern to note was the fact that some of the deplorable conditions previously reserved to migrants, such as wage theft, have been generalized to the rest of the population. Unlike the previous tables, which measured the statistical significance of differences across group proportions within each year, Table 10 compares across years within group proportions. Differences across groups did not shift considerably, but conditions for both groups appeared to deteriorate over time, with all workers approximating conditions among undocumented workers. Table 10 indicates those

TABLE 10. Poor Conditions Generalized from the Undocumented to All (%)

	Undocumented			Other		
	2006	2009	Difference	2006	2009	Difference
Received less money than promised	37.7	48.2	10.5	25.4	33.3	7.9
Unfair treatment from employer	15.4	34.5	19.1**	9.7	30.4	20.7***
Problems being paid for work	32.1	41.1	9.0	20.8	38.6	17.8***
Problems with employer payment	21.2	50.9	29.7***	11.4	31.9	20.5***

Source: Author-administered survey and statistical calculations.
**Difference in year proportions significant at $p < .05$.
***Difference in year proportions significant at $p < .01$.

items in which survey respondents indicated that poor conditions were increasingly generalized across the entire workforce. For these items, statistical tests indicate the significance in the growth in the proportion of workers from each category experiencing these forms of wage theft at $p < .01$ and $p < .05$.

In 2006, 37.7 percent of undocumented workers received less money than promised at least some of the time, as compared to 25.4 percent among other workers, but this increased to 48.2 percent and 33.3 percent in 2009. Another question asked whether workers experienced unfair treatment from an employer, and 15.4 percent of undocumented responded affirmatively in 2006, compared to almost a third fewer, 9.7 percent, among other workers. By 2009 the affirmative response rates had increased and were almost the same across groups, 34.5 and 30.4 percent. In response to a question about problems with employer payment, 21.2 percent of the undocumented and 11.4 percent of other workers responded affirmatively in 2006. In 2009 these figures more than doubled among the undocumented, to 50.9, and almost tripled among others, to 31.9 percent. When the question was asked another way, 32.1 percent of undocumented workers reported problems being paid for work at least some of the time in 2006, as compared to 20.8 percent of other workers, increasing slightly among the undocumented in 2009, to 41.1, with others practically catching up, at 38.6 percent.

Finally, although police are the main public authority charged with protecting individuals from crime, survey results suggest that police harassment is an increasing problem for all workers. In 2009 a total of 29.9 percent of respondents reported police harassment, in contrast to 6.1 percent in 2006. Harassment at the hands of police affected 20 percent of undocumented workers and 38.8 percent of other workers in 2009. When we explored these results by race, we found that police harassment was especially directed at African American workers, with 68.0 percent reporting police harassment, a statistically significant difference from white respondents, at 27.3 percent, and Latino respondents at 19.8 percent, with pickup-site Latino workers reporting a slightly higher 30.6 percent.[29] Among the kinds of harassment reported, many workers reported being violently treated at gathering places like hardware stores, parking lots, and grocery stores, including being shoved, kicked, and punched in the chest.

It is worth considering some of the reasons why conditions could have deteriorated for all construction workers. One explanation is that in the immediate aftermath of Hurricane Katrina, employers and state actors experimented with mistreatment on undocumented workers and found that there was no sanction, so they extended mistreatment to other workers in subsequent years. A second explanation is that the combination of the recession and the slowdown of rebuilding several years after Katrina meant that there was simply less work in residential construction, creating slimmer margins for employers, who became more likely to deny payment to workers and cut corners on safety and health precautions.[30] Finally, it is possible that the survey was picking up a more general deterioration of work in residential construction, which is more informal than more highly regulated infrastructure construction (Fussell 2009). Whatever the explanation, the implication is worrying—secondary labor market conditions now affect more workers, in more jobs, than ever before.

Abuse and Resistance

A booming and transnational construction sector has segmented workers according to national origin and gradually extended secondary-sector conditions to an increasing number of workplace activities and categories of worker. Complete control of the workplace by employers and government inaction (except harassment) enables these dynamics. Yet, even as vulnerable workers, especially the undocumented, experience abuse, they are gradually building the capacity to resist. The courage and occasional victories won through resistance deserve attention and examination, though the structural and organizational limits of a dominant dual development project have blocked the articulation of a viable joined-up workplace and community alternative.

According to the survey, most workers faced difficulties organizing, and few were active. Levels of affiliation were above 20 percent only in sports leagues and religious organizations for the worksite-surveyed workers. Yet, the one portion of the workforce in which there was a statistically significant difference in worker activity was among pickup-site workers active in ethnic and worker organizations, with 30.2 percent of these workers claiming affiliation with a worker organization as compared to only 8.7 percent of the rest of the workers. These were the most put-upon workers, suffering rates of wage theft as high as 80 percent (according to the Southern Poverty Law Center [2006]) and around 50 percent according to the survey performed for this project.[31]

A few anecdotes of workplace violations have been recorded in a Southern Poverty Law Center report titled "Broken Levees, Broken Promises: New Orleans Workers in Their Own Words." Similar anecdotes were commonplace in the cases taken by the Loyola Workplace Justice Clinic, where every Thursday as many as forty workers sought legal assistance to recover stolen wages. One group of Brazilian workers worked eighty hours per week for three months but never received overtime. Another worker described the predicament faced by workers on the job:

> When the company didn't pay us when they had promised they would, I heard of people who didn't have food to eat. I saw people cry as well. I don't know if it was out of desperation or out of hunger. . . .
>   . . . When three weeks had passed, people looked thinner and looked tired as if they didn't have the hope of anything except to keep waiting for their first paycheck.
>   They didn't know whether to continue working or to quit. They said, "If I leave they won't pay me and, if I stay, who knows what will happen?" There wasn't any other option. . . . And, because of all this, they had to continue. They were forced to do it. (SPLC 2006, 5)

Other workers reported health and safety violations:

> They gave us masks with filters, and they changed the filters in the first and second weeks, but after a couple of weeks, the company didn't change them anymore. The masks were only good for seven days. If a worker lost his mask, he couldn't get a new one. He had to work without one until the end of the seven days. There wasn't anyone to ensure that everyone had a mask—no one from the government, from the public health agency, or anyone, to take care of us. (SPLC 2006, 14)

As workers faced dangerous conditions, injuries were common, but employers took no responsibility for care. Said one worker:

> I was working in a church. I slipped and fell off the ladder. I broke my arm and cut my face. There was so much blood. My boss left me at a hospital in New Orleans where no one spoke Spanish. I was then taken to a hospital in Baton Rouge. There, they told me to come back in four or five days when they would fix my arm. I was totally alone and without any place to sleep or anyone to help me. I have a metal pin in my arm. I'm never going to be able to work as hard as I could before. How will I pay my hospital bills? (SPLC 2006, 9)

These experiences were especially common among day laborers, the most vulnerable among the construction workforce. Yet, it was the day laborers who were among the most organized. One factor was the effort of local and national organizers. One local movement, the New Orleans Worker Center for Racial Justice, formed the Congreso de Jornaleros (Congress of Day Laborers), and sent organizers to day-laborer pickup sites to recruit members, educate workers about their rights, and mediate relations with employers, police, and other government authorities. They hold weekly meetings with members and encourage members to develop organizing skills and take on leadership positions.

Honduran worker Denis Soriano is one such worker who graduated to organizer. His experience is illustrative. One employer worked him for three weeks and failed to pay, and another refused to offer any assistance after a trailer came loose and crushed his hand. He received care from a hand surgeon but accrued thousands of dollars of hospital bills that his employer refused to recognize. "There comes a moment as a worker when you get dumped on too much," said Soriano. "And so these bastards are screwing me over, screwing me over, you ask 'what are we going to do?' But if you don't have support from anyone, if you don't have [immigration] papers, you say, 'What do I do?' And this was when I started to meet organizers from the Center. They started coming to the corners and talking with the people. When the workers were having problems with the police, they were there to intervene, to offer support to those who were arrested" (quoted in Gorman 2009, 25).

The Congreso model of direct organization by and for workers also included efforts to reach out to allies. They received assistance from the National Day Laborer Organizing Network, a national member-based coalition of day laborer advocacy groups, as well as funding from major donors, such as the Open Society. Locally, the Congreso pursued alliances with programs run by the Catholic Archdiocese (Catholic Charities) and legal-aid projects against wage theft run by Loyola University.

Among the most significant victories of the Congreso was to secure a commitment from Sheriff Marlon Gusman that he would not submit to federal Immigration and Customs Enforcement (ICE) hold requests. Such requests call for local authorities to hold immigrant inmates until ICE has reviewed their immigration status, resulting in the extended detention of immigrants, even on minor infractions, and eventual deportation. Gusman announced his acquiescence to Congreso demands in a raucous Congreso meeting, joining chants of "sin papeles, sin miedo" — "no papers, no fear."[32]

Most importantly, the Congreso has built support among other groups from working classes and popular sectors. From unions, the Congreso has rallied support to raise standards for all workers. One such effort was a wage-theft ordinance they pressed at the City Council. In a council hearing, union allies explained why their members sought to uphold basic standards in the workplace. "No payroll taxes; no social security; no federal taxes—how can our contractors compete?" asked Herbert Santos of the International Union of Painters and Allied Trades (Rodriguez 2009).

The Congreso has also joined forces with working-class African American organizations, sharing offices with Stand with Dignity, an organization of primarily African American public-housing residents. In a rally with Stand with Dignity, Daniel Castellanos, another worker who has graduated to organizer, explained to his audience, "We understand that African slaves were the first immigrants to be brought here without rights. Now, we Latinos are denied civil rights in the same way." The alliance between day laborers and African American working-class residents gained particular energy around issues of police harassment. When immigration raids targeted Congreso members in 2007, the New Orleans Survivor Council, an organization of African Americans, posted bail. In return, "the day laborers formed a volunteer crew to renovate the lower Ninth Ward flooded home of Ora Green, a member of the [Survivor] Council" (Downes 2007).

The Worker Center for Racial Justice, with its Congreso and Stand with Dignity branches, evidenced cross-ethnic organizing among working classes. Further, their efforts around immigration, police abuse, and working conditions and wages targeted extraction and exclusion as they occurred in the workplace and in the community. Yet, even in victory the difficulty of working-class and popular organizing was evident—workplace demands for jobs and wages were occasionally juxtaposed with community demands to preserve non-market provision of basic services. As the city knocked down complex after complex of public housing to make space for mixed-income market developments, the Worker Center engaged in years of advocacy and pressure to force the Housing Authority of New Orleans to accept workforce agreements promising jobs to public-housing residents and certified union job training.[33] Yet, housing advocates noted that projects had survived Katrina and served the city for generations, and demolition, even under the best possible workforce agreement, was still a form of accumulation by dispossession that would undercut existing community and turn previously public assets to the private sector for accumulation (Nathan Martin 2014).

The Congreso de Jornaleros represent the most vulnerable and exploited workers within the construction sector, yet they have shown remarkable capacity to organize and to form alliances with groups within the community. This building of organization and alliance articulates an alternative development model for the construction sector, in which people can earn a livelihood, work safely, and address issues of racial and ethnic discrimination that segment the workplace and divide communities.

Yet, these efforts stand in contrast and opposition to the overwhelming trend within construction. The sector has received an unprecedented boom as a result of the private and public reconstruction occurring after Hurricane Katrina. While the infusion of capital could raise incomes for all in the sector, address critical human needs for infrastructure such as housing, and spill over to other sectors, this has not been the case. Instead, global firms and developers integrated with global markets have captured the benefits of construction and have collaborated with policymakers to preserve a sector with high rates of profit, segmented labor markets, and poor conditions for workers.

CHAPTER SIX

Racial and Gender Segmentation in Tourism and Services

In New Orleans, tourism and services are among the most important emerging sectors adapted to globally integrated production and markets. The city has always marketed its unique combination of Caribbean calypso, southern hospitality, and the vice associated with a seedy seaport, and this brand took on new significance as the city lost the port, petroleum, and manufacturing base that began its accelerated decline in the 1980s. Hurricane Katrina punctuated the shift away from traditional sectors and propelled local elites atop the tourism and services sector into dominant alliances with political leaders to reshape development in the city.

Tourism and Service Dual Development

Tourist development includes casinos, convention centers, hotels, cruise lines, and sports facilities, all of which are predicated on selling a specific brand of New Orleans culture. To develop this brand, tourism entrepreneurs marketed jazz, Mardi Gras, historic neighborhoods, and French Quarter vice (Stanonis 2006), and by the post–World War II period a host of government policies had emerged to promote tourism and tap into the connectivity of transportation infrastructure and marketing technologies. By 1975 they had developed a rationalized strategy and institutional architecture, indicated by an expansion and deepening of economic infrastructure—doubling the number of hotels, tripling the number of sightseeing and tour operators, a sixfold increase in the number of travel agencies and tourist information centers, and 114 new convention services, facilities, and bureaus (Gotham 2007, 108). During the 1980s and 1990s, public-policy strategy emphasized tourism as the leading sector of development. The city and the state established the New Orleans Tourism Marketing

Corporation and a Mayor's Office of Tourism and Arts, earmarked hotel-motel taxes for the New Orleans Sports Foundation, set aside taxes for the Greater New Orleans Tourist and Convention Commission, and legalized gaming—first on the river and eventually granting Harrah's Casino a monopoly on land-based casino gaming in the city (Whelan, Young, and Lauria 1994).[1]

This thickening tourism infrastructure brands New Orleans and maximizes its exposure to global markets. Part of this process is homogenization, simplifying the complexity of the city into a "holy trinity" of food, music, and history, a strategy of "tourism from above . . . a mix of the extralocal processes of globalization, commodification, rationalization, Disneyization, and branding" (Gotham 2007, 10).[2] This entails at once stimulating locally authentic expressions, such as jazz, and then homogenizing them for the purpose of marketing to external visitors and local "as if tourists," that is, high-income residents who consume the same things (Gotham 2007, 135).

Homogenization arouses the opposition of preservationists, cultural innovators, and others who defend the city's specificity and authenticity, and the decades since the 1970s have pitched conflict between "top-down" homogenization and "bottom-up" hybridity and diversity (Gotham 2007). In the post-Katrina period, however, the top-down project has achieved dominance, especially in its economic guise of concentrating and privatizing tourism revenues.

The top-down project builds alliances between local political elites, local tourism entrepreneurs, and external capital. External allies provide capital, cutting-edge technologies of dissemination and cultural production, and understanding of and linkages to international markets. Local capital disciplines local production processes to expand profits, for example, by segmenting workers and squeezing wages and working conditions. Local capital also mediates access to local political elites, who deregulate the industry, use public power to concentrate ownership, and pump public resources into tourist enterprise. As these alliances intensify, New Orleans tourist and service elites can replicate their enterprises externally, selling a recognizable New Orleans/Creole/Cajun/Mardi Gras brand outside the geographic limits of the city itself.

Typical of trends within the tourism and services boom are the trends occurring within food-service and drinking establishments, where a number of the observations for this chapter have been made. As the food third of the tourism "holy trinity," restaurants are one of Louisiana's most important economic sectors, and their growth has far outpaced that of other sectors. For example, despite a decline in population, the city in 2015 had more restaurants than it did before Katrina, with more than twenty-five hundred food-service and drinking places.

The census category of "leisure and hospitality" is the single largest sector for employment in the city, providing 13.2 percent of all private-sector jobs. Almost two-thirds of these jobs are in food-service and drinking establishments, and employment in food services grew 160 percent between 2001 and 2010, three times the rate of overall job growth.[3] After Katrina and the 2007 recession, restaurants lost fewer jobs than other sectors, and restaurant employment recovered both faster and to a greater degree, even as other sectors continued to decline. Much of Louisiana's tourism is accounted for by the city of New Orleans, which provides slightly over 10 percent of all restaurant jobs in the state, and slightly over 30 percent if one takes the metropolitan area (U.S. Census Bureau 2010).

In terms of revenues, restaurants make up over half of the metropolitan tourism and hospitality sector and accounted for $2.6 billion of the city's revenues in 2008. State sales tax in city restaurants is close to $150 million per year, and the city collects over $300 million in taxes on the more than $5 billion generated in tourist dollars per year (ROC 2009).

At the pinnacle of the restaurant sector are the gourmet fine-dining restaurants, defined by the Restaurant Opportunities Center (2009) as those with price points above $40 for each meal. These are the segments most prepared for insertion into globalized value chains as they cater to cosmopolitan tastes and incomes. To make local restaurants attractive enough for large-scale and globalized enterprise, local capital concentrates into mini-empires of three or more fine-dining restaurants, often located in or connected to high-end hotels (ROC 2009, 5). These mini-empires hold together through networks such as family and financial ties, with examples such as the Brennan family—led by siblings Ralph, Dickie, and Lauren—and their host of high-end establishments.[4]

To smooth the insertion of high-end New Orleans restaurants into global processes, owners use several strategies. One is to tap into the official tourism branding strategy, hiring celebrity chefs who combine international recognition with local roots—at once both homogeneous and authentic.[5] Local owners can also surf the wave of New Orleans branding into external markets, locating locally named restaurants in far-flung sites, as in the Dickie Brennan–owned Commander's Palace in Las Vegas and the Ralph Brennan–owned Jazz Kitchen in Disneyland—literal disneyization.

To guarantee their access to international capital and markets, owners of mini-empires work themselves into political networks that provide access to key decision-making entities. Ralph Brennan, one of the brother owners of Brennan's Business Group, has served as the president of the chief association of restaurant owners in New Orleans, the New Orleans Restaurant Association, as well as at the state level, in the Louisiana Restaurant Association (LRA). Among other functions, restaurant associations lobby, and Brennan contributed an average of $20,160 per year in the election years from 2004 to 2010.[6] As an organization, the LRA collects the resources of more than seventy-five hundred paying members and donated almost thirty thousand dollars to state and federal campaigns in 2008 ($28,600). The LRA employs a lobbyist, Jim Funk, who reported nearly ten thousand dollars of lobbying expenses in 2008 ($9,520.12).[7] Rising local stakes attracted the attention of the D.C.-based National Restaurant Association, which made contributions to state campaigns of $25,000 in 2006 and $33,500 in 2008.[8]

Concentrated power at the peak of the sector and deepening ties to political actors advance a top-down restaurant agenda that includes three core aspects: minimal regulation, international integration, and a high-profit/low-cost model that rests on segmenting workers and workplaces. Statements on the LRA website indicate the deregulatory agenda: "Your membership strengthens our impact both in the state Legislature as well as the national arena in Washington, D.C. Our professional lobbyists fight for you and your rights to operate in a profitable manner with fewer restrictions."[9]

An additional expression of the deregulatory agenda appears in the kinds of services the LRA offers to members. A workers' compensation insurance fund turns a program to protect workers hurt on the job into an additional source of profit, as the LRA website trumpets the amount of money it has returned to participating restaurant owners in the form of unused premiums and interest income: "In 2007, The Louisiana Restaurant Association Self Insurer's Fund returned $4.1 million in unused premium and interest income to eligible participants. For 25 years, the LRA/SIF had more than $75 million in dividends—more than any other workers' compensation provider in the state."[10]

Deregulation creates an enabling environment for higher profits and lower costs. The LRA seems well aware of the practice, as indicated by the Employment Practices Liability Insurance offered to protect against "many kinds of employee lawsuits, including claims of: Sexual harassment, Discrimination, Wrongful termination, Failure to employ or promote, Wrongful discipline, Mismanagement of employee benefit plans." The LRA website goes on to explain that "employees have a 63% success rate of winning employment suits that go to verdict. According to the 2006 edition of Jury Verdict Research, the average verdict in an employment suit is greater than $600,000. The average verdict if discrimination is alleged is a whopping $656,000 and can increase to more than $1 million if the suit goes to a state court. By the way, these figures don't include legal fees! One way to mitigate such a catastrophic loss is to protect yourself with Employment Practices Liability Insurance."[11]

Finally, the LRA undertakes investments to shift the priorities of public institutions toward tourism priorities by allying with the internationally oriented elites of other sectors. Its website notes that "the LRA's Greater New Orleans Chapter planned to donate $100,000 to the University of New Orleans' Kabacoff School of Hotel, Restaurant and Tourism Administration."[12] The University of New Orleans is the main public institution of higher education in the city, and Pres Kabacoff is a leading real estate developer.

The restaurant sector is at the heart of the tourism and services sector of New Orleans, a sector that has boomed after Katrina. At least part of that boom is attributable to international adaptation, as local elites link to globally integrated capital and markets. Economic elites concentrate control at the peak of the sector, navigating political and social networks to shift local priorities toward their top-down development strategies, structuring the sector around an internationally integrated, high-profit, low-cost, deregulated development model.

Impact on Workers

This development model has particular impacts on working people. Deregulated tourism offers some opportunities for livable incomes, but these jobs are allocated on the basis of ascriptive characteristics such as race, gender, and ethnicity. As a result, good jobs are out of reach for those workers who are not native-born and white, and generally male. Women, people of color, and immigrants tend to be relegated to jobs and segments where incomes are low, working conditions poor, and opportunities for mobility limited. In general, work in tourism and services is difficult, dangerous, insecure, and low-paying. A shocking number of workers earn low wages, lack benefits such as vacation days or health insurance, do not receive regular raises or promotions, face violations of workplace and health and safety regulations, and face intimidation or reprisals if they attempt to organize.

Among all traded sectors serving external markets, hospitality and tourism had the third-lowest average wages in 2014, at $30,431.[13] Only performing arts and video production were lower, and they accounted for fewer than 5,000 jobs each. By contrast, hospitality and tourism accounted for more than 80,000 jobs, was the largest single sector for employment among traded clusters, and was the fastest growing. Hospitality establishments serving local markets were second only to health services in the number of jobs provided, close to 60,000, but had the single lowest average wages for local-serving clusters at $18,019 (Plyer, Shrinath, and Mack 2015, 16–19).

To paint a more detailed picture of worker experience, two sets of surveys and interviews provide observations of working lives in food services. The first survey attempts a comprehensive exploration of restaurant work through surveys undertaken in 2008 and 2009 and ongoing interviews and contacts with organizers in the sector. Students assisted staff and restaurant worker-members of the national advocacy organization Restaurant Opportunities Center (ROC) to conduct closed-ended interviews of 535 workers and approximately 30 open-ended qualitative conversations. The author has also maintained ongoing contact with the staff of ROC as a local advisory-board member and research associate.[14]

The second set of observations draws on surveys undertaken between September 2011 and May 2012 of food-service workers with the global contractor Sodexo on the campus of Tulane University. Student volunteers interviewed fifty-one workers after their shifts or during breaks, identifying workers by their uniforms and using convenience sampling methods to select respondents.

For each set of respondents, a relatively similar set of questions was used, exploring the availability of benefits, working conditions, hiring and promotion practices, the existence of job-specific training opportunities, and employer discrimination. The similarity of methods of data collection triangulates the information on working conditions from different perspectives, but there are good reasons to limit direct comparisons across the two surveys. Only the restaurant worker survey attained a relatively large number of respondents using a randomized sampling strategy. For this reason, the results for the two sets of surveys are presented separately, and only the results for restaurant workers are extrapolated to the entire population of metropolitan restaurant workers. Conclusions based on the results for the other survey are limited to the sample population surveyed. The second survey remains of particular relevance as it targets a demographic relegated to a particularly exploited corner of food services: African American women.

Restaurant Workers

In general, restaurant workers work for low wages, receive few benefits, and face obstacles to mobility. There are frequent violations of workplace regulations, and conditions vary significantly according to segment of the industry and job in the workplace. Across these segments and jobs, workers appear allocated on the basis of ascriptive characteristics of race, gender, and national origin. In spite of and in opposition to these conditions, workers find ways to resist, forming organizations and making alliances with other members of the community.

In general, restaurant workers are low-wage workers, with a median wage of $8.92 per hour.[15] Among survey respondents, 9 percent of the workers earned less than minimum wage; 87 percent earned below the wage calculated as a living wage ($18.31/hour) given the cost of living in New Orleans (Economic Policy Institute 2008);[16] and nearly one-third (31 percent) earned below the more conservative federal poverty line of $17,500 per year. Over time, average restaurant worker incomes have remained virtually flat: $15,435 in 2001, $16,870 in 2008, and $18,560 in 2012.

In addition, the survey revealed that workers receive few or no workplace benefits. Very few workers (15.5 percent) have health insurance through their employers, and over half (53.2 percent) reported no health insurance at all. Almost none have paid sick days (88.6 percent) and three-quarters of respondents have no paid vacation days (74.2 percent). Workers on low wages cannot afford to take unpaid days off, and they have no insurance to pay for care. As a result, nearly one-third (32.2 percent) went to the emergency room without being able to pay, and almost three-quarters (72.3 percent) had worked while sick. One worker reported, "I've seen broke down servers, bartenders, who just keep working because they can't afford not to and they got a sprain or whatever or pulling their back. . . . They have some condition of some kind and they just work through it." Another explained, "If you leave for a month you really hurt the job; they might find somebody else to take your position." A third worker elaborated, "They don't care. You gonna be sneezing over people's food and stuff like that and if you wanna put a mask on or try to cover yourself up or whatever then it's bad for the business. That's why you should have allowed me to stay home. I told ya'll I was sick. That's how it is right now; they just don't care" (Schneider and Jayaraman 2014, 13).

There are also few opportunities for mobility. Most workers receive no regular raises (69 percent), almost three-quarters had never received a promotion (73.6 percent), and more than half (53 percent) reported that they did not receive the on-the-job training needed for promotion. In the absence of opportunities for promotion or higher wages through seniority, workers circulate from one restaurant to the next, averaging 2.8 years at their current employer, and still most (72.9 percent) reported that they did not consider their current job a step up from the previous one.

The respondents to the survey reported multiple and various types of workplace violations: 38.1 percent reported failure to receive overtime wages, 27.8 percent had worked off the clock without pay, 9 percent earned less than a minimum wage, and 18.8 percent of fine-dining servers reported that management took a share of worker tips. One way management cuts pay is by requiring workers show up early to set up, or to clean after they have clocked out. "We're all required to go in at 4 pm but not clock in because the restaurant doesn't open until 6 pm. We got to clock in after a meeting and other work, so we always work one and a half to two hours extra," said one worker.

Another pattern is to divide worker hours among multiple establishments owned by the same company: "They have you running all over the place like really slave driving. And then how they do you is they will work you extra hours, they will work you overtime, but what they do is they separate you. So you got there, here, and they split you up and they give you a different time card for every place that you work. Each one is separate so that you never really work overtime" (ROC 2009, 26).

Some establishments simply undercount hours to avoid paying: "They would adjust the hours so they didn't have to pay me. For every hour that you don't make minimum wage, they are supposed to supplement your income to bring you to the minimum wage. But, what this restaurant would do is change my hours so that it looked like I worked less so they wouldn't have to pay me the extra money. They would give me my tips, but they wouldn't pay me for all the hours I worked" (ROC 2009, 25).

In addition to wage and hours violations, health and safety violations are common. For example, 24 percent report missing guards on cutting machines, 29.3 percent report doing something that put their own safety at risk, 86.3 percent report working when the restaurant was understaffed, and 86.1 percent perform several jobs at once.[17] As a result, 43.5 percent have been burned, 42.4 percent have been cut, 15.4 percent have slipped and injured themselves on the job, 39.9 percent have come into contact with toxic chemicals, and 16.4 percent have chronic pain caused or worsened by the job (ROC 2009, 20–21).

Other workplace violations include verbal abuse and sexual harassment, frequently based on race, gender, ethnicity, or sexual orientation. Nearly one-third (29.4 percent) reported that they or a co-worker had experienced verbal abuse, with one-third (33.6 percent) reporting that race had been a factor, 22 percent gender, 15.1 percent language, and 14 percent sexual orientation. One server reported, "The floor manager smacking my ass and grinding me when I tell him 'stop it,' and he still don't stop, and nobody says nothing. . . . I see our floor manager grabbing on everybody's ass, talking about how we'd sleep together outside of work and this that and the other" (ROC 2009, 47).

While restaurant work is generally low-wage, with few benefits, and subject to frequent violations, there are also variations according to segment of the industry and position within the workplace. Front-of-the-house jobs in fine-dining establishments provide the few livable-wage jobs in the industry, with higher benefits, more potential to increase income with tips, and less risk than in back-of-the-house jobs and in family-style and quick-service segments. With data disaggregated, statistically significant differences emerged across segments of the industry and position in the workplace. For example, one-quarter (24.5 percent) of all front-of-the-house workers earn wages above $18.31 per hour, compared to only 2.1 percent of back-of-the-house workers, generally head chefs. Front-of-the-house workers are more likely to receive benefits such as health insurance (51.6 percent versus 39.1 percent), and they are less likely to experience risky working conditions (20.1 percent versus 29.7 percent), leading to fewer workplace injuries (33.2 percent versus 47.9 percent for burns).

There were also differences between fine-dining, family-style, and quick-service restaurants. Fine-dining restaurants were more likely to allow increasing incomes through tips—60.1 percent in fine dining, 56.7 percent in family style, and 18.9 percent in quick service—and were more likely to produce incomes above $400 per week—49.2 percent versus 38.4 percent and 27.4 percent.[18]

While decent jobs were concentrated in the fine-dining and front-of-the-house jobs, these jobs were not accessible to all workers. Workers appeared to be assigned to segments of the industry and positions in the workplace on the basis of ascriptive characteristics such as race and gender. Among front-of-the-house jobs, white workers accounted for 58.3 percent of the workforce, and 79.9 percent of all white workers worked in the front of the house. By contrast, African American workers accounted for only 21.8 percent of front-of-the-house workers, and only 41.4 percent of black workers were in the front of the house.[19] Similar patterns emerged throughout this industry segment, as 57 percent of fine-dining workers were white, and 39.8 percent of white workers are in fine dining. By contrast, only 20.1 percent of African American workers are in fine dining, and they make up only 22.1 percent of fine-dining workers.[20] Similarly, twice as high a proportion of African Americans (36.5 percent) were in limited service establishments, as opposed to only 18 percent of white workers.

When gender and race are considered together, additional patterns of segmentation also appear. About one-half (49.1 percent) of all African American women in the restaurant workforce are in quick service, compared to 30.3 percent of African American men, 14.9 percent of white women, and 21.4 percent of white men.[21]

The assignment of workers to jobs and segments of the industry happens in subtle and not-so-subtle ways. One fine-dining restaurant owner related, "Well, I don't have any black people working here. They never came to apply. The black people have their thing and the white people have their thing." In a separate conversation, an African American worker stated, "At fine dining establishments in the French Quarter, you can be as smart as this book right here but they won't hire people like me for certain positions" (Schneider and Jayaraman 2014, 252).[22]

Table 11 shows some of the statistically significant differences that emerged from the survey. Using Pearson chi-squared tests to measure the significance of differences in proportions across groups, the respondents

TABLE 11. Few Good Jobs, Many Bad Jobs in Food Service

	Front	Back	Pearson Chi^2
Living wage	24.5	2.1	138.26***
Below poverty line	14.3	22.4	12.3**
Tipped	68.5	14.6	149.19***
Health insurance	51.6	39.1	9.38***
Felt at risk	20.1	29.7	6.52**
Burned	33.2	47.9	11.20***
Toxic chemicals	25.1	36.5	7.72***

	Fine Dining	Family Dining	Quick Serve	Pearson Chi^2
Hourly wage	13.40	12.10	8.50	
Weekly earning <$400	49.2	38.4	27.4	13.84**
Tipped	60.1	56.7	18.9	68.16***
Health insurance	63.2	36.3	46.7	30.87***
Toxic chemicals	27.6	25.8	38.5	6.62**

	Black	White	Pearson Chi^2
Front of the house	41.4	79.9	66.80***
Fine dining	20.1	39.8	60.06***
Limited service	36.5	18.0	22.82***
Weekly earning >$400	26.4	41.6	14.64*

	Black Female	Black Male	White Female	White Male	Pearson Chi^2
Quick serve	49.1	30.3	14.9	21.4	55.04***

Source: Author-administered survey and statistical calculations.
* Difference in groups significant at $p < .10$, ** Difference in groups significant at $p < .05$, *** Difference in groups significant at $p < .01$.

were categorized according to front- and back-of-the-house workers, fine dining/family dining/quick service, black/white, and black female/black male and white female/white male. For example, while 14.3 percent of front-of-the-house workers were below the federal poverty line, the proportion reached 22.4 percent of back-of-the-house workers. While the average hourly wage in fine dining was $13.40, the average wage in quick service was $8.50. While 26.4 percent of black workers earned over $400 per week, that number reached 41.6 percent among white workers.

The survey of restaurant workers revealed a generally difficult life for working people. There was only a small proportion of good jobs, and those would appear to have been allocated on the basis of race and gender characteristics that make it difficult for workers to move from bad jobs and bad segments of the industry into good ones. White workers can access the few good jobs; black workers cannot. Black women are particularly segmented into quick-service restaurants.

Limited-Service Workers

To characterize the work that African American women particularly do within food service, a second survey targeted limited-service workers, specifically those who staff cafés, cafeterias, and other eating establishments on the Tulane University campus. These workers are employed by Sodexo, a useful workforce to target for several reasons, in addition to the fact that the author was working at Tulane at the time. Sodexo employs more than a thousand people in New Orleans, including workers at Tulane, Loyola, Xavier, and Dillard Universities, as well other corporate and medical complexes in the city. On Tulane campus, Sodexo employs 250 workers, 130 on a part-time basis.[23]

The most important reason to survey this workforce was related to the demographic characteristic of limited-service work highlighted by the restaurant survey—it is dominated by African American women. The survey on Tulane campus confirmed this observation, as 74.5 percent of the workers were women and 86 percent were black.[24] For these workers, work was poorly paid, with few benefits, and many had to depend on public assistance even though they worked. Workers reported frequent workplace violations, especially a high level of verbal abuse, and there was little possibility of mobility.

A total of fifty-one workers were surveyed.[25] The average age was 38.4, with a minimum of 18, a maximum of 64, and around one-third between 40 and 64.[26] Average tenure was five years, with a maximum of thirty. Slightly over half, 52 percent, did not consider their move to their current job as a step up, and more than 60 percent started at or below $8 per hour.

A plurality of workers, 40.5 percent, earn between $8 and $9 per hour, with 19.6 percent at $8 per hour.[27] Average weekly earnings after taxes were $314.40, with a minimum of $150, and 19.4 percent of respondents earn less than $200.[28] At these levels of income, since starting work on campus, 26.6 percent had received food stamps, 17.2 percent had received Medicaid, 15.6 percent had received Section 8 housing assistance, and 7.8 percent had received WIC assistance.[29]

Among all respondents, three-quarters had never received a promotion with a change in title (74.5 percent), though 87.5 percent reported having the skills they would need for a promotion and 45 percent said they did not receive the training they needed for a promotion from their employer. Slightly over half (54.9 percent) reported they did not receive regular raises, and of those who reported a raise, 46.9 percent received raises of 21 to 40 cents per hour.[30]

As reported by the Louisiana Justice Institute:

> The main complaints from the workers regarding working conditions are a total lack of respect from management (one woman has been working for Tulane food service for 40 years and must ask permission to go to the restroom), inadequate healthcare benefits (for most employees the healthcare plan provided would cost two weeks of their salary), and poverty wages (many Sodexo workers are paid under $9 hourly while the federal government reports living wage in New Orleans as $9.68 hourly for one individual). Many workers have waited over a year for raises, only to receive a raise of $0.20 or less while others who have worked on Tulane's campus for more than 3 decades work for $9.50 per hour and without healthcare. Many were hired being told they could rise to management, only to realize they would be unable to do so because Sodexo would never provide training—they prefer to hire outside management. Many others were hired with the promise of full-time employment only to receive part time hours. (Elliott and Ford 2010)

Among the respondents to the survey, slightly under one-quarter (24.4 percent) work more than one job, with 11.1 percent working two other jobs, and the total average hours in all jobs at 42.2 per week, with a maximum of 75 hours per week.[31] In terms of the characterization of their employment on campus, 56.8 percent described their work as either temporary or terminating each summer.[32] Of those laid off each summer, the company reports rehiring 75 percent.

Among the benefits received with work, 40 percent reported not having guaranteed vacation or paid sick days.[33] Over one-third (35.4 percent) have no health insurance, and only 31.3 percent of those who do have insurance get it from their employer. As a result, 68 percent reported having to go to work sick and 31.3 percent reported that they or a family member had gone to the emergency room without being able to pay at some point in the last year.

A Sodexo employee, Shaquille Taylor, penned the following words in a letter to the editor:

> After four years at Bruff, I make $8 an hour. For the summer months, I remain on contract, but there is no work, and no money. I'd like to get another job to save money to go to college myself, but it's hard to find a good job just for the summer and during the year my schedule is constantly changing. My job can be tiring and dangerous. In one incident I cut my finger and was out of work for a whole year recovering. But what I want to change the most is the way that managers treat workers like me. I feel they treat us like children, and they ignore our suggestions to make our jobs better. They know our work can be dangerous so they require us to use hairnets, cutting gloves, and slip resistant shoes, but we have to pay for protective gear out of our wages. This is especially hard to take when we earn so little. There are no opportunities for promotions—and raises are few and far between. We want to have a career path so we can live a decent life. Most of all we just want to be treated with respect. (Taylor and Freimuth 2011)

With respect to conditions on the job, 26 percent of our respondents reported frequently or sometimes doing something that put their own safety at risk, and 12 percent sometimes did something that might have harmed the health or safety of customers because they were under time pressure. With respect to doing something they were not trained to do, 34 percent reported frequently or sometimes, and three-quarters, 76.4 percent, reported having to do several jobs at once. Nearly one-third (29.4 percent) had been burned on the job, 35.3 percent had been cut on the job, 8 percent had slipped and injured themselves on the job, and 9.8 percent had some other injury on the job. There were 13.7 percent of respondents who came into contact with toxic chemicals, and 25.5 percent who had chronic pain caused or worsened by their job.

In terms of abuse on the job, 31.4 percent had experienced verbal abuse and 5.9 percent had experienced sexual harassment. Of those who answered affirmatively to experiencing abuse, equal proportions attributed it to race or ethnic reasons (46.7 percent), and 6.6 percent attributed the abuse to religion.

When workers raised issues, they felt intimidated. The student news-paper, the *Hullabaloo*, reported from eight-year employee Maria Osario that "the managerial staff is consistently unresponsive to workers who voice concern about safety in the workplace and the fairness of their wages and that workers are intimidated about unionizing. 'They trick us; they say you'll lose your job'" (Shoup 2011).

Worker Resistance

Even in the context of workforce segmentation and exploitative practices, workers in food services sought allies across the community to advance an alternative to New Orleans dual development. The most important organi-zation of restaurant workers is the Restaurant Opportunities Center (ROC), which began in New York in 2001 and has an affiliate in New Orleans (R. Sen and Mamdouh 2008). ROC builds worker power along three tracks: research and policy, direct campaigns, and facilitation with owners. The first track, research and policy, includes the survey cited here, as well as other studies that diagnose the sector and offer policy solutions. In New Orleans, among the policy initiatives supported by the research was legis-lation to ease conditions for workers forced to evacuate after a hurricane, a not uncommon experience in New Orleans. Nationally, the research has fed into efforts to raise minimum wages for restaurant workers.

The second track, direct campaigns, involves action to achieve jus-tice for individual workers and to have a demonstration effect on the sec-tor. To date, there has been one high-visibility and successful campaign against a particularly unscrupulous owner, Yousef Wafiq Salem Aladwan. "J'obert," as he is known, owns the fine-dining Italian restaurant Tony Moran's in the French Quarter, as well as several other French Quarter eating and drinking establishments. At Tony Moran's he wrote paychecks that bounced, paid workers in cash, failed to pay overtime, made employ-ees work off the clock, and stole their tips. He assigned workers of color to the upstairs dining area, where there were fewer customers and there-fore fewer tips.[34]

An African American worker had been working as floor manager until the management decided he "was not Italian enough" (ROC 2009, 25). He was demoted to regular server, his hours were cut, and he was moved to the upstairs overflow, where earnings potential was only one-third the first-floor dining room. He was asked to show up early but could not clock in until the first customers arrived, working an average of an hour per day without pay. Eventually, he complained, but his hours were further cut, the house took 20 percent of his tips, and he was relegated exclusively to the upstairs overflow. He discussed the situation with other workers, but they were too scared to confront management.

He contacted ROC and eventually filed suit for over $500,000 in wages and penalties, including a complaint with the Equal Employment Opportunities Commission.[35] The campaign began with the slow collection of claimants from among the many workers who had been wronged—a difficult task, as most had quit and moved on rather than confront management. Eventually, eleven workers joined the suit, and they worked for over two years to move the case through the courts. To increase pressure, they staged protests in front of the restaurant, and management responded by taking pictures, calling the police, and standing bouncers menacingly on the sidewalk to intimidate protesters. Some protests involved just a few workers trudging through the rain, but at other times as many as fifty marchers paraded, including other ROC members and allies.

Among the allies who demonstrated support were middle-class students and professors, clergy, and other low-wage workers. Students and academics had begun their contact with ROC through participation in the restaurant survey, and ROC maintained contact by appointing academics from several local universities, including the author, to a local advisory board. Other allies were drawn from local clergy, especially faith leaders with a particular commitment to social justice. They turned protests into prayer sessions, sang spiritual protest songs, held candlelight vigils, and offered sermons and reflections on the lives of working people.

The largest rallies were filled by allies drawn from undocumented day laborers. They recognized in the struggle against abuse in the restaurant sector the same patterns of abuse that occurred in their workplaces, and they arrived as members of the Congreso de Jornaleros (Congress of Day Laborers), one of the member organizations of the Worker Center for Racial Justice, an organization that organizes day laborers, guest workers, and public-housing residents.

The Worker Center and ROC collaborate often, as ROC staff and members attend rallies to protest immigration raids and police abuse against Worker Center members, and the executive director of the Worker Center, Saket Soni, articulated a shared understanding of the challenges facing worker organization across sectors:

> People like guestworkers and farmworkers and domestic workers and day laborers, they're the next wave of the movement. That's not just something that exists in my head. . . . I think there's an aspiration to figure out what organizational forms, what laws, what movement will get us to the point where workers have a voice in the economy and in

democracy. We know our country is in a crisis of democracy. Right now, democracy is under attack. From time to time in the history of this country, there is a vision of the next phase of our democracy that is fueled by the energy and the imagination of workers. That's the role that the Mississippi Delta played in the '50s and the '60s. I think it's the role that low-wage workers in the South will play in the next decade. (Dean 2014)

After almost two years of litigation and countless protests, the workers finally won. To avoid payment, J'obert had filed for bankruptcy and switched lawyers repeatedly, but he was eventually forced to pay more than $260,000 in unpaid wages and penalties. In the process of negotiations, ROC demanded an employee handbook to establish best practices in the restaurant and ROC oversight to ensure implementation of the agreement. Among the best practices demanded are clear rules for promotion, as well as basic standards to prevent discrimination in the workplace.

The ROC campaign against J'obert fed into their efforts to pursue the third track, facilitation with owners. With the threat of legal action and direct campaigns, facilitation strategies involve meeting with owners to share "high-road" strategies that combine business success with decent wages and working conditions (ROC 2009). Some owners have welcomed the opportunity, meeting in roundtables with ROC staff and accepting strategies to improve productivity, minimize turnover, and offer regular raises. Together, roundtables have established policies for review and promotion and handbooks for employees, among other best practices.

Eventually, ROC New Orleans hopes to model the success of a high-road strategy with a worker-owned cooperative restaurant.[36] The cooperative would be a fine-dining establishment and would follow high-road practices, including training for workers to increase productivity and map paths for mobility within the cooperative and into fine-dining establishments throughout the sector. Currently, ROC offers training to workers, with high-skill fine-dining servers and bartenders training other members to give them the capacity to move into fine-dining and front-of-the-house jobs.[37]

While direct-action campaigns have scored important victories, the high-road strategies generate more ambiguous results. While a number of owners have been eager supporters, the Louisiana Restaurant Association put active pressure on owners not to engage ROC roundtables, handing out threatening flyers at a restaurant convention event to dissuade owners from participating. ROC efforts to reach out to corporate and more establishment allies produced similar ambiguity. At the last moment before ROC's

2010 launch of its survey results, Catholic Charities withdrew and blocked the participation of one of the restaurants they support. When asked for comment, a member of the Catholic Church noted that they wanted no problems with the LRA and thought it best to steer clear of ROC. Despite these limitations, ROC scores occasional victories by building alliances across segments of the working class and into the community. Similar strategies have been pursued by the workers in limited-service food establishments, where mostly African American women were relegated to jobs with low pay, difficult conditions, and little prospect for mobility. Workers responded by advancing an alternative model for the sector, forming alliances especially with two key groups. The first ally was the Service Employees International Union (SEIU), who provided an organizer to assist workers, and the other was the portion of the community with whom they had the most contact in their work—the largely middle-class and white students of Tulane.[38] A student-administered survey of on-campus service workers picked up some of this contact, as almost four-fifths of respondents, 78.3 percent, supported some informal activity in which campus workers and their families could interact with students.[39] On a scale of 1 to 10, respondents rated student appreciation of workers at 7.29, with about a third of the responses (30.6) between 6 and 8. On a scale of 1 to 5, with 1 "very bad" and 5 "very good," the average characterization of the relationship between students and workers was 3.84, with approximately half (48 percent) responding "good." About 29.2 percent reported coming together with other workers or students to discuss relations between students and workers, and 42.9 percent reported coming together with workers or students to discuss workplace issues.[40]

The student organizations that joined Sodexo workers included Tulane University Solidarity Committee (later Tulane Peace Action Committee), African American Congress, Men of Color, University Students against Sweatshops, and Amnesty International. They organized worker appreciation events, sit-ins, worker speak-outs, and public actions.

In a letter to the Tulane student newspaper, Tulane student organizer Mat Freimuth demanded a labor code of conduct: "The university can no longer ignore unfair pay, disrespect, and rights violations of community members on campus. We have asked the university to adopt a labor code of conduct, but it's languished for months. Offer a code of conduct that covers all employment at Tulane, including the employees of contractors. That code of conduct should guarantee that everyone earns a living wage, everyone can work safely, and everyone is treated with respect. It seems like the university sees us as children, just as SODEXO sees the workers as children" (Taylor and Freimuth 2011).

The demand for the code of conduct was widely supported by workers (Tulane USAS 2011). In response to a survey question as to whether Tulane should have a set of minimum standards in a labor code that applies to all workers on campus, including subcontracted ones, 90.9 percent responded affirmatively. A draft code was written by students with the help of workers and the SEIU, and it was submitted to the university senate in the spring of 2010. There, it was assigned to a Social Issues Committee, where it sat without resolution.

To put pressure on Sodexo and the university, students marched to the Sodexo administrative offices on campus and presented a list of demands (Coll 2010). Sodexo accepted the demands but offered no negotiations, issuing only a statement affirming its high standards for working conditions and its support for worker rights to organize.[41] On April 13, workers, students, and the SEIU presented their concerns to the City Council, where "Helene O'Brien, president of SEIU Local 21LA, said Sodexo managers systematically erased overtime hours worked by 150 employees last year, denying them a total of $22,000 they had earned" (Eggler 2010).

Workers also organized a strike at the main cafeteria dining hall. According to two of the student organizers of the event, Lauren Elliott and Brian Ford, "This walk-out was a large and loud public outcry against the injustices of Sodexo. For the first time, the Tulane and Loyola Sodexo workers seized the opportunity to be public, vocal, and united. . . . The day of the strike they stood at the picket line and said, 'Look at us, we are human!' to their managers as they walked by. After months of silence and fear, the workers were able to find courage in each other that day and the community of support around them, collectively demanding that management see them, hear them, and treat them with the respect and dignity they deserve as humans" (Elliott and Ford 2010).

The response from the university was harsh. Four student leaders were charged with code of conduct violations, including intimidation or harassment, abusive or disorderly conduct, interference with the freedom of expression of others, interference with the educational process or other university-sponsored activities, and failure to comply with university officials acting in the performance of their duties. One of the accused, Brian Ford, wrote: "We were kind of shocked and surprised. We couldn't believe that the administration would take this response to a very nonviolent and orderly demonstration. They had to make the argument that clapping and cheering was intimidation, that encouraging students not to use the dining facilities was interfering with school-sponsored affairs or the education process. They basically took the position that part of the educational process was eating lunch" (Elliott and Ford 2010). As a result of the charges, two of the students who graduated that spring were subsequently banned from campus to participate in any unauthorized protests and/or rallies and threatened with arrest for criminal trespass (Rothschild 2010).

Despite the intimidation, workers staged another strike on October 7 (Nolan 2010), and in April 2011 they held a sit-in at the university president's office. They explained, "The legitimacy of our claims was constantly being questioned by President Cowen and the administration—the very people who should have been *helping* to get a code of conduct in place, not *resisting* it." The sit-in was covered in the *Chronicle of Higher Education*, among other places (Bousquet 2011).

In 2011, a case filed by the SEIU reached the National Labor Relations Board, winning back pay and an offer to rehire a worker terminated for organizing. Tulane also factored into the settlement, required to apologize to workers and organizers who had been "expelled, harassed, and intimidated by the university, as well as postings and notifications to all workers." These were important victories, but the settlement included a neutrality agreement, and the union pulled its organizer from campus. The university posted its apologies but allowed the labor code of conduct to die in committee. Eventually, the experience of mobilizing, intimidation, and the sense of abandonment took its toll. One of the worker leaders fell ill and was unable to continue working, blaming her illness on the stress of organizing and intimidation. When asked why SEIU had apparently abandoned a fight that appeared to be making progress, one union organizer observed, "I don't know. I've seen unions do it before. They allocate resources for a certain amount of time. If they don't think they can secure a union outright, they win a few battles, declare a victory, and get out."[42] In the face of a university and corporate attack, unions abandoned the worker organizing that showed such promise, and on-campus student, faculty, and worker alliance dissipated.

This chapter has presented observations on the food-service sector in New Orleans. Economic elites oriented to globally integrated models of accumulation have used their networks, resources, and influence to design a high-profit, low-wage, and segmented model of restaurant development. This is expressed in a restaurant sector with great dynamism in terms of producing wealth but offering only a few good jobs. Worse, good jobs appear allocated on the basis of ascriptive characteristics such as race, gender, and ethnicity, and most jobs available to workers of color, women, and the non-native born are characterized by low wages, few benefits, unsafe and abusive conditions, and little chance for mobility.

A closer look at the limited-service sector provides detail on the experience of African American women. This hugely important demographic in the city dominates the workforce of limited-service workers, and their conditions on one campus display difficulties such as low wages, insecurity, lack of safety, and abusive conditions. The workers attempted to resist their conditions and formed alliances with unions and students, the portion of the community with whom they had the greatest contact. Their efforts at organizing were inspiring for their bravery and won a number of victories, though they did not win their demand for a union.

Slightly more durable organizing has occurred in a sectorwide effort, led by the Restaurant Opportunities Center, an organization of restaurant workers seeking allies among a variety of community groups, including students and academics, clergy, and other workers from low-wage sectors. ROC has maintained an organization and a membership, buoyed in part by a national organization, and has won campaigns against specific employers as well as ongoing research and facilitation strategies including roundtables with willing employers and training for workers. Still, even ROC has achieved only limited success in advancing alternatives for development in the food-services sector, testament to the dominance and influence of elite strategies.

This chapter focuses on food service as a window into the tourism and services sector more generally. While the sector is rising and has been the focus of elites oriented to globally integrated accumulation, they have structured the sector according to a top-down project of limited regulation, high profits, low wages, and an industry segmented according to ascriptive characteristics that assign workers to good and bad jobs within establishments and good and bad portions of the industry. To advance dual development, economic elites have sought political influence and market power, forming powerful trade associations, linkages to local and national politicians, and mini-empires that control high-end fine-dining establishments held together through financial, family, and other social ties.

CHAPTER SEVEN

Deindustrialization versus Joined-up Workplace and Community Struggle

The only sector that has provided a reasonable number of good jobs for people with the educational and demographic characteristics of the majority of New Orleanians is manufacturing, and only some manufacturing jobs can be considered good. The pivot of manufacturing work in the New Orleans area has been the port, inspiring industrial processing of goods coming in and out and manufacturing activities associated with transportation machinery and infrastructure. Manufacturing received a boost with petroleum and petroleum-related activities, especially after World War II, but elites directing port- and petroleum-associated manufacturing neglected to produce linkages to other sectors, and manufacturing began a steady decline in the 1970s. Oil price shocks caused additional disruptions, and the area suffered rates of deindustrialization similar to other cities characterized as "rust belt" (Hirsch 1983).

Within the arc of industrial boom and bust, one of the key manufacturing sites has been Avondale Shipyards, at one time the biggest single employer in the state. Avondale did not begin as a good place to work, especially for the largely African American workforce, but the shipyard was transformed through worker efforts to link workplace and community struggle. By organizing, workers improved safety and livelihoods, and this had reverberations in the vibrancy of surrounding communities and businesses. The years before Hurricane Katrina marked steady victories for workers, but their efforts existed in spite of and in opposition to the elite dual development model. Katrina turned the table, and by 2013 the shipyard had shuttered for good.

Still, Avondale and the manufacturing sector more generally are worth considering within this study, as they offer a glimpse into potential alternative development trajectories rooted in worker-community power.

Development led by joined-up worker and community struggles offers reasonable livelihoods to typical New Orleanians. The Avondale experience demonstrates that such livelihoods will only be possible again if workers and communities can overcome unregulated globalization of production, the shift of U.S.-based firms into financial sources of accumulation rather than production and employment, and local elites who prefer to jettison sectors in which they have to share control with workers and communities.

This chapter begins by exploring the trajectory of manufacturing in New Orleans, tracing it from its post–World War II peak through its 1970s and 1980s decline. Within the sector, the chapter emphasizes the alternative development model that appeared episodically when workers and communities joined forces to structure patterns of production and distribution. The chapter looks particularly at the case of the Avondale shipyard, where workers embedded their organizing efforts in the community, secured some control over their livelihoods, but were ultimately discarded by local elite strategies of dual development.

Role of Manufacturing in New Orleans

New Orleans sits at the mouth of the Mississippi River and therefore offers a prime location for industrial activity associated with the port. As goods come in and out, the area around the port offers an opportunity to add value to the agricultural products originating in the U.S. heartland and destined overseas and processing the raw materials arriving from abroad to be sold domestically. Oil refineries, petrochemical plants, and industrial facilities line the Mississippi between New Orleans and Baton Rouge, testament to the advantages of an inland deep-water port. Government incentives in the form of tax benefits and subsidies to industrial activity built the region as a manufacturing hub, booming particularly after World War II.

Yet, transformations shortly after World War II indicated that industrial prominence required not just advantageous geography but continuous innovation to protect against low-cost competitors. Technical transformations such as containerization lowered the costs of handling seaborne transport by reducing the amount of machinery and labor necessary to handle cargo. Smaller Gulf of Mexico ports such as Biloxi absorbed some New Orleans traffic, and New Orleans port jobs peaked in 1970 with 12,764 water transportation service jobs, falling 78.1 percent between 1980 and 2003. Marine cargo handling also peaked in 1970 with 12,141 jobs, falling 80.7 percent between 1980 and 2003 (Brunsma, Overfelt, and Picou 2007, 69). In tonnage, the port has dropped to the fifty-third-largest in the world and sixth-largest in the United States, handling 61,804 tons in 2009.[1]

While the port lost some of its primacy over time, manufacturing received a temporary boost from the oil and gas sector, as oil was discovered in Louisiana in 1906. Even in 2015, seven of eight U.S. rigs in the Gulf of Mexico lie in Louisiana coastal waters, making New Orleans well placed to house the industries supported by the extraction, refining, and processing of petroleum products. Still, just as in the case of the port, New Orleans failed to upgrade its oil- and gas-related bonanza and suffered when the sector underwent changes. Although the 1970s oil price rise pumped money into the local economy, the 1980s price crash prompted consolidation, and New Orleans was unable to keep its oil and gas jobs. Most major companies moved to Houston, which has approximately 56,101 jobs in mining, quarrying, and oil and gas extraction, as compared to 5,193 in New Orleans (U.S. Census 2013).

In 1965, 18.2 percent of New Orleans non-farm employment was in manufacturing, and this fell to 14.6 percent by 1970, 10.2 percent by 1980, 7.8 percent in 1990, and 4.5 percent in 2000 (Brunsma, Overfelt, and Picou 2007, 64). Data available from the Bureau of Labor Statistics indicate that the city lost a large number of manufacturing jobs in the 1980s but that the percentage held steady during the 1990s at around 8 percent, employing close to 50,000 workers. In 2000 the city began to shed manufacturing jobs once again, with the number of manufacturing workers dropping steadily to 29,000 in 2014. Figure 10 shows the decline in both the number and the proportion of manufacturing jobs in the city.

To give an idea of the loss implied by the disappearance in manufacturing jobs, it is worthwhile to consider the average wages in manufacturing

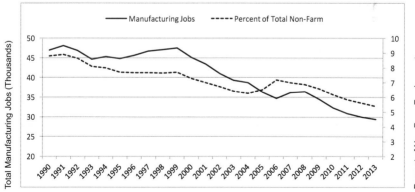

FIGURE 10. Declining New Orleans manufacturing. Source: Bureau of Labor Statistics, State and Area Employment, Hours, and Earnings. https://www.bls.gov/sae.

($43,000 in 2003) versus the accommodation and food services sector ($16,000). According to one estimate, "If New Orleans had retained its manufacturing jobs, its labor force would have earned $571 million more in 2003" (Ross 2011). The next section considers the sector that had been at the heart of regional manufacturing: shipbuilding.

The Global Shipbuilding Regime

Before turning to the specific case of Avondale, it is worthwhile to consider the nature of the global shipbuilding regime. Ships are in fact the largest items produced in factories, with normal-size commercial ships including 5,000 tons of steel and 2,500 tons of other components, including the main engine. These materials add up to almost one-third of the total cost of the ship (steel 13 percent and the engine 16 percent), and labor costs add another 17 percent. Shipyards bring these massive resources together in operations that require technological and managerial coordination to construct the hull, outfit the machinery, equipment, and furnishings simultaneously for assembly in one massive plant located near deep waterways.

The major obstacle facing shipbuilding markets is the extended time frame between the order and production of vessels (Stopford 2009). This time frame, combined with the significant resources required, means that

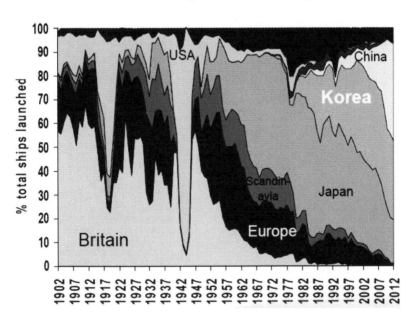

FIGURE 11. Share of global shipbuilding. Source: Stopford 2009, 616.

orders follow a boom-and-bust cycle. Orders accumulate when long-distance trade is expanding and demand is high, but by the time a yard has worked through its orders, demand has often fallen, and shipbuilders face problems of overcapacity.

To ride out such cycles, government support has been necessary, and global production has allowed for only a few dominant producing countries. Figure 11 displays the share of global shipbuilding in different countries, and the sequence of dominant producers reads like a geopolitical history of industrialization. The UK dominated in the 1850s, followed by the United States during the two world wars, then Japan and subsequently South Korea in the 1970s (OECD 2007). In recent years, China has rapidly accelerated its market share, increasing deliveries by 500 percent between 2006 and 2010 (G. Collins and Grubb 2008).

One reason countries are eager to occupy dominant positions in the sector is that shipbuilding produces a number of economic and national security benefits. In economic terms, shipbuilding involves spillovers to sectors such as iron and steel, electronics, and machinery manufacturing; it also absorbs large numbers of workers and produces clusters of activity and accumulation that expand regional development. Further, shipbuilding has the geopolitical attraction of creating goods with utility for economies as well as military power (OECD 2007).

To sustain national shipbuilding capacity, most governments attempt to manage the sector. In some cases, governments offer subsidies or directly own shipbuilding enterprises, as occurred in the UK in the 1970s (Jamieson 2003; Johnman and Murphy 2005). Other countries offer privileged financing in an attempt to manage crises of overcapacity (Stokes 1997), while others offer guaranteed orders, especially for vessels with the potential for both military and industrial uses (Todd and Lindberg 1996). Many countries, including the United States, have cabotage laws regulating the origin of freight ships allowed to sail between national ports. In the United States the Merchant Marine Act of 1920, also known as the Jones Act, requires all goods transported by water between U.S. ports to be carried on ships built in the United States (Strath 1987; Lorenz 1991).

Still, at least since 1981 the United States has steadily removed its efforts to sustain a national, commercial shipbuilding capacity. In 1981, at the same time President Reagan announced an increased order for military vessels (which never fully materialized), he removed loan guarantees, tax incentives, and subsidies to commercial shipbuilding.[2] Ongoing deregulation allowed further deterioration of commercial U.S. shipbuilding, with most yards becoming dependent on military orders that provided three times more revenue than commercial shipbuilding (IBIS *World* 2012). For the Gulf Coast, the commitment to deregulation was only exaggerated with the temporary waiver of the Jones Act in response to Hurricane Katrina (Department of Homeland Security 2005). Deregulation has encouraged a globally integrated shipbuilding regime. Because the main adjustable cost in shipbuilding is the price of labor in production and repair, production shifts to countries that keep labor costs low, such as China and Vietnam (Cho and Porter 1986). The other main mechanism of competition is government support, especially to ride out booms and busts. As we will see, New Orleans shipbuilding suffered on both counts. Even when federal government largesse was available, local elites were unwilling to preserve the New Orleans shipyard.

Across the world, shipbuilding workers and the communities they support have organized and won victories to orient shipbuilding toward more human concerns for wages, safety, and community benefit. In fact, with their strategic importance and large numbers, worker organization in shipyards has provided the core of successful national working-class movements (Varela and Van der Linden 2011). Yet, as the Avondale case indicates, these victories have too often been temporary.

Avondale

The Avondale shipyard outside New Orleans is a microcosm of the struggle for worker-community control against a globally oriented set of elite priorities. At its peak, Avondale provided more than nineteen thousand jobs, and almost four thousand people worked there in 2011. Their work produced barges, commercial supertankers, cruise ships, steamboats, destroyers, and even a floating jail for New York when the state government sought to relieve prison overcrowding. After a lengthy struggle, the workers in the yard secured union protections and built a shipyard with good wages, decent benefits, safe working conditions, and career stability.

Avondale closed its doors in 2013. Starting after Hurricane Katrina in 2005, Northrup Grumman, the owners of the yard, took steps to shut down activities. New orders were not booked, machinery and upgrades were shifted to other yards, ownership was restructured, and layoffs gradually accelerated until by the end there was only a skeleton crew conducting environmental remediation. In 2014 the shipyard came to be used as a parking lot for a local speedway (WGNO Web Desk 2015).

The Avondale shipyard did not have to shut down. The federal government and the state government made more than $500 million available to transform Avondale into a commercially viable yard (R. Thompson 2012). Workers and community members were committed to saving the yard. Yet the globally oriented elite of New Orleans did not see shipbuilding as part of their dual development strategy. They discarded Avondale.

The sections that follow tell the story of Avondale through information gathered from surveys and focus groups.[3] The focus groups included workers chosen with the help of the local union, and the survey included eighty-two questions applied to eighty-four respondents in take-home and in-person interviews.[4] The following sections analyze the responses in terms of the good jobs at the shipyard; workers who were good neighbors, members of the community, and model citizens; and the risk facing New Orleans as the yard closes.[5]

Joined-up Workplace and Community Struggle at Avondale

Avondale manufacturing was not always a good place to work.[6] It was known as a racially divided place a worker went to get hurt. Said one focus group participant, "The safety record was just horrendous; people were getting killed. . . . Before, this was just plain a bad place to work. People would ask me, 'How can you stay there?' Before the union, the reputation was that Avondale was a place you went to die" (Focus Group, June 8, 2011). Another focus group participant remembered, "Back in the 1960s, if you were black, you could work here but you wouldn't ever be anything higher than a helper." Another worker observed, "Before, the foreman could hold you down. They told me straight out—you will never make top money here. . . . When I started, I was making $2.30 an hour, and the only way you could survive was to work overtime, 45 or 50 hours a week, just to get those extra hours to make ends meet. The yard grew; the number of docks increased; but, we didn't see the benefits" (Focus Group, June 8, 2011).

What changed things for Avondale workers was the struggle for the union, and that struggle began anew in 1993, fifty-five years after Avondale was established.[7] There had been other attempts to form a union, but these had fallen short, and as the biggest non-union shipyard in the country, Avondale had the lowest wages, miserable pensions, and ongoing safety issues, with rates of death more than double those of its closest competitors.

When the Metal Trades Council of the AFl-CIO sent a veteran organizer to evaluate conditions at Avondale in the early 1990s, workers responded immediately. In the space of a few days, more than 1,500 unionization cards were signed, and workers approved the union 1,954 to 1,632 in a National Labor Relations Board (NLRB)–approved election. The NLRB recognized the Metal Trades Council, but Avondale refused to recognize the union or bargain with it. They faced little pressure to cede, as the U.S.

Navy continued to award new contracts, including a contract for amphibious assault craft valued at $685 million.[8]

The case dragged on for eight years, with Avondale owners appealing the case to the U.S. Supreme Court, even as the NLRB found they "had violated the law more than 70 times, dismissing, for example, 28 workers because they supported the union . . . suspending 5 others, issuing 18 warning notices, denying benefits to 8 employees and assigning 'onerous' work to 8 others" (Greenhouse 1998).[9] Veterans of the struggle remembered the discipline and patience it took: "You have to understand that during the union drive we had to be strong. This was our third try, and we had lost the first two. We lost before because the company fired us, intimidated us, told lies and tried to sweet-talk us out of the union. 'What would it take,' they asked me, and I told them, 'I want for my kids the same thing you give to your kids. When you can offer me that, then we can talk.' The manager just turned around and walked away" (Focus Group, June 8, 2011).

Given the drawn-out nature of the effort, workers turned to friends and neighbors outside the yard.

> People look at me and they see a hard-nosed, six foot five 250-pounder, and they know I had my confrontations. But, as we were organizing the union, we needed help from the community. We organized marches, went to the churches, we took action with them. We sent our younger members out into the neighborhoods to talk to people, get them involved, so they would understand and stand by us. Winning the union was something we all had to do together; we knew that unionizing to make our jobs better would make our community better. . . . The union picked up this community and carried it on its back. We held this community together, and we were known around the world. (Focus Group, June 6, 2011)

Ultimately, the union struggle was successful in getting recognition in 1999. "I remember the fliers we used said 'Justice at Avondale,' and that was what it was, 'Justice at Avondale.' . . . Making this a good place to work was the struggle of the union, so all of us would be able to make it on the earnings we took home. . . . I knew right and wrong, and the union was right for the people" (Focus Group, June 8, 2011).

Benefits of Worker-Community Struggle

As a result of unionization, wages and pensions rose, safety improved, and career progression became more regularized. One worker noted, "With the apprentice program, they start to recruit people from within, move them up and eventually even into management. Imagine, from the street and all the way up to white collar. This was a real career, a route into the middle class. All of this was because of the union" (Focus Group, June 8, 2011).[10] Responses from the surveys and focus groups demonstrate some of the benefits of unionization. Where available, Table 12 below presents comparisons to national averages.[11]

TABLE 12. Avondale Workers and the Community

	Avondale (%)	National (%)
Own home	63.0	47.0*
Involved in union	65.5	12.4**
Involved in church or religious establishment	53.6	15.0+
Involved in political party	21.4	71.3+
Involved in neighborhood association	19.0	9.0+
Involved in veterans affairs group	11.9	2.0+
Involved in civil rights organizations	9.5	1.8++
Involved in environmental protection group	9.5	2.7++
Involved in ethnic cultural organization	6.0	2.0+
Attend meetings	52.4	20.0++
Get others to attend meetings	32.1	17.4+
Distribute information	32.1	17.5+
Recruit others	28.6	17.4+
Vote in an election	71.4	62.0+
Past year, attend government meeting/other public meeting	39.3	14.0+
Past year, attend march, rally, demonstration, or protest	20.2	4.1++
Past year, attend meeting to discuss labor issues	36.9	8.4+
After Katrina, rebuild home or replace lost items	67.5	
After Katrina, help a family member	76.2	
After Katrina, help a friend	70.2	
After Katrina, help another member of the community	58.3	
After Katrina, help a coworker	52.4	

Source: 2008 National Election Survey and 2010 National Election Survey. Available at https://www.icpsr.umich.edu/icpsrweb/ICPSR/series/3#studies.
*Home ownership in New Orleans area (Ortiz 2011).
**National rate of unionization (Bureau of Labor Statistics 2010).
+2008 National Election Survey.
++2010 National Election Survey.

On average, respondents had worked at Avondale for thirteen years, with a third of the workers working fewer than five years and a quarter working more than twenty years. The data showed a somewhat curious pattern among the workers in terms of length of time worked, with a large number of workers between zero and ten years, a slight dip in workers between eleven and twenty years, and another large concentration of workers with more than twenty years of experience.[12]

An anecdote portrays the typical working life. A fifty-five-year-old welder described his work trajectory as one in which he joined the shipyard at twenty-two after serving four years in the military. At the yard he apprenticed to upgrade his skills and worked as a welder for five years, only to leave to enter the welding trade at another firm when work slowed at the yard. After being called up to military service and returning, he rejoined Avondale once again. Since then he has worked at Avondale for stretches of six to ten years when there is a demand for workers, and in between he has been able to turn the skills he gained at Avondale into work in other large-scale manufacturing firms (Focus Group, June 1, 2010).

This career pattern provides a stream of relatively steady income. Almost all the workers asked owned a car (89 percent), and more than half owned their homes (60 percent), well over the New Orleans area average rate of home ownership of 47 percent (Ortiz 2011). Most workers appear to stay in the same home for long periods, with an average of fifteen years at the same address and a maximum of fifty-nine years at the same place. In the focus groups, workers described the access to credit that Avondale provided, supporting a credit union and a general infusion of liquidity that kept things moving in housing and other long-term purchases. One worker remarked, "It used to be that all you had to do was go to the bank and tell them that you work at Avondale and they would write you a loan right then and there" (Focus Group, June 6, 2011).[13]

With access to income and credit, workers patronized local businesses.[14] When asked what they would do if the shipyard closed, workers in the focus group described cutting back on eating out, extracurricular activities for their kids, new appliances, and home improvements (Focus Group, June 8, 2011). "That's what you get with good jobs," said one worker. "You get teachers, military vets, people with degrees, women. All of them know that this is a place where you can have a career and be the breadwinner for your family. . . . Take my youngest son, for example. He started as a welding apprentice. He came here and he has been steadily getting educated, paid to go to college through our cooperative program. I mean, once he gets all the way through, he's gonna be an engineer—first one in the family to go to college" (Focus Group, June 6, 2011).

Their impact on the community went beyond economics. In the month of the survey, they reported an average of eight days caring for a family member or friend who has a "health problem, long term illness, or disability." For 14 percent of the workers, they offer such care every day, and over half of the workers, 51 percent, offer care at least one day a month. For one participant in the focus groups, the ability to care was a product not only of work but of the way work was managed within a unionized shop. "Seeing the transition from a non-union to a union shop was huge. As a minister, I even see it as an improvement of religious ethics. As a result of my work at Avondale, I learned to minister to my people in the community differently. I could take my lessons from the union to help minister to people outside" (Focus Group, June 8, 2011).[15]

The role of Avondale workers as pillars of the community was even more evident after Katrina, when most workers and their neighbors had to evacuate. More than two-thirds of workers (67 percent) rebuilt their own home, and 43 percent helped a family member. Exactly half helped another member of the community, and 52 percent helped a co-worker.

The civic impact of workers also took form in membership and associational activity. More than half (54 percent) of workers are members of a church, donating an average of $150 per month to their place of worship. The most contributed by any individual was $1,000, and 31 percent of respondents contributed over $200 per month. The churches of the region recognize their close relationship with Avondale, as more than two hundred churches signed a pledge to pray for Avondale, lifting the spirits of the workers with a day of prayer dedicated to saving the shipyard.

The thick networks of communication built up through union activism produce high levels of political interest and information. Workers read the newspaper, watched local television news, listened to radio newscasts, or went online to get news, with 73 percent of workers seeking news every day, much higher than the national average of 50 percent who watch television news (NES 2010). As indicated in Table 13, Avondale workers also displayed high level of political engagement.

More than two out of three workers, 68 percent, "strongly agreed" or "agreed" with the statement that they were "very interested in politics," and more than 65 percent agreed or strongly agreed that they were "as well informed about politics as most people," compared to a national average of only 23 percent (NES 2000). Forty-five percent disagreed or strongly disagreed with the statement that politics and government seem so complicated that "a person like me can't really understand what's going on," higher than the national average of 31 percent (NES 2008).

As politically interested and informed individuals, workers demonstrated high rates of interaction with others when it came to sharing and

TABLE 13. Avondale Workers and Politics

	Strongly Disagree or Disagree (%)	Neither Disagree nor Agree (%)	Agree or Strongly Agree (%)
Very interested in politics	17.3	14.8	67.9
Politics so complicated	47.6	23.8	28.8
As well informed about politics as most people	12.4	22.2	65.4
Don't have any say	47.5	13.8	38.8
Pretty good understanding	9.9	17.3	72.9
Public officials don't care	25.0	20.0	55.0
I'm well qualified to participate	28.8	25.0	46.3
Can't do much to affect government	46.2	20.5	33.3
	Not/Slightly	Moderately	Very/ Extremely
When you think about the work you have done at Avondale, how proud does that make you feel?	4.8	13.1	82.2
When you think about the closing of the shipyard, how angry does that make you feel?	18.3	6.1	75.6

Source: Author-administered survey.

cultivating political and social knowledge. Workers discussed politics frequently, with 86 percent "discussing politics" at least once a week and 23 percent discussing politics between five and seven days a week. They also discussed labor issues at high rates (71 percent), and 62 percent of workers reported discussing civil rights or women's rights in the last year.

Avondale jobs also produce workers who feel like their efforts made an impact, both for personal development and for political efficacy. In one focus group, a younger worker explained, "I really look up to these old guys. Like them, I want to progress myself, to learn new skills, to make myself better like they've improved themselves. I learned to understand work and life in a different way; if someone says I can't do something, now I just want to do it more, do it better. I took this job thinking that I was taking a career, a place I could work for twenty, forty years and more" (Focus Group, June 8, 2011).

The confidence that comes with this kind of empowerment translates also to political efficacy, with workers showing rates of political efficacy higher than national averages. When presented with the statement that "I don't think public officials care much what people like me think," 55 percent agreed or strongly agreed, and workers strongly disagreed or disagreed 46 percent of the time when presented with the statement that "there is not much someone like me can do to affect what the government does." When asked if they agree that they "don't have any say about what the government does," 48 percent strongly disagreed, higher than the national average of 41 percent (NES 2004). When presented with the statement that "I consider myself well qualified to participate in politics," workers agreed or strongly agreed 46 percent of the time, as compared to the national average of 33.6 percent (NES 2000–2004).

These rates of political information and efficacy produced real action. In the year prior to the survey, which included the midterm elections of 2010, Avondale workers reported voting at a rate of 71 percent, far higher than the national reported voting rate of 41 percent, and higher even than the national turnout for the presidential election of 2008, 62 percent, which was the highest percentage of the population voting since 1968.[16]

Worker power within the shipyard benefited not only workers and the community but also productivity in the yard. Production prior to unionization included cross-training of employees across ninety-one classifications, a practice workers blamed for informality, poor training, and accidents. According to one worker, "The yard used to just run around like a stirred up ant pile. . . . Then when the union got in there . . . people were more satisfied about what they were doing and the skill level got better also" (Baxter et al. 2011).[17]

Closing Avondale

Joined-up struggle in the workplace and community had been sufficient to win the union and improve the shipyard, but it could not stop closure in 2013. Structural factors such as the concentration of firms in the shipbuilding industry and the incentive to seek profit through financial innovation coincided with the dual development emphasis of the local elite.

As early as the 1980s, emphasis on military shipbuilding increased requirements for capital, financing, and technology, leaving room for only a few large producers, consolidating national production into two parent firms, Northrop Grumman and General Dynamics. In 1999, Litton Industries, which also owned Ingalls Shipbuilding in Pascagoula, Mississippi, bought Avondale for $529 million, leading to early worries that one of the two yards would be shuttered (Albright 2010), and in 2001 Northrup Grumman bought Litton for $5.1 billion (including $1.3 billion in debt).[18]

Under Northrup Grumman management, machinery and capital up-grades began to be withheld, a practice that began to be noticed after Hurricane Katrina, even as Avondale was largely undamaged by the storm. Pascagoula, which suffered more damage, received upgrades, and even some advanced machinery shifted over from Avondale, while a new panel line was left in the Avondale warehouse to avoid the cost of having to install it. The company received $835 million in insurance claims, but it was subsequently accused of using the money for shipbuilding costs instead of repairing shipyards, and Avondale fell farther behind in terms of ability to compete for new contracts (Baxter et al. 2011).

By 2010 the company had declared its intention to shut down Avondale and get out of the shipbuilding industry, and in 2011 they spun off a new company, Huntington Ingalls, as the holder of Avondale. The spin-off allowed Northrop to "offload 40% of its debt ($1.88 billion) onto Huntington Ingalls, part of which funded a $1.43 billion cash contribution that Huntington Ingalls had to pay Northrop Grumman as part of the deal" (Baxter et al. 2011, 8). That same year, the Northrop board of directors authorized a plan to buy back $4 billion of their own stock, leaving Northrop Grumman with a minimal debt-to-equity ratio, while Huntington Ingalls holds debt equal to double shareholders' investment in the company (Baxter et al. 2011, 9).

At this point, the workers and their union initiated the Save our Shipyard campaign, rallying churches, academics, and other allies to prevent the closure. A potential buyer for the shipyard was identified, American Feeder Lines, a commercial ship producer specializing in boats plying inland waterways, hoping to capitalize on increasingly clogged road and rail networks.

More than two hundred regional churches signed up for a "Pray for Avondale" commitment, and workers joined activists, neighborhood organizers, and community members in a march through downtown. Popular pressure led Louisiana representative Cedric Richmond to transform a $300 million federal subsidy to shut the shipyard into funding to keep the yard open, and Governor Bobby Jindal offered an additional $214 million for any new use of the site.

Notably absent from these efforts was any movement by local elites to support Avondale. Manufacturing, especially the large-scale industrial activity associated with a shipyard, was mis-fit to their globally integrated services and tourism model. American Feeder Lines went bankrupt before a deal could be made, and potential Korean investors backed out without a local partner to help them get around cabotage laws. New Orleans leadership did little to prevent the closing of the shipyard, and have seemed to forget about it once it was gone. Business interests from Jefferson Parish demonstrated greater attention; Jefferson Business Commission chairman Jerry Bologna commented on the 2015 governor race, "We hope the governor will . . . use the strength of the position to assist Jefferson Parish in bringing the Avondale Shipyard back into commerce" (LaRose 2015). By contrast, the New Orleans Business Alliance declined to form a new industry council, and director of human capital and culture Ken Weatherup noted, "Since it is in Jefferson Parish and not in Orleans, the New Orleans Business Alliance has not been engaged in any efforts to return it to use." Shipbuilding, especially as a sector with strong unions exerting worker power, does not seem to be part of their dual development strategy.

While help from local elites might not have been expected, the union also failed to build worker power beyond its boundaries. Given Avondale's size, the union might have had some success extending its unionization efforts into other firms and sectors. The disruption of Katrina in 2005, just two years after the union finally won recognition, may have short-circuited any such broader working-class project.

While the union recognized that part of its victory owed to joined-up struggle with communities, opportunities to maintain and deepen workplace-community ties were missed. Issues such as protecting public housing, saving Charity Hospital, and defending public schools focused struggle in communities, and they could have benefited from mobilized worker power. However, Avondale, and building trades unions more generally, tended to provide only lukewarm support to struggles to preserve common resources and public assets, especially when there was room for them to bargain for union benefits within development projects (MacDonald 2014). Layoffs accelerated until only a skeleton crew was left. In 2013 the yard closed. One respondent expanded on his answers to the survey: "I'm buying a gun. If the shipyard dies, the community dies, and when communities die, there is crime. It's gonna be bad."[19]

The Avondale shipyard represents a failed opportunity to chart an alternative path for New Orleans. Through struggle joined with allies in the community, workers secured a voice in the management of the shipyard, improving their lives, creating benefits for the community, and adding productivity to the firm. Yet joined-up worker and community struggle could not overcome the structural forces of a concentrated manufacturing sector and the urge to secure profit through financial mechanisms rather than production. As a result, shipbuilding in New Orleans went the way of other manufacturing activity, discarded by a local elite interested in a globally integrated services model and unwilling to find a solution to prevent deindustrialization. Said one of the focus group participants, "The union picked up this community and carried it on its back. . . . I want to know, where are our people now? Where is the support from public officials?" (June 8, 2011).

These missed opportunities and the overall structural and political power of globally oriented elites give the impression of little hope for an alternative to dual development. Globally oriented elites have discarded sectors they do not need or cannot control, and they have used newfound political dominance to drive expansion of tourism and services in ways that accelerate accumulation but exacerbate poverty. In response, working classes and popular sectors have resisted, attempting to forge joined-up struggle to oppose exploitation in the workplace and in the community and to articulate an alternative strategy of development. This chapter and previous ones have traced the dynamics of this conflict between elite and working-class and popular struggle as it plays out in governance, construction, services, and manufacturing. The Conclusion will explore the lessons when these struggles are considered together.

CONCLUSION

The trajectory of New Orleans since 2005 highlights issues of political economy in urban development. Hurricane Katrina unbalanced an existing stalemate among rival factions of economic and political elites, and the aftermath mobilized a globally oriented faction of local elites into power. They were able to work their way through fragmented local institutions to consolidate control over key areas of public policy, and control over political power allowed them to reorganize sectors strategic to their model of dual development focused on tourism and services. Several characteristics of this dual development strategy stand out. First, while tourism and services were rejuvenated after the hurricane, they offer few linkages to the rest of the local economy. Second, one of the ways local elites have promoted strategic sectors is by deregulating to allow concentrated ownership and unfettered control of production processes, which have been segmented according to ascriptive characteristics such as race, ethnicity, and gender. Third, while this strategy of dual development has created impressive growth, most New Orleanians have been relegated to a life of poverty of multiple forms. In response, working people and popular sectors have experimented with joined-up workplace and community struggle, articulating a new kind of class struggle that addresses exploitation as it occurs at work and in the home.

The lessons of New Orleans are important because they reflect fundamental issues relevant to the kind of economic development we desire and the kind of society we wish to build. In addition, while the New Orleans case is exaggerated, punctuated, and on display as a result of Katrina, many other cities share the experience of a globally oriented dual development project that distributes privilege to the few and poverty to most.

New Orleans also highlights the class struggle inherent in debates over development strategy. Interestingly, it is in the sectors that globally oriented elites discard and in the interstices and gaps of the sectors they control that lower-class formation occurs. The examples outlined earlier highlight struggle that bridges workplaces and communities, articulating an evolving lower-class identity constituted by workers and popular sectors. Joined-up struggle maximizes the strength of workers reclaiming production and of communities reclaiming social order, and it is necessary because elites extract surplus by controlling the production process and by marketizing and appropriating the lived experiences of popular sectors in their communities. In response, joined-up struggle addresses discrimination that divides communities and segments the workplace on the basis of race, ethnicity, and gender. By bridging workplace and community struggle, workers and popular sectors forge a new kind of lower-class project, offering an alternative to the poverty inherent in dual development.

The sections that follow will review core conclusions about politics, development, poverty, and resistance. Previous chapters present comparisons across time and across sectors, and this conclusion gathers implications for further research and activism. In particular, it considers the potential for an alternative development strategy that builds on worker-community struggle to produce more democratic and more just political and economic outcomes.

Politics

Popular understandings of New Orleans politics paint it as unique and even carnivalesque, but the current study considers the city within a more generalizable politics of medium-sized, centuries-old urban centers. While Deep South and Gulf Coast particularities make New Orleans history interesting and important, the generalizable questions of urban regimes make for a useful tracing of New Orleans politics over time: to what degree and how do local governments "get things done" (C. N. Stone 1993)? This approach focuses on urban regimes as combinations of social coalitions, state capacities, and public-policy agendas that guide state-society relations at the local level.

In New Orleans, the trajectory of urban regimes was shaped by the structural and geological conditions of a Gulf Coast port city following an arc of industrialization and deindustrialization. On top of these structural conditions were also layered a sequence of electorally dominant political machines, culminating in a series of black urban regimes that ended in the first decade of the twenty-first century (Reed 1999). The sequence of regimes, shaped as they were by the structural conditions in which they operated, produced institutional legacies that can be read in the structure of a fragmented New Orleans local state characterized by a large number of quasi-public satellite entities exercising public authority.

A few observations emerge based on the analysis of evolving regimes and the institutional architecture of New Orleans. The structure of satellite governance handicaps the local state by distorting public finance, weakening total revenues, forcing government to manage with a smaller budget, and interrupting democratic mechanisms of accountability by making putatively public functions more difficult to monitor and oversee.

Satellites also record in institutional terms the legacy of past political conflicts. In the current period, conflict is especially expressed in terms of the distinction between institutional legacies of declining black urban regimes and the institutions convenient to newly emerging globally oriented elites. African American incorporating entities are left over from the black urban regime period and available as remaining points of access for the African American professional and political class.

Even as they attempt to roll back and constrain the African American incorporating entities, globally oriented elites appear to have sought to deepen their own networks by joining ring-fencing, privatizing, and dual development entities. Ring-fencing entities create club goods for members, defined usually by geographic boundaries and coinciding closely with white, upper-class efforts to protect their resources from black urban regimes. Privatizing entities make public assets available for private accumulation, an institutional manifestation of the limited response to deindustrialization and economic slowdown since the 1970s and 1980s. Finally, dual development entities explicitly promote the tourism and services dual development strategy.

The institutional conflict expressed in satellites highlights ongoing political transition and is relevant to many other urban centers. In New Orleans and elsewhere, black urban regimes incorporated portions of African American society but were encumbered by a toxic combination of white flight, deindustrialization, and post-1980s federal neglect, as well as contradictory internal coalitions and agendas (Reed 1999). As a result, they offered little to working-class African Americans or working classes in general, who have only been further excluded with the passing of black urban regimes.

The decline of black urban regimes coincides with a transformation of the international economy, namely, the global integration of production, in which North American cities compete to act as strategically placed nodes within international processes of accumulation. The combination of black urban regime decline and international integration has propelled globalized-growth coalitions that link local to international capital in support of gentrification, financial and property speculation, and a services orientation. In New Orleans this process was facilitated by the disruption of a disastrous hurricane, which dispersed and disorganized African American electoral machines in neighborhoods uprooted by flooding. While other cities may not experience the suddenness of a transition driven by disaster, globally oriented elites seek to take over all similarly positioned cities to advance their development strategies and do little to include working-class residents.

One of the more worrying aspects of contemporary urban politics is that it creates a distorted and unbalanced political arena. On one side sits a decaying African American political class that never fully incorporated members beyond a narrow professional and political elite. On the other side sits an emergent globally oriented faction of local capital, allied with and subservient to major international actors. Instead of open conflict, these two factions of the local elite would appear to be reaching an accommodation in which globally oriented elites open limited space to African American elites who come to share their dual development agenda.

This coalition represents in the clearest terms an upper-class alliance with little interest in resolving the problems facing working-class and popular sectors. While subordinate actors attempt to build class power in joined-up workplace and community episodes of resistance, they have yet to identify a vehicle to carry their class interests into politics. Without an established political vehicle, resistance necessarily attempts to access the public sphere outside normal channels of politics, as in the Black Lives Matter and other protest movements.

It is worth reflecting on the absence of a political vehicle for working classes in New Orleans. In fact, the same questions might be asked of the United States more generally. For pluralists, the many channels for interest groups to gain access to power obviate the need for a unified Left project, and the availability of surplus makes it possible for excluded groups to eventually secure a share of the wealth (J. M. Berry 1999). Observers of the distortions of foundation funding voice a more damning critique, noting that funds donated by corporations and channeled through foundations dampen and fragment potential working-class projects, whether intentionally or not (Arena 2012). To these obstacles must also be added the reality of repression, as the state repeatedly reacted brutally to working-class attempts to form labor and socialist parties in the 1890s, 1920s, and 1930s (Archer 2010). Finally, the response of establishment officials, especially dominant political parties, has been to erect overwhelming institutional obstacles to potential challengers. The strategy was perfected as far back as the late nineteenth century, when U.S. workers and farmers attempted to form a "populist vision," leading the Democratic and Republican Parties to change ballot rules, electoral processes, and voting procedure to ensure a monopoly on office (Postel 2009). Indeed, the United States is perhaps the only party system in the world in which no new major party has emerged for over 150 years.

At the level of organized politics, New Orleans and other U.S. cities face a challenge of representation. Existing political actors fail to address the concerns of working people and popular sectors. Worse, there is little incentive to break out of the current impasse, as political conflict between decaying black urban machines and rising globally oriented elites is most likely to be settled in favor of an upper-class dual development project that offers a division of spoils to both. While protest movements engage direct action in streets and on social media, there has yet to emerge an alternative organization that can channel these demands into the political arena, and resistance that occurs outside the boundaries of normal politics is exposed to institutional exclusion, co-optation, and outright repression.

Development

The dual development project described here outlines a globally oriented strategy of local elites seeking to connect with international processes of production and accumulation. This strategy is now common in U.S. cities seeking to transition in a more integrated global economy, and in New Orleans dual development has focused on tourism and services. The strategy is dual because it promotes a highly profitable set of internationalized sectors while remaining delinked from the majority of New Orleans residents.

Leading sectors in dual development are characterized by concentrated ownership in the hands of leading local factions of capital, who use their local control to attract larger international allies and ensure a smooth integration with international processes of production and accumulation. In exchange for intermediating the entrance of larger players into local politics and markets, local elites accept smaller projects and the opportunities for profit that come from their brokerage role. Their central function is to brand and reshape the city as an attractive place to do business.

To preserve their dominance and increase profit margins, local elites segment their production processes and allocate work on the basis of ascriptive characteristics of race, ethnicity, and gender. This reproduces the poverty experienced by working classes and popular sectors and infects communities with ascriptive divisions. By dividing workers along ascriptive lines, local elites exercise control in the workplace to drive down wages and erode working conditions.

Dividing communities along ascriptive lines also plays into local elite efforts to control policy and regulatory regimes. With institutional access through satellites and emerging electoral power, ascriptive divisions among popular sectors and working people block lower-class coalitions against elite development designs. These designs increasingly operate not only in the workplace but also in communities.

Extraction occurs through social processes that operate in the workplace and in the community: expanded reproduction, social reproduction, and accumulation by dispossession. Expanded reproduction is the ever more intense squeezing of workers in the workplace. In New Orleans, the emerging tourism and services sectors are perhaps most defined by the highly unequal distribution of benefits between high profits and low wages. By squeezing workers, capital turns the workplace into a site of privilege for some and poverty for others.

Extraction also occurs through social reproduction, in which society consumes commodities in order to survive. To turn the process of consumption into an opportunity for accumulation, capital raises prices and secures public subsidy, with basic needs goods providing especially attractive targets as communities cannot survive without them. In New Orleans, privatization and the rapid increase in the cost of housing, education, health, and recreation turns the very act of survival into an opportunity for accumulation. By distorting the process of social reproduction, capital turns communities into sites of privilege for some and poverty for others.

A third strategy of extraction is accumulation by dispossession, the term David Harvey (2007) uses to describe the privatization of what used to be commonly held, such as environmental assets, community outputs, or public-sector assets. In New Orleans, the communal production of art has no exchange value when practiced in Mardi Indian celebrations and second-line parades, but art becomes commodity when someone sells tickets, runs a tour bus through a neighborhood, or uses a stolen image to brand a product. By dispossessing communal producers of their collective product, capital turns the community into a site of privilege for some and poverty for others.

In New Orleans, privilege accumulates in the workplace and in the community. There is no area of life untouched by the concentration of privilege. In making the links between the extraction that occurs in communities and the exploitation that occurs at work, working people and communities in New Orleans organize across sectors and across ascriptive groups, and in the process they expose expanded reproduction, social reproduction, and accumulation by dispossession as social relations that reproduce privilege and poverty. Further, these social relations appear as integral to the elite project of dual development. In response, workers and popular sectors form alliances and offer alternatives, and in the process form a lower-class project of resistance.

Poverty

The experience of poverty is built into a dual development model that boosts elites within sectors linked to the international economy but leaves out most of the people of New Orleans. In particular, New Orleans dual development segments into poverty those groups defined by ascriptive racial, ethnic, and gender characteristics. To understand the experience of working people and popular sectors, different conceptualizations highlight absolute, relative, multidimensional, probabilistic, intersectional, and social exclusion aspects of poverty. Such a complex and nuanced approach to poverty offers a complete, if depressing, impression of the limits of dual development.

Comparison across sectors shows how ethnic segmentation on the basis of national origin is pronounced within construction, and racial and gendered segmentation appears most pronounced in tourism, at least within food services. In manufacturing, workplace-community struggle addressed racially defined inequality at the same time as it confronted workplace injustice. Unfortunately, resistance could not alter the structural realities of a consolidating and military-industrial-dependent shipbuilding sector, and ultimately it could not develop an alternative to the high-profit, low-regulation globally integrated sectors that were the priority of emerging elites.

The distinct pattern of segmentation that operates in each sector raises methodological questions and has implications for questions of class formation. In terms of analysis, sensitive study of each sector requires a mix of quantitative and qualitative methods to identify, measure, and test the nature of segmentation and poverty (Bowman, Lahoucq, and Mahoney 2005). In fact, the approach might best be considered an effort in authenticity (Guba and Lincoln 1989), in which the researcher only approximates complex concepts such as poverty by speaking directly to workers and members of the community. Such an inductive construction of poverty concepts designs more valid and reliable quantitative measures and analyses and, most importantly, reflects more authentically the beliefs and experience of people who live poverty (Farmer 2004).

In studies of this sort, authenticity is as important as quantitative and qualitative criteria of validity and reliability. To achieve authenticity, the analyses presented here have been returned to workers and popular sectors for them to digest, consider, and reflect on. If the analysis resonates for them, is meaningful in terms of their understanding, and aids them in their action, it can be considered authentic. The iterative process of moving back and forth from qualitative to quantitative and inductive and deductive analysis not only triangulates by bringing different kinds of information and perspective to bear; it also grants agency to poor people, turning them from subjects of research to active participants.

Active participation is especially important for class formation, as dimensions of ascriptive segmentation vary by economic sector and the experience of poverty varies across groups. Latinos made vulnerable in construction experience poverty differently than African American women made vulnerable in quick-serve restaurants and poor white workers losing their jobs in manufacturing. These differences are not inherent to Latino or African American or white identity, but rather derive from the overlap of workplace exploitation and community marginalization, and therefore require active construction of a shared lower-class project.

The preceding chapters have emphasized multiple examples of New Orleans coalitions that incorporate Latinos, African Americans, and white workers, not to mention middle-class and mostly white students, professors, and advocates. Such alliances go beyond poverty, a concept useful to characterize the poor, and focus attention on social relations, the interactions of individuals and groups that create poverty for some and privilege for others. As workers and popular sectors turn their lived experience of poverty into a social relation of struggle, they engage in the process of class formation.

Resistance

The preceding chapters emphasize the way workers and communities in New Orleans resist. In the sectors that globalizing elites ignore, such as manufacturing, and even in the sectors central to the dual development project, such as construction and tourism, working people and communities build alliances that contest social relations of poverty.

In each of the sectors examined, workers faced exploitation that bridged workplace and community. In the workplace, workers experienced poverty as a result of generalized pressure on wages and working conditions and segmentation on the basis of ascriptive characteristics. Ascriptive segmentation drew on and exacerbated racial, ethnic, and gender divisions reproduced in communities, reifying segmentation within the workplace. When transposed into communities, such segmentation complicates popular-sector solidarity, opening communities to strategies of extraction that accumulate by dispossessing communities of their commonly held or publicly provided resources. Further, profiteering on the basic needs of social reproduction generates additional sources of extraction from communities.

Because of this close link between workplaces and community extraction, resistance was most successful when it bridged these two sites. Joined-up struggle gave workers and communities a shared target for mobilization and a shared identity of resistance. Shipyard workers identified their families and their parishioners as the beneficiaries of their workplace organizing and targeted the owners who decided to close the shipyard as the threat to their communities.

Joined-up struggle begins with an acknowledgment of and confrontation with the segmentation that plays such a prominent role in dual development. For Latino workers in construction, alliances across sectors and ethnic divisions called for a sophisticated understanding of segmentation as a historical and contemporary reality. They sought African American worker allies by stressing their inherent solidarity with the first workers to be brought to North America and denied rights, African slaves.

Joined-up struggle also includes enjoining worker power to confront extraction occurring through accumulation by dispossession and social reproduction. For the African American and Latino workers of the Worker Center for Racial Justice, confronting the sheriff and convincing him to stop facilitating Immigration and Customs Enforcement deportation was as much about protecting families as it was about protecting workers.

Bridges from workplace to community take on added complexity as they go beyond working classes. African American workers—mostly women—organizing on an elite college campus had to translate their struggle into terms that middle-class and mostly white students could understand. Workers stressed the satisfaction they felt feeding hungry students and the systematic reasons why a twenty-year-old working-class African American and a twenty-year-old white middle-class student would find themselves on opposite sides of a cafeteria counter. In New Orleans and elsewhere, there can be no bridge between workplace and community without confronting the reality of ascriptive segmentation, and this segmentation varies by sector and across groups.

While building bridges across workplace and community is difficult, it may be the most powerful weapon that movements in New Orleans have developed. The power comes not just from necessity but also because joining workplace and community targets the social relations that reproduce poverty: expanded reproduction, accumulation by dispossession, and social reproduction.

Workers and communities confront expanded reproduction by building worker power. While elites offer social entrepreneurship or corporate social responsibility and other charitable acts as ways to benefit the poor, they never give up power over how to organize the workplace or distribute the benefits of production. Such elite strategies leave intact the basic social relations of expanded reproduction. Instead, worker power demands control of the workplace and a more equitable distribution of benefits. When New Orleans shipyard workers unionized, they achieved a say in the organization of work, cutting mortality and cultivating careers by altering the rules for training and promotion. New Orleans movements show that the only antidote to the poverty doled out by expanded reproduction is worker power.

In response to extraction through social reproduction, New Orleans movements insist on social guarantees. Rising prices empty the accounts of working families, so resistance seeks to ensure non-commodified access for basic needs. This begins with the right to return, as families dispersed by the storm refuse to accept that only those who can pay the price of rebuilding on their own have the right to return. They won a court case against the discriminatory practices of the Road Home program; they demand participation in the rebuilding of their homes and the city's infrastructure; they return land to public trust rather than make it available for speculation.

Finally, in response to accumulation by dispossession, New Orleans movements demonstrate a commoning approach to public goods. While accumulation by dispossession imposes a profit logic on communal outputs and other goods previously outside the market, commoning insists on protecting and expanding non-market provision. In the halls of the charter schools that capitalize on a service that used to be public, New Orleans students organize to demand quality education, an end to excessive discipline, and fair treatment of teachers. By reclaiming what the dual development model privatizes, New Orleans movements impose common values over profit.

New Orleans movements connect the exploitation experienced in workplaces to the extraction experienced in communities by building alliances across sectors and groups. In the process, they slowly articulate a lower-class alternative to the dual development project. While dual development entails social relations that reproduce poverty, the lower-class project of New Orleans movements offers worker power, commoning, and social guarantees.

Some of the movements advancing this project have been the focus of discussions in preceding chapters, such as the Community Evaluation Commission, Congreso de Jornaleros, Stand with Dignity, the Worker Center for Racial Justice, the Restaurant Opportunities Center, Tulane and Loyola Sodexo workers, and the Save our Shipyard campaign of the Avondale Metalworkers Council. There are myriad others that could have occupied an equally central role in the narrative, as New Orleans has become a center of "innovative, progressive organizing" (Flaherty 2015), and the same story of competing development projects could be told about all major cities where ferment and mobilization confront racist police brutality, property speculation, and low wages.

By articulating the politics of the dual development project and the social relations of poverty and privilege that it allocates, the current study attempts to make clear what is at stake in New Orleans and elsewhere. In highlighting resistance that forms alliances across sectors and groups, the project attempts to articulate the lower-class project that bridges workplaces and communities. New Orleans and other cities are sites of class struggle. Only a lower-class project forged through joined-up worker and community struggle promises a more democratic and just future.

ACKNOWLEDGMENTS

Prior to my arrival in New Orleans, my work concentrated on the study of developing countries, especially in Latin America. It would be easy to say that I turned to New Orleans because it exhibits many of the foibles of Latin American cities, such as a difficult history of inequality, racial oppression, and political corruption. Yet academic work in New Orleans means also engaging social struggle, a task difficult and underrewarded, even occasionally punished by the academy.

Part of the reason engaged academic work is rare is the long road to achieve tenure. Graduate school is five to ten years of learning the rules to secure a tenure-track job, and the path to tenure is no easier, requiring another five to ten years. Assistant professors learn to master the norms of collegial university service, and they learn to soften the bite of published outputs to pass peer review in which senior scholar gatekeepers protect against work that strays from the status quo they have established. Academia socializes a preference for conflict avoidance.

Still, like everyone else, I had watched as Katrina televised racial and economic exclusion, and I felt the added shame of having escaped to teach in faraway UK at the time. A radio interview with New Orleans human rights lawyer Bill Quigley reminded me of the folly of guilt; solidarity, not charity, is the appropriate response to injustice. Though my work on developing countries continues, my arrival in New Orleans in 2007 forced me to reconsider my role as an academic. I made myself available to social justice advocates, drawn first to Latin American immigrants rebuilding the Gulf Coast, many of whom were subjected to workplace abuse, unpaid wages, and threats of deportation. I provided translation assistance for Hiroko Kusuda, Laila Hlass, and Father Tom Greene, law school professors from Loyola University who offer counsel to immigrants detained in the privatized rural jails of Louisiana without the right to legal representation. I assisted colleagues Luz Molina and Vanessa Spinazola, who pursued the cases of workers who had been cheated of their wages by unscrupulous employers. Father Tom would later guide me on an exploratory research trip accompanied by four graduate students, Marcelle Beaulieu, Jennifer Boone, Lori Dowell, and Bradley Hentschel, in which we retraced the path migrants travel as they make their way from Central America through Mexico to the U.S. border, braving criminal abuse, corrupt authorities, and life-threatening conditions. To tell the stories of migrants who had arrived in New Orleans, Phuong Pham and Patrick Vinck, now of Harvard University, generously agreed to partner with me in undertaking a second wave of a construction worker survey they first undertook immediately after Katrina. On multiple afternoons and weekends, I canvassed far-flung neighborhoods interviewing construction workers with the help of collaborators such as Rosanna Eugenio, Neil Hendrick, Michael Hornsby, Molly Kai, Jonathan Kim, Keri Libby, Johanna Nice, Molly Thomas, Linda Tran, Scott White, and Lea Yu. This work evolved further when the Louisiana Legislature considered anti-immigrant laws, offering the opportunity to report the results of the survey at the request of organizers from the Worker Center for Racial Justice, including Jacinta Gonzalez, Jacob Horwitz, Lorena Murga, J. J. Rosenbaum, Saket Soni, Dennis Soriano, and Collette Tippy.

The construction worker survey was the first survey I had ever done, and the skills I learned opened another opportunity to contribute to the work of the Restaurant Opportunities Center (ROC). ROC was started by workers from the restaurant at the top of the World Trade Center who had lost colleagues on duty on September 11. Those who survived were fired when the restaurateur opened at another location and employed new workers without seniority and at lower wages. The displaced workers organized for the rights of restaurant workers and eventually extended their efforts to other cities, including New Orleans, where I offered my assistance surveying workers. This collaboration came to the attention of the president of the Louisiana Restaurant Association and local restaurant magnate Ralph Brennan, who asked the president of my university to shut me down. It was my first, but not only, introduction to the harsh environment facing workers in New Orleans, where the enemies of worker rights are also the enemies of academic freedom. I could never have survived without the help of ROC New Orleans organizers Darren Browder, Claudia Muñoz, Le'Kedra Robertson, and Abi Thornton, and of national ROC organizers Fekkah Mamdou, José Oliva, and Saru Jayaraman. Through them, I came to know other local organizers, such as Keron Blair and Ilana Scherl, and the work eventually evolved into a parallel survey of food-service workers at Tulane, where I was inspired by brilliant student organizers such as Lauren Elliott, Brian Ford, Mat Freimuth, Derek Rankins, and Benjamin Zucker.

The next occasion in which I could listen to workers and give them a chance to tell their stories came at the Avondale shipyard. Journalist Abdul Aziz took the cover photograph. The yard once employed nineteen thousand workers in unionized jobs with decent wages, but it closed at the end of 2013. An organizer from the AFL-CIO, Nick Unger, was not about to let that happen. He called for a worker-community effort and brought together researchers from local universities and community organizations, including Thomas Adams and Jana Lipman of Tulane University; Vern Baxter, Michael Mizell-Nelson, and Steve Striffler of the University of New Orleans; Ron Macoske and Jill Murray from the Southern University of New Orleans; Ted Quant and Petrice Sams-Abiodun of Loyola University; and Bryan Cassagne of United Way. Special thanks are also due to Tiger Hammonds and Louis Reine from the AFL-CIO, Andrew Croom from the Metal Trades Council, and student activists and research assistants Mike Barr, Andrew Brooks, Tasneem Chowdhry, Leslee Dean, Katie Lucky-Heard, Sarah Mandel, David McCoy, Anna Schumacher, Kyle Shepherd, Stephanie Sullivan, Zach Ulrich, and Yao Wu.

Even as the Avondale struggle began to bear fruit, I was drawn deeper into another project, exploring the myriad boards, commissions, public-benefit corporations, special districts, and other entities that exercise power in New Orleans but are subject to confused and weak accountability. A conversation with outgoing inspector general Bob Cerasoli had excited my interest as he described a wall in his office covered in Post-its, one for each entity, which accumulated so rapidly that he lost track. My attempt to document the entities grew exponentially, and I could never have made sense of them without the help of David Marcello of the Tulane Public Law Center and support from different departments at Tulane, especially the Gulf Coast Center, led by Lawrence Powell, as well as civic groups such as the New Orleans Coalition on Open Governance. With David's help we raised enough funds to launch a website and employ several students and professionals in its upkeep, including Chelsea Douso, David Martin, Luke Nowlen, Ariana Spiros, and Adrienne Wheeler. As the project moved forward, the background detail on entities and the power they hid required deeper knowledge, and it was provided by local activists and brokers such as Jacques Morial, Bob Tucker, and Wade Rathke. To understand and describe the relationships that joined entities, I benefited from conversations with Cassy Dorf, and Carlos Schönerwald taught me to build and analyze networks using statistical tools.

Finally, as my work filled some gaps, others became apparent. Latina immigrant women are a growing population, following male migrants who arrived in post-Katrina reconstruction to fill essential but insecure work, such as cleaning hotels and casinos. An impressive group of immigrant women asked for my help establishing the group Feminas in Biloxi and organizing events and support for the women who work, live, and raise families along the Gulf Coast. I was honored to help them stage a few events, raise funds, survey their members, and dress as Santa for their kids at Christmas. Through Feminas I met people like Iveth Diaz, Lorena Diaz, Rosa Herrin, and Yinette Valencia.

My colleagues at Tulane also provided support and guidance, including political science colleagues Martin Botelho-Mendoza, Brian Brox, Mary Clark, Patrick Egan, Ludovico Feoli, Chris Fettweis, Melissa Harris-Perry, Khaled Helmy, Casey Kane-Love, Sally Kenney, Tom Langston, Celeste Lay, Nancy Maveety, Vicki Mayer, Eduardo Silva, Ray Taras, Tor Tornqvist, Mark Vail, Justin Wolfe, and Dana Zartner. The Provost Office, Murphy Center, Stone Center, Newcomb College Institute, Center for Public Service, and Center for Engaged Learning and Teaching all provided monetary support for this project at one point or another.

I encountered many others in New Orleans who helped me and deserve my thanks. The best I can do is name a few, such as Jordan Flaherty, Jonathan and Holly Friedman, Leo Gorman and Nikki Thanos, Mario and Allison Padilla-Goodman, Shana Griffin and Brice Nice, Khalil and Renata Shahyd, and Jonathan and Amy Tabak. Other friends read the text and offered suggestions, such as Jeremy Levin, Ben Rankin, and Stuart Turner. Their wisdom as I tried to make sense of my experiences shows true friendship and patience. To keep me from getting too bloated on all the New Orleans food, the Ipswich soccer team put up with my attempts to play fullback on Sundays.

Three years ago, I left New Orleans after accepting a post at the University of Denver. As I integrated into life in Denver, I began compiling this book as a reflection on my New Orleans experience. On its surface, Denver is a shiny gem of abundance, but colleagues here have helped to reveal struggles that shaped and continue to shape this city's own Katrina moments. I owe a debt of thanks to new colleagues Erica Chenoweth, George DeMartino, Tom Farer, Rebecca Galemba, Alan Gilbert, Ilene Grabel, Nader Hashemi, Minsun Ji, Devin Joshi, Oliver Kaplan, Haider Khan, Frank Laird, Danny Postel, Martin Rhodes, Tony Robinson,

Tim Sisk, Margie Thompson, Ernesto Vigil, Jim Walsh, Karin Wedig, and Sam Zhao. Thanks to Joe Ryan and the Statistics and Visualization Center, who aided in the presentation of the results of network analysis.

Thanks must also go to Susan Clarke, editor of the Globalization and Community series, and Pieter Martin, my editor at the University of Minnesota Press. I am honored to be included in the impressive series you have shepherded to publication, and this book is far better as a result of your encouragement and prodding. Jay Arena reviewed the manuscript and dared me to confront head-on the contradictions of New Orleans capitalism. This book emerges more accurate and more inspired as a result of your careful reading, suggestions, and challenges.

While New Orleans may drift into my past, it will never leave my memory; my daughter was born there in 2013. Luna Serena Schneider-Zúniga, this book is for you, so that you may know a bit about the place where you were born and the wonderful and important struggles that will always surround you. I fell in love with you the second you were born, and your arrival made me fall in love in wholly new ways with your mother, Rebeca. You two are the loves of my life, and I only hope that the struggles described in this book will someday make a world worthy of you.

Satellite Entities

A. P. Tureaud Elementary
Akili Academy
Alcoholic Beverage Control Board
Algiers Development District
Algiers Economic Development Foundation
Algiers Technology Academy
Alice M. Harte Charter School
Andrew Wilson Charter School
Arise Academy Elementary Charter School
Arthur Ashe Charter School
Arts Council
Audubon Area Security District
Audubon Commission
Audubon Nature Institute
Audubon Nature Institute Foundation
Batiste Cultural Arts Academy
Benjamin Banneker Elementary
Benjamin E. Mays Preparatory School
BioSciences District
Board of Building Standards and Appeals
Board of City Trust
Board of Electrical Examiners
Board of Examiners of Operating Engineers

Board of Liquidation, City Debt
Board of Mechanical Examiners
Board of Trustees of Firemen's Pension and Relief Fund
Board of Zoning Adjustments
Broadmoor Neighborhood Improvement District
Business Resource Capital Specialty
Canal Street Development Corporation
Central City Economic Development District
City Civil Service Commission
City Planning Commission
Civil District Court Clerk
Criminal Justice Coordinating Council
Crocker Arts and Technology School
Delgado Albania Plantation
Dock Board, Port of N.O.
Downtown Development District
Dr. Charles R. Drew Elementary
Dr. Martin Luther King Charter School
Dwight D. Eisenhower Academy of Global Studies
East N.O. Neighborhood Advisory Commission (ENONAC)

Source: Author compilation from www.nolasatellitegovernment/tulane.edu.

Economic Development Advisory Committee

Edgar Harney Elementary

Edna Karr High School

Edward Wisner Advisory Board

Eisenhower Academy of Global Studies

Enterprise Funds

Ernest N. Morial-N.O. Exhibition Hall Authority

Esperanza Charter School

Ethics Review Board

Fairgrounds Citizens Advisory Committee

Fannie C. Williams Charter School

Film and Video Commission

Finance Authority of N.O.

First City Court Constable

Fourteenth and Sixteenth Wards Neighborhood Development District

French Market Corporation

French Quarter Festival, Inc.

French Quarter-Marigny Historic Area Management District

Friends of Lafitte Corridor

Garden District Security District

Gentilly Development District

Gentilly Terrace Elementary

George Washington Carver High

Great Expectations Foundation, Inc.

Greater N.O. Sports Foundation (Executive Committee)

H.C. Schaumburg Elementary

Harriet Tubman Elementary

Historic District Landmarks Commission, Central Business District

Historic District Landmarks Commission, N.O.

Housing Authority of N.O.

Human Relations Advisory Committee

Huntington Park Subdivision Improvement District

Hurstville Security and Neighborhood Improvement District

Independent Police Monitor

Industrial Development Board

Institute of Mental Hygiene

Intercultural Charter School

James Johnson Elementary

James Singleton Charter School

Jazz and Heritage Foundation

John Dilbert Community School

John McDonogh High

Joseph Craig Elementary

Joseph S. Clark Preparatory High

Kenilworth Improvement District

Kingswood Subdivision Improvement District

KIPP Believe College Prep

KIPP Central City Academy

KIPP Central City Primary

KIPP McDonogh 15 Elementary School for the Creative Arts

KIPP McDonogh 15 Middle School for the Creative Arts

KIPP N.O. Leadership Academy

KIPP Renaissance High School

L.B. Landry High School

Lafayette Academy

Lafitte Greenway Steering Advisory Committee

Lagniappe Academies

Lake Area New Tech Early College High School

Lake Barrington Subdivision Improvement District

Lake Bullard Neighborhood Improvement District

Lake Carmel Subdivision Improvement District

Lake Forest Estates Improvement Associates, Inc.

Lake Oaks Subdivision Improvement District

Lake Terrace Crime Prevention District

Lake Vista Crime Prevention District

Lake Willow Subdivision Improvement District

Lake Willow Taxing District

Lakeshore Crime Prevention District

Lakeview Crime Prevention District

Lakeview Street Maintenance District

Lakewood Crime Prevention and Improvement District

Lakewood East Security and Neighborhood Improvement District

Langston Hughes Academy Charter

Law Enforcement District

Louisiana Biomedical Research and Development Park Commission

Louisiana Stadium and Exposition District

Louisiana Technology Council

Magistrate Court

Maple Area Residents Security Tax District

Martin Behrman Charter Elementary

Martin Behrman High School

Mary D. Coghill Elementary

McDonogh #32 Elementary

McDonogh #32 Literacy Charter School

McDonogh #42 Charter School

McDonogh #City Park Academy

McKendall Estates Neighborhood Improvement District

Medard Nelson–UNO Charter

Metropolitan Human Service District

Metropolitan Youth Commission

MetroVision Economic Development Partnership

Mid-City Security District

Miller-McCoy Academy for Math and Business

Milneburg Neighborhood Improvement District

Morris Jeff Community School

Mosquito and Termite Control Board

Municipal Court

Municipal Employee's Retirement System

Music and Entertainment Commission

N.O. Charter Science and Math Academy

Neighborhood Conservation District Review Committee (NCDC)

Neighborhood Housing Improvement Advisory Committee

N.O. Access Television Board

N.O. Affordable Homeownership

N.O. Aviation Board

N.O. Building Corporation

N.O. Business Alliance

N.O. City Park Improvement Association

N.O. City Park Taxing District

N.O. College Prep

N.O. Coroner's Office

N.O. Council on Aging

N.O. Medical Complex, Inc.

N.O. Metropolitan Convention and Visitor's Bureau

N.O. Multicultural Tourism Network

N.O. Museum of Art

N.O. Public Library Foundation

N.O. Recreation Development Commission (NORD)

N.O. Recreation Development (NORD) Foundation

N.O. Redevelopment Authority

N.O. Regional Business Park (formerly NOBID)

N.O. Regional Loan Corporation

N.O. Research and Technology Advisory Committee

N.O. Tourism Marketing Corporation

N.O. Traffic Court

O. Perry Walker College and Career Preparatory High School

Oak Island Neighborhood Improvement District

Office of the Inspector General

Office of the Recorder of Mortgages

Orleans Levee District

Orleans Parish Assessor's Office

Orleans Parish Civil District Court Judges

Orleans Parish Communication District

Orleans Parish Criminal District Court Clerk of Court

Orleans Parish Criminal District Court Judges

Orleans Parish District Attorney

Orleans Parish Juvenile Court

Orleans Parish Landmarks Commission

Orleans Parish Law Library Commission

Orleans Parish Public Administrator

Orleans Parish School Board

Orleans Parish Service Hospital District

Orleans Parish Sherriff's Office

Paul Habans Elementary

Piazza D'Italia Development Corporation

Pierre A. Capdau Charter Elementary

Police Pension Fund, Board of Trustees

Pride College Preparatory Academy

Public Belt Railroad Commission

Public Library Board

Recovery School District (RSD)

Reed Elementary

Regional Planning Commission

Regional Transit Authority

Register of Conveyances Office

ReNEW Accelerated High School, City Park Campus

ReNEW Accelerated High School, West Bank Campus

Revenue Estimating Conference

Rivergate Development Corporation

S. J. Green Charter School

Sarah T. Reed Elementary

Sarah T. Reed High

Schwarz Academy (Alternative School)

SciTech Academy at Laurel Elementary

Seabrook Neighborhood Improvement and Security District

Second City Court

Seventh Ward Neighborhood Development District

Sewerage and Water Board

Sojourner Truth Academy

Sophie B. Wright Charter School

Southeast Regional Airport Authority (SERAA)

Spring Lake Subdivision Improvement District

Success Preparatory Academy

Tamaron Subdivision Improvement District

Total Community Action

Touro-Bouligny Security District

Treme Historical Development Corporation

Twelfth and Thirteenth Wards Neighborhood Development District

Twinbrook Security District

Upper Audubon Security District

Upper Hurstville Security District

Upper Pontalba Building Commission

Upper Pontalba Building Restoration Corporation

Vieux Carre Commission

Walter L. Cohen High

William J. Fischer Academy

Workforce Investment Board

Yacht Harbor Management Corporation, Municipal

Millages, Special Tax Districts

Property taxes are commonly expressed in mills. Each mill is calculated at .001 of the value of the property; for example, a $100,000 property taxed at 10 mills would owe $1,000.

Mill	Rate
General municipal purposes	10.85
Interest and redemption of city bonds	25.5
Special tax for construction and operation of drainage system	16.43
Special tax dedicated to maintenance of double platoon system in the Fire Department and triple platoon system in the Police Department; increase in pay of the officers and men in the Police and Fire Departments	4.66
Special tax for establishng and maintaining a zoological garden in Audubon Park	0.32
Aquarium	2.99
Public library	3.14
Special tax for support of police protection services	3.98
Special tax for support of fire protection services	3.94
Special tax to fund the Neighborhood Housing Improvement Fund	0.91
Special tax to fund the New Orleans Economic Development Fund	0.91
Special tax paying for the operations and improvements by the Parkway and Parks Commission	1.09
Special tax paying for the operations and improvements by the New Orleans Recreation Department	1.09
Special tax for street and traffic control device maintenance	1.38
Capital Improvements and Infrastructure Trust Fund	1.82
City services	0.87
Orleans Law Enforcement District	2.9
Constitutional tax for operating and maintaining a separate system of public schools	44.12

Source: City of New Orleans, *Annual Operating Budget*, 2010.

Citywide Mills	126.9
Special tax for benefit of New Orleans Regional Business Park	20.85
Special tax on all taxable real property within the Garden District's Security District	11.62
Tax on taxable property within the Touro Bouligny Security District except parcels qualifying for Special Assessment Level	7.8
Total Special Millages	66.7

Special Fees

Property Type	Rate ($)
All improved parcels situated within the Lakeview Crime Prevention District	100
All taxable real property within the Spring Lake Subdivision Improvement District	200
All taxable real property within Lake Carmel Subdivision Improvement District	250
All taxable real property within the Audubon Areas Security District	475
All improved parcels within the Lake Terrace Crime Prevention District	300
Each improved parcel with three (3) or more family units within the Lake Terrace Crime Prevention District	700
All taxable real property within the Lake Forest Estates improvement District	385
All taxable real property within the Huntington Park Subdivision Improvement District	175
All parcels within the Upper Hurstville Security District	485
All parcels within the Lakewood Crime Prevention and Improvement District	450
All parcels of land within the Lakeshore Crime Prevention District	360
All parcels within the Kenilworth Improvement District	200
All taxable real property within the Lake Oaks Subdivision Improvement District	350
Each improved parcel of land within the Twinbrook Security District except parcels qualifying for Special Assessment Level	440

Source: City of New Orleans, *Annual Operating Budget*, 2010.

All taxable real property within the Kingswood Subdivision Improvement District	240
Each improved parcel of land within the Hurstville Security and Neighborhood Improvement District	455
Each parcel of land within the Tamaron Subdivision Improvement District	185
Each parcel of land within the McKendall Estates Neighborhood Improvement District	250
Each improved parcel of land within the Lake Bullard Neighborhood Improvement District	250
Each parcel of land in the Upper Audubon Security District	500
Each improved residential parcel of land within the Mid-City Security District	200
Each improved commercial parcel of land within the Mid-City Security District	300
Each parcel of land in the Audubon Area Security District	500

Introduction

1. The Big Four are Lafitte, B. W. Cooper, C. J. Peete, and St. Bernard.
2. Reckdahl (2015) quotes Professor Bill Quigley of Loyola University: "HUD and HANO always go back on their promises. They always end up saying, 'Oh, we have less money than we thought,' or 'We will do more later.' The fact is that poor people were living on property which could be more profitably developed by and for other people."
3. Rental costs rapidly increased also, with 37 percent of renters paying more than 50 percent of their pretax income on rent and utilities in 2013, compared to 24 percent in 2004 (Sayre 2014; Plyer 2015).
4. Hurricane Katrina was even more costly than Hurricane Sandy, which hit the Northeast in 2012.
5. The rapidity with which the media loses interest in serious and necessary conversations about race and class injustice has been observed by Klinenberg (2002).
6. The decision was especially tragic in that the New Orleans levees were never under threat, but local financial elites wanted to assuage the fears of external financial backers and sacrificed areas populated mostly by African Americans to indicate their resolve (Barry 1997).
7. While a court case eventually corrected this obvious discrimination, it took five years, by which time a predictably small number of poor evacuees were able to wait out the case and return (Cohen 2008).
8. While Hurricane Katrina affected all neighborhoods and homes, block-by-block analysis suggests that half of the city's white residents experienced flooding as compared to three-quarters of black residents (see Brazile 2006). This is consistent with other studies that show a disproportionate impact of the hurricane on African American residents (see Brunsma and Picou 2008).
9. There had already been a long-term trend of decreasing resources and actions by the Department of Labor, as department actions decreased by one-third from

2001 to 2007, enforcement hours by the Wage and Hours Division fell by approximately 100,000, and the number of cases concluded fell from 38,051 to 30,467.

10. These steps received favor from some. Representative Charlie Norwood appreciated the "quick action to strip away unnecessary bureaucracy that may hamper our ability to recover. . . . [The country] can't afford that kind of inefficiency, red tape, and inflated costs when we have an entire region to rebuild, largely at taxpayer expense." M. Kirk Pickerel, chief executive of Associated Builders and Contractors, noted that "certain special interests and their allies in Congress are more concerned about reinstating this wasteful and outdated act than they are with fairly and expeditiously reconstructing the devastated area" (Witte 2005). Others took the opposite view. In a letter to Congress, union leaders from the Carpenters and Joiners of America, Laborers International Union, and International Union of Operating Engineers noted that workers "have gone through so much and now the administration wants them to sacrifice decent pay. . . . We don't hear contractors being asked to work for a reduced profit" (Bureau of National Labor Affairs 2005).

11. The Economic Policy Institute website includes a Family Budget Calculator that can be used to determine the living wage for different jurisdictions: http://www.epi.org/resources/budget.

12. One evolution of the multidimensional approach was Sen's capabilities approach (A. Sen 1985; Nussbaum and Sen 1993) and his "development as freedom" argument (A. Sen 2000). For Sen and others, income and other dimensions of poverty are important not for their intrinsic value but because they serve instrumental ends: "The usefulness of wealth lies in the things that it allows us to do—the substantive freedoms it helps us to achieve" (A. Sen 2000, 14).

13. "It was only when these apparently separate movements of labor and women joined, took to the streets, and, through intense direct action as a public discussion, captured public opinion that sections of the liberal middle class and intelligentsia became convinced it was in their interest to support these demands and the ruling bourgeoisie yielded" (Aronowitz 2004, 143).

14. "Joblessness among women remains higher than that of men; their living and working conditions tend, in growing numbers, to veer toward economic and social disaster. . . . Unemployment among blacks remains twice that of whites, millions are stuck in deindustrialized urban areas where wages revolving around federal minimum wage still predominate and schools have become the institutional sites of the stigmata to ensure that most black youth will remain poor" (Aronowitz 2004, 169–70).

15. "Americans are right that the bonds of our communities have withered, and we are right to fear that this transformation has very real costs" (Putnam 2000, 402). Technological explanations include changes in information, as people no longer need associations to secure information, make interests known, or even provide social support (Ridlen Ray 1999). Others emphasize the role of powerful, single-issue, and narrow-interest groups that form slick national organizations while marginalizing local citizens and community debates (J. M. Berry 1999). Further, mass media dumbs down issues; millionaire funders finance campaigns; advocacy

organizations and lobbyists dominate the decision process; and political parties eliminate the uncertainty of elections by turning every district into a safe district (Bullock 2010). Together, these factors lower citizen ability to engage politically.

16. This takes seriously Aronowitz's call for an analysis "sundering the traditional sociological distinction between class and social movement. . . . Genuine social movements are struggles over class formation when they pose new questions concerning the conduct of institutional and everyday life" (2004, 52).

1. Dual Development, Segmented Labor Markets, and Urban Regimes

1. "A conservative patrician past may hinder development, as old families with social pedigrees suffocate dynamic growth initiatives. This sort of situation, quite unusual in the U.S., seems to have characterized New Orleans up to the 1970s" (Molotch 1988).

2. The result for firms is that they can adopt management techniques that respond more quickly to market demands. Firms set up production chains with tight turnarounds, minimal inventories, and quick outputs so that production can occur "just in time" for each link in the production chain. Workers are trained and machines are designed to be specialized but flexible, allowing them to switch quickly from production of one output to another to meet rapidly changing consumer tastes (Piore and Sabel 1986).

3. These investments have been termed by some the actions of the "competition state" (Cerny 1997).

4. Harvey also notes also notes that cities serve not just to generate surplus product, but also to dispose of it. Excess surpluses generated by capitalist competition have to be absorbed somewhere, and investment in urban renewal and speculation in urban property offers an outlet. Further, these uses possess the added advantage of delayed returns; capital invested at one period brings inflated returns later. "This means that capitalism is perpetually producing the surplus product that urbanization requires. The reverse relation also holds. Capitalism needs urbanization to absorb the surplus products it perpetually produces" (Harvey 2012, 5–6). Yet this faces an inevitable contradiction, as the delayed realization of surplus only replicates and exaggerates at a later date the original problem of absorbing excess. The very act of capturing surplus value from rent is its own contradiction, as it requires trading on what had been distinct, and in the process turning it into something homogeneous, as seen in the "disneyification" of culture and gentrification of neighborhoods (Harvey 2012, 99–100).

5. Lewis's work was particularly important because it offered a way to understand development as movement from dualist to balanced economy. This entailed two processes of moving workers into the higher-productivity economy and raising productivity in the subsistence economy. Multiple potential intermediate stages contributed to an effervescence of development economics research into the "stages of development" (Ranis 2006).

6. Lewis suggested that productivity differences drove duality. Subsequent development thinkers of the dependency tradition built on his observation and argued that the abundant supply of underutilized workers held wage rates down, as did the repressive apparatus that had established this type of linkage to the international economy in the first place (Amin 1976). This implied a development challenge more than simply allocating workers to high-productivity activities; it was a fundamental homogenization of the economy around advanced techniques and practices (Singer 1999).

7. Some argue that the rise of the tourism and convention industry positioned local officials and business elites alongside civil rights leaders in opposing segregation, especially when it came to integrated accommodations (Souther 2003), but the bitter fight over desegregating schools displayed all the rancor of other southern cities and had similar demographic effects on white flight and educational disinvestment (Crain 1969, 250–322).

8. Indeed, most portrayals of New Orleans tell a story of Katrina washing away the low-wage and low-productivity population of the city to allow a boom in cosmopolitan sectors such as nonprofits, education, and medical research, evidenced by an influx of individuals with high levels of human capital, concomitant increases in average income, and a rising percentage of residents with college degrees (Plyer, Ortiz, and Horwitz 2011).

9. The work done in the secondary market is necessary to the functioning of the entire economy. Dirty, difficult jobs that few people see or acknowledge bring food to market, prepare products for consumption, and reconstruct buildings for inhabitance. These jobs are often informalized, deregulated, and poorly remunerated (Piore 1980, 17). Some observers have gone so far as to suggest that it is the hyper-exploitation in secondary labor markets that allow better conditions and greater earnings in the primary labor market (Castells and Portes, 1989).

10. Racism and xenophobia also undermine attempts to ameliorate the effects of workplace segmentation by undermining support for the welfare state and economic regulation (Alston and Ferrie 1999).

11. This contrasts with liberal traditions that view racism as an exception or aberration within liberalism (De Toqueville [1832] 2001), what Gunnar Myrdal (1944) describes as an "irrational" sentiment within a national character of individualism, democracy, tolerance, and opportunity (Huntington 1981; Walzer 1992).

12. Within that prison-industrial complex, Louisiana is the state that imprisons the highest percentage of its population and in which African Americans account for 93% of those sentenced to life without parole for nonviolent offenses (Frymer 2004; Alexander 2012). These observations have driven a tradition calling for more radical construction of Black power and more fundamental change to social and political institutions (Katznelson 1976; Reed 1999; Walton 1972, 1973).

13. This has been a historic dimension of exclusion in the United States. Chinese and Filipino immigrants, for example, were explicitly prohibited from citizenship,

and limits were placed on chain migration to slow the rate and pattern of absorption of non-European immigrants in the nineteenth and twentieth centuries (Zhou 1997; Ramakrishnan and Espenshade 2001; Rana 2010). Some consider immigration status to be a temporary problem for liberal traditions, as assimilation is assumed to be an inevitable and generational sequence, with second- and third-generation descendants of immigrants living out the American dream and moving fluidly within the dominant culture. For some this was a "straight line," with assimilation occurring steadily generation by generation (Park 1928). Others posit rates of assimilation that vary across groups and time periods (Zhou 1997), with some especially focusing on the racial and ethnic obstacles to assimilation embedded within American culture (Katz, Stern, and Fader 2007), and others presuming that some ethnicities could never assimilate U.S. culture (Huntington 2004).

14. In one study of low-wage work in major urban centers, half of all immigrant workers who told their employers about an injury were reported to immigration, fired, or instructed not to file claims (Bernhardt et al. 2009).

15. In 1891, Italian immigrants in New Orleans were the victims of the largest mass lynching by a mob in the United States (Moses 1997).

16. The regimes approach carves a middle ground between pluralist approaches, which assume an open and inclusive polity, and Marxist approaches, which assume capitalist dominance. Pluralists, joined by public choice theorists (Peterson 1981), argued that urban politics is characterized by the relatively unordered competition of rational individuals and interests. Different social forces concatenate to produce public policy, with interests mobilizing more forcefully around those issues of concern to them and always finding sufficient room in fragmented institutions to secure at least some access and influence. As a result of this relatively open and competitive notion of politics, resulting political outcomes approximate the general will, expressed as the sum of the various interests mobilizing in the public space (Dahl 1961). Marxists argued that the threat of capital flight and monetary influence over easily captured local political classes give dominant capitalists hegemony over local politics: "Conflicts in the living space are, we can conclude, mere reflections of the underlying tension between capital and labor. Appropriators and the construction faction mediate the forms of conflict—they stand between capital and labor and thereby shield the real source of tension from view. The surface appearance of conflicts around the built environment—the struggles against the landlord or against urban renewal—conceals a hidden essence that is nothing more than the struggle between capital and labor" (Harvey 1973, 289).

17. Part of the critique of pluralism came from its reductive, simplistic understanding of power. The pluralist approach theorizes power in terms of the open display of resource mobilizing potential. According to Lukes (1974), while pluralism addresses the open decision-making process evident in what he calls "the first face of power," pluralism ignores the second face of power embedded in the institutional mechanisms that prevent certain options from getting on the agenda in the

first place. Further, Lukes recognized a third face of power in the hegemonic ideas that constrain what political options will be considered legitimate. Elaborated by John Gaventa in studies of community organizing in Appalachia, the third face considered the power of manipulating symbols and ideology to constrain interests and rule out alternative options as illegitimate (Gaventa 1982).

18. "It must be able to mobilize resources commensurate with its main policy agenda" (C. N. Stone 1993, 21).

19. Much of Stone's work emerged from his close study of Atlanta, where governing elites allied to local business in a coalition articulated a development regime oriented toward growth (C. N. Stone 1976, 1989).

20. San Francisco has been taken as an example of this kind of coalition (Beitel 2004).

21. The last two types, though theoretically feasible, are unlikely, as they tend to be resisted by the local business elites who control resources (C. N. Stone 1993, 19–22).

22. "First, the dynamics that make possible the empowerment of black regimes are the same as those that produce the deepening marginalization and dispossession of a substantial segment of the urban black population. Second, the logic of progrowth politics, in which black officialdom is incorporated, denies broad progressive redistribution as a policy option and thereby prohibits direct confrontation of the problem of dispossession among the black constituency. Third, the nature of the politics that black regimes govern is such that the relation between the main components of their electoral and governing coalitions is often zero-sum" (Reed 1999, 88–89).

23. Reed actually outlines four factors: "the conceptual bias in black political discourse against accounting for intraracial stratification, the sociological circumstance that black officials themselves are members of upper-status communities and social networks and therefore are more likely to identify with upper-strata agendas, the pragmatic imperative to give priority to the most politically attentive constituents and most active supporters, and the relatively low fiscal and political costs of defining black interests around incorporation into an existing elite allocation framework" (1999, 98–99). He adds: "Therein lies the central contradiction facing the black regime: It is caught between the expectations of its principally black electoral constituency, which imply downward redistribution, and those of its governing coalition, which converge on the use of public policy as a mechanism for upward redistribution" (102).

24. Those closely involved with this balancing act labeled it "managed growth" (Mumphrey and Moomau 1984; M. P. Smith and Keller 1983).

25. "I have argued that virtually all U.S. cities are dominated by a small, parochial elite whose members have business or professional interests that are linked to local development and growth. These elites use public authority and private power as a means to stimulate economic development and thus enhance their own local business interests. They turn their cities, as active, dynamic units, into instruments

for accomplishing the growth goals that will enhance their fortunes. The city becomes, for all intents and purposes, a 'growth machine.' The operation of cities as growth machines has an impact on the quality and distribution of growth within and among urban areas" (Molotch 1988, 25).

26. "The role of the local rentier elite links daily life and mundane politics, on the one hand, to the larger economic and political structures of constraint and support, on the other" (Molotch 1999, 248).

27. "Place entrepreneurs attempt to create conditions that will intensify future land use in an area. . . . Unlike the capitalist, the place entrepreneur's goal is not profit from production, but rent from trapping human activity in place. Besides sale prices and regular payments made by tenants to landlords, we take rent to include, more broadly, outlays made to realtors, mortgage lenders, title companies, and so forth. The people who are involved in generating rent are the investors in land and buildings and the professionals who serve them. We think of them as a special class among the privileged, analogous to the classic 'rentiers' of a former age in a modern urban form. Not merely a residue of a disappearing social group, rentiers persist as a dynamic social force" (Logan and Molotch 1987, 32).

28. For Manuel Castells (1983), cities offer the potential for a popular coalition against capital, forged in defense of the collective consumption of infrastructure such as housing and urban services, cultural integrity of community and identity, and political autonomy for local democratic decision making. "The three goals that are crucial factors in the fulfillment of urban social movements are precisely the three alternative projects to the modes of production and modes of development that dominate our world. The city as a use value contradicts the capitalist form of the city as exchange value. The city as a communication network opposes the one-way information flow characteristic of the informational mode of development. And the city as a political entity of free self-management opposes the reliance on the centralized state as an instrument of authoritarianism and a threat of totalitarianism. Thus the fundamental themes and debates of our history are actually the raw material of the urban movements" (Castells 1983, 326).

29. "This deep and broad permeation of locality allows growth elites to prepare the ground for capital, thus coupling local agendas with national and international systems of production" (Molotch 1988, 42).

30. These are labeled "up-links" (Gotham 2000; Molotch 1999) or "vertical linkages" (Humphrey 2001). In the United States, local jurisdictions opt into or attract federal infrastructure projects, such as the 1950s Federal Highway Act, the housing and poverty programs of the 1960s Great Society, and downtown redevelopment and megaprojects of the 1980s and 1990s.

31. Growth machines must also engage the ideological work legitimating their position within global processes, acting as boosters, with local media playing an important role pumping up localities as amenable places to live, work, and do business (Boyle 1999). "When asked why he had consistently favored development on beautiful orchard lands that turned San Jose into one of the largest cities in

California within a period of two decades, he replied, 'Trees do not read newspapers' (Downie 1970, 112, as quoted in Domhoff 2009, 168).

32. "The number of special district governments has seen a nearly three-fold rise, from 12,340 in 1952 to 35,356 in 2002" (U.S. Census Bureau 2002).

33. "Special districts are created primarily because existing general-purpose local governments are unable or unwilling to provide needed services in a timely manner" (Porter 1992, 6).

34. Also, for an early indication of alarm at the proliferation of special districts, see ACIR (1964).

35. Marx values struggle over wages in the formation of a working class, but urges revolutionary action: "They ought, therefore, not to be exclusively absorbed in these unavoidable guerrilla fights incessantly springing up from the never ceasing encroachments of capital or changes of the market. They ought to understand that, with all the miseries it imposes upon them, the present system simultaneously engenders the material conditions and the social forms necessary for an economical reconstruction of society. Instead of the conservative motto: 'A fair day's wage for a fair day's work!' they ought to inscribe on their banner the revolutionary watchword: 'Abolition of the wages system!'" (Marx [1898] 1974, 29).

36. In the words of Schlozman, Verba, and Brady, the participating in politics is difficult for working people because "they can't, they don't want to, and nobody asked" (1999, 427–60). By definition, poor and working people lack the money that might buy them influence, and they lack time as they are too busy trying to survive. This means that they rarely develop the civic skills necessary to engage, and they fail to develop an interest in politics. Ultimately, they are isolated from the social and political networks that might overcome these obstacles to mobilize people into collective action.

37. To illustrate his argument, Aronowitz notes that women's suffrage was the result of labor recognizing that voting rights for women were class issues: "It was only when these apparently separate movements of labor and women joined, took to the streets, and, through intense direct action as a public discussion, captured public opinion that sections of the liberal middle class and intelligentsia became convinced it was in their interest to support these demands and the ruling bourgeoisie yielded" (2004, 143).

38. "This divide is characterized by the demonization and privatization of public services, including schools, the military, prisons, and even policing; by the growing use of prison as our primary resolution for social contradictions; by the degradation and even debasement of the public sphere and all those who would seek to democratically occupy it; by an almost complete abandonment of the welfare state; by a nearly religious reverence for marketized solutions to public problems; by the growth of a consumer culture that repeatedly emphasizes the satisfaction of the self over the needs of the community; by the corruption of democracy by money and by monied interests, what Henry Giroux refers to as 'totalitarianism with elections'; by the mockery of a judicial process already tipped in favor of the powerful;

by the militarization of the police; by the acceptance of massive global inequality; by the erasure of those unconnected to the Internet-driven modern economy; by the loos of faith in the very notion of community; and by the shrinking presence of the radical voices, values, and vision necessary to resist this dark neoliberal moment" (Hill 2016, 29).

39. "The changing productive relations and working conditions of the Industrial Revolution were imposed, not upon raw material, but upon . . . the inheritors of Bunyan, of remembered village rights, of notions of equality before the law, of craft traditions. . . . [T]he working class made itself as much as it was made" (E. P. Thompson 1966, 194).

40. Rosa Luxembourg similarly criticized trade union and social democrat leaders for self-congratulations over workplace gains while not confronting "the simultaneous and immense reduction of the proletarian standard of life through such methods as land usury, by the whole tax and customs policy, by landlord rapacity which has increased house rents to such an exorbitant extent, in short by all the objective tendencies of bourgeois policy which have largely neutralized the advantages of the fifteen years of trade-union struggle" (1971, 285).

41. For Marx, the appropriation of communal lands and natural resources was a form of "primitive accumulation," occurring at early stages of capitalism to concentrate wealth in the hands of incipient capitalists (Marx [1894] 1993, vol. 1, chap. 26). For Lenin, this process took place not only at early stages but also at the "highest stage" of capitalism, as developed capitalist countries responded to declining profits by engaging in imperial wars to claim for themselves the last opportunities for primitive accumulation (Lenin [1917] 2011). Rosa Luxembourg (2003), by contrast, recognized primitive accumulation as a strategy repeated each time capital faces a crisis of reproduction.

42. "Struggles against the recuperation and realization of surplus value from workers in their living spaces have to be given equal status" (Harvey 2012, 140).

43. "Urbanization is about the perpetual production of an urban commons (or its shadow-form of public spaces and public goods), and its perpetual appropriation and destruction by private interest" (Harvey 2012, 80).

44. As a professor at Tulane, I was given a chair in social entrepreneurship, an experience that led me to pen an article on the relationship between social entrepreneurship and other, related concepts (Schneider 2016).

45. Yet, without the ability to bargain collectively and sustain themselves through dues deduction from members, worker centers depend on external funding, frequently foundations supported by elite charity (Jenkins 2002).

46. Collaboration was most successful among skilled screwmen and longshoremen, was less successful at the bottom of the port hierarchy of freight handlers, roustabouts, yardmen, and other unskilled workers, and was occasionally interrupted by episodes of mob violence and racist division encouraged by employers.

47. Katrina foregrounded once again the racial dimensions of class inequality. As entertainer Kanye West observed in a television fund-raiser, "George Bush doesn't care about Black people."

48. http://www.plessyandferguson.org.

49. Amartya Sen (2005) translates the concept of human capital into the notion of capabilities, the ability to do things, the result of combining endowments and assets to pursue goals.

50. For Coleman (1988), social capital was constituted by the social ties and shared norms that fill in the gaps in individual behavior, for example, the bonds of trust that allow market operations to function.

51. Putnam (1994) brings the same logic to the study of political life in his comparison of northern and southern Italian democracy. He argues that "making democracy work" in northern Italy depends on a set of shared associations and overlapping bonds that allows individuals to collaborate in governance.

2. The Rise of a Globally Oriented Elite in a Fragmented City

1. A searchable, first-of-its-kind database is available for research and civic use at http://nolasatellitegovernment/tulane.edu. Most of the data from this chapter are available at the site, and the qualitative methodology underlying it will soon be available through the Qualitative Data Repository—https://qdr.syr.edu.

2. A monument erected to commemorate the battle and celebrate white supremacist victory sparked ongoing conflict, including a city council decision in 1991 to move the monument to a less conspicuous site with the "tepid" inscription, "In honor of those Americans on both sides of the conflict who died in the Battle of Liberty Place. . . . A conflict of the past that should teach us lessons for the future" (Reed 1993).

3. The Shakespeare government also coincided with the vicious 1891 mob lynching of eleven Italians. Though they were innocent, the men were blamed for the murder of the police chief (Powell 1990).

4. In fact, the city had amassed quite a quantity of debt, estimated at $22 million, leading to a default in 1874. A historian of the Board of Liq noted: "The history of the finances of a great municipality ordinarily is a dry and uninviting subject. To it turn none but those who, for professional or technical reasons, have a special interest in an intricate subject. But New Orleans in this respect, as in many others, is exceptional. Her financial history is of exceptional interest. . . . Since then its problem has been to meet the requirements of this debt without overwhelming the taxpayers and without impairing its credit at home and abroad. How this has been done is a record of which any city might well be proud" (Smith Kendall 1922, 481).

5. Similar satellites were initiated during another interruption in Old Regular dominance, 1896 to 1900, under Walter C. Flower. In the aftermath of a bungled Cotton Exposition at the 1894 World's Fair, in which the city ended deep in the red and the director fled the country, Flower rode a wave of dissatisfaction, carrying a middle-class and business-elite coalition into government. Flower adopted civil service reforms and depoliticized the police department, setting an agenda for

technocratic governance by professionals instead of political appointees. Two boards initiated during the period, the Sewerage and Water Board and the Port of New Orleans Commission, or Dock Board, parceled seats to relevant business chambers and granted appointment power to the Board of Liquidation. Other entities included requirements for professional certification, such as engineering or medical degrees, for membership.

6. Among the emblematic boards and commissions of the period was the Public Belt Railroad Commission, which took over transportation along the port of New Orleans, building a rail network to move freight along the river and eventually including service across the Mississippi River and to Lake Pontchartrain. All sixteen members of the commission were appointed by the mayor, and the commission modernized the port, offering lucrative opportunities for private-sector involvement and large numbers of jobs. It should be noted that while the public works offered opportunities to distribute benefits to working-class immigrants, the mayor maintained an ambiguous relationship with unions. While union members frequently voted for the Old Regulars and unions occasionally lent their support, the Behrman machine and its commissions refused to recognize any debt to the unions. A union secretary reported, "Behrman told the union that he did 'not owe any allegiance to organized labor . . . and that he would place men to work in the Public Belt only when he saw fit. This fact alone will demonstrate what an enemy to organized labor Martin Behrman has been" (*Times-Picayune*, August 17, 1920, quoted in Arnesen 1994, 338).

7. It was in this period that major New Orleans public works were undertaken, including investments in public spaces such as City Park and Audubon Park, numerous public-housing developments, as well as the reconstruction of the French Market. As in all such Old Regular accelerations in government activity, the projects expanded opportunities for contracts to local business, employment for ethnic working classes, and corruption that allowed Maestri to penetrate and absorb the Old Regular network.

8. Morrison was limited to cautious reforms (Haas 1974), as he faced challenges from within the CCDA, the statewide machine run by Governor Earl Long, and the residue of the Maestri regime, as well as pressure from competing local elite interests in the port, associated manufacturing, a speculative and services elite interested in tourism, and a vocal faction of historical preservationists. Three times Morrison attempted to win the Democratic nomination for governor, but Long used his statewide machine to defeat him each time, and Morrison ultimately had to settle for the 1961 nomination as ambassador to the Organization of American States by John F. Kennedy (Morrison 1965).

9. While Schiro could muster support to set in motion a shift toward a tourism and major events economy with the construction of the Superdome, he was unable to push through efforts to remake the whole of the downtown with the construction of an expressway along the river (Baumbach and Borah 1981).

10. As a state representative, Landrieu had been a staunch advocate for school integration, and this was remembered by a majority of African American voters,

who joined with a minority of white voters to elect him mayor in 1970 and 1974. Like previous mayors, Landrieu was forced to accommodate the interests of rival factions among the white elite, and he took steps to integrate City Hall and diversify the beneficiaries of city patronage and jobs to African American constituencies. This balancing of white elite and aspiring black interests earned Landrieu's administration the label of "pluralist"—respectful of white elites but also open to a long-excluded African American middle class and political elite (Whelan 1987, 221–23).

11. "When Chep Morrison became mayor of New Orleans in 1946, he claimed that he discovered three thousand 'rat catchers' whom Maestri and the Old Regulars had hired" (Kurtz and Peoples 1991, 95). Of course, Morrison was quick to replace Old Regular personnel with loyalists to his CCDA machine, which he built quickly into dominance using much of the same patronage used before (Kurtz 1971).

12. Theories of long-term planning called for setting goals, designing programs to achieve those goals, and allocating resources to the programs, in which entities like the City Planning Commission promised to improve performance through innovations in management and efficiency (Schick 1966).

13. In total the city went from 845,000 in 1960 to 593,000 in 1970 and to 496,000 in 1980, changing from 68 percent to 54 percent to 34 percent white over the same period (U.S. Census Bureau 2010).

14. Morial came out of the Seventh Ward, a traditional heart of Creole African American organizing and power, and occupied a putative middle ground, according to some, within the city's three-tiered racial hierarchy of African American, Creole, and white (Hirsch 1992, 316–19).

15. SOUL (Southern Organization for United Leadership), BOLD (Black Organization for Leadership Development), and COUP (Community Organization for Urban Politics) had traditionally organized in different wards of the city from the Seventh Ward, where Morial had his deepest roots.

16. Subsequent Bush and Clinton rollbacks of the welfare state meant that by the 1990s African American urban political machines had lost most of their already limited ability to extend patronage (Fuchs 1996, 62–63).

17. Barthelemy was backed by traditional African American neighborhood political brokers, BOLD and COUP, but faced an opponent who articulated a more redistributive agenda and mobilized a majority of working-class African American voters. As a result, Barthelemy won his first election with a minority of African American votes and a majority of white votes. His opponent in the runoff, William Jefferson, would go on to build the Progressive Democrats, a vote-mobilizing machine that would return him to congressional office seven times. The organization has crumbled in a series of corruption scandals, including Jefferson's 2009 conviction after $90,000 was famously found in his freezer, as well as convictions of family members and associates. Jefferson lost reelection to Republican Joseph Cao in 2008 (Morris 2009). Notably, Barthelemy won his second election with a majority of the African American vote, facing off against a white challenger, Donald Mintz.

18. Morial exercised his influence to direct the bidding process to the Pres Kabacoff–led Historic Restorations Incorporated, where former mayor Barthelemy now also works (Arena 2012, 125, 139).

19. Many such programs have their origins in Johnson's War on Poverty and Great Society programs and the Kerner Commission Report of 1968, which identified racism as the cause of 1960s urban uprisings: "White society is deeply implicated in the ghetto. White institutions created it; white institutions maintain it; and, white society condones it" (Kerner Commission 1968, 2).

20. The "soft state" was a "public/private governing apparatus" that was "dependent on soft money from grants, on soft power from private and non-profit organizations, and on concern about the soft spaces of the human mind. Its growth came from manipulating white fear of black disorder, encouraging social stability through therapeutic solutions, and reshaping the relationships between white and black leaders" (Germany 2007, 8).

21. A club good is one that is non-rival, meaning that availability does not decrease with use, as in the case of other public goods like cable television, safety, a good business climate, etc. What differentiates a club good from a public good is that club goods are excludable; their use can be limited to members, contributors, or some other criteria (Buchanan 1965).

22. Most levy flat per-parcel fees, though some assess millage-based fees according to property values. While Improvement Districts might seem like they have additional functions besides security, both kinds of district allocate over 80 percent of their revenues to security (OIG 2013, 16).

23. A precursor and ongoing ring-fencing parallel to the security districts was the Downtown Development District (http://www.legis.state.la.us/lss/lss.asp?doc =89989). Through legislation at the state legislature, the city created the Core Area Development District, which is denoted geographically by the major boulevards bounding the downtown business district. The bill authorized the approval of property taxes levied on businesses within the district as well as the issuance of bonds, both of which would have to be approved by voters. The use of Downtown Development District funds is decided by its board, whose members are appointed by the mayor, the state legislature, and the local chamber of commerce from among those who reside or have businesses within the district. Tax authority has been repeatedly renewed and ceilings raised, most recently for a twenty-five-year term of up to 22.9 mills until 2030. In addition, the Downtown Development District issued $7.3 million in bonds in 2001 for projects within the district and backed by tax revenues. These funds complemented an additional $10 million raised by the Canal Street Development Corporation, another satellite entity, established in 1989 (Ord. No. 13,325 MCS). There are no limits on spending, and the entity does not have to obey civil service rules.

24. Much of this discussion comes from the 2013 Inspector General report "Review of New Orleans Security Taxing Districts." The executive summary of that report concludes: "Security districts were only available to those able to pay additional taxes for increased services, which raises the question of whether public

safety should be treated as a private good at the neighborhood level, or as a public good at the city-wide level" (OIG 2013).

25. They also contract with private companies, typically run by retired police officers.

26. Nagin would eventually be embroiled in his own corruption schemes, convicted in 2014 of bribes and preferential contracting in the building of a Central City hardware store, as well as kickbacks involved in technical upgrading of City Hall. As of this writing, he is serving a ten-year prison term (Grimm 2014).

27. The candidate was Bobby Jindal, who lost in 2004 but won in 2008.

28. The challenger was subsequent mayor Mitch Landrieu, son of Moon.

29. The polarizing effect of the hurricane and the failure of the African American political machines to present their own candidates allowed Nagin to fill the vacuum (Lay 2009).

30. The *Times-Picayune* columnist James Gill writes, "If there is another city where one encounters as much inefficiency and incompetence, I don't know it" (Gill 1997, 196).

31. http://likesuccess.com/38132.

32. http://www.nola.gov/mayor/priorities.aspx.

33. http://www.nola.gov/boards.

3. Satellite Governance, Public Finance, and Networks of Power

1. http://nolasatellitegovernment.tulane.edu.

2. Other predictors of public finance might include whether the city is a state capital, the age of a city, and the number of large cities nearby (Clark and Ferguson 1983), but these variables provided inconsistent statistical results and the simple model presented here is preferable.

3. In conducting its own investigation, the State Legislative Auditor's Office also found its own difficulties: "During our review, City records were not always accessible. They were maintained in multiple locations or missing. It was extremely difficult, time consuming and, in some cases, impossible to obtain some records. . . . We were constantly confronted with limited access to records and slow responses to our requests for documentation" (Louisiana Legislative Auditor Office 2010, 3).

4. All totals are from the New Orleans annual budget, *Comprehensive Annual Financial Reports* obtained from the State Legislative Auditor's Office, and annual financial reports provided directly by boards, commissions, public-benefit corporations, and other entities associated with the city of New Orleans.

5. http://nolasatellitegovernment.tulane.edu/index.php.

6. One advantage of the website is that scrolling closer can make the names of entities visible: http://dataviz.du.edu/projects/schneider/new_orleans.

7. Other measures of centrality, such as closeness, betweenness, eigenvalue, and Katz, produce slightly different descriptive statistics, but degree centrality is the most straightforward to characterize different networks (Miura 2012).

8. For a network with vertices v1. . . . vn and maximum degree centrality cmax, the network degree centralization measure is S(cmax−c(vi)) divided by the maximum value possible, where c(vi) is the degree centrality of vertex vi.

9. The clustering coefficient of node i in graph g is the share of network contacts N_i(g) who are directly connected. The average clustering coefficient for the network is: Cluster_i(g) = # {kj in g | k,j in N_i(g)} / # {kj | k,j in N_i(g)}.

10. The categorization was done on the basis of current characteristics (What functions does the satellite perform?) as well as historical considerations (In what context was the satellite initiated?). For example, the Audubon Nature Institute Foundation (initiated in the 1970s) was placed into the privatizing category, while the New Orleans Recreational Development Foundation (initiated in 2010) was placed in the dual development category. While they serve similar functions, they emerge in different contexts, and it makes sense to place them in different categories.

11. Other criteria were "health, safety, and security" and "transparency, monitoring, and compliance" (Community Evaluation Commission 2014b, 2–3).

12. "STAND is a grass-roots organization of low-income residents and workers in New Orleans. As survivors, we believe unity and self-determination are our most viable solutions. Now more than ever, when City, State, and Federal government have turned their backs, we believe grassroots leaders must come together to take collective action to change our condition. We seek to transform all systems of exploitation and racism through organizing the power of the working poor. To this end, we pledge to ensure the rights of workers and residents to return and recover." http://nowcrj.org/about-2/stand-with-dignity.

13. Two original proposals were submitted, one by Hunt-Gibbs-Boh-Metro and the other by Parsons-Odebrecht. The first proposal did not have a certified Disadvantaged Business Enterprise (DBE) partner at the time of proposal, while the second was reported to include a company with a history of alleged racial discrimination and harassment. The Aviation Board scrapped the original evaluation and reissued a request for proposals (McLendon 2014a).

14. Commissioner Perry said, "My goal is due process. . . . There was nothing in the first Aviation Board call that protected due process, but we put it in there. They say they are going to recruit workers from Job One. We got them to say they would listen to community voices. They added an addendum to the call in which they said they would listen to community voices" (Interview, August 2014).

15. Stand with Dignity organizer Collette Tippy said, "This effort came out of the B. W. Cooper, C. J. Peete, and Iberville organizing. At Iberville, there were health and safety problems, and we learned how to fix those" (Interview, August 2014).

4. The Post-Katrina Political Transition

1. Clarkson had served on the council before and was one of the few members of the council to oppose the 1992 anti-discrimination law that barred public funds

from all-white Carnival krewes that excluded African Americans (Gotham 2007, 183).

2. "Despite the fact that grievances or competition within the consensual framework of governance still may be expressed in more or less muted racial terms, perception that deep racial cleavage remains the key fault line around which elites align is a badly out of date vestige of the tense politics and structural conflict that were especially salient during the period of racial transition" (Reed 2016, 12).

3. Perry is married to academic and TV personality Melissa Harris Perry, showing some of the ambiguousness of class position and representation.

4. Divergence in support for the City Council was also pronounced in terms of levels of education. Respondents with high school or less disapproved of the City Council at 31.4 percent, while those with a graduate or professional degree disapproved of the City Council at only 21 percent (UNO 2013).

5. This section draws particularly on P. Burns and Thomas (2015, 26–61).

6. Organizations included the Bureau of Governmental Research, the Public Affairs Council, Citizens for 1 Greater New Orleans, the Council for a Better Louisiana, the World Trade Center, the Jefferson Business Council, the Northshore Business Council, the Young Leadership Council, and the New Orleans Chamber of Commerce.

7. http://nordc.org/about.

8. Fully one in fourteen African American men from New Orleans are behind bars (Chang 2012).

9. http://www.clearinghouse.net/chDocs/public/JC-LA-0003-0025.pdf.

10. https://www.youtube.com/watch?v=E_rRZ9ejTqU.

11. http://www.wdsu.com/news/4562307/detail.html.

12. https://opprcnola.org/about.

13. https://www.splcenter.org/seeking-justice/case-docket/jones-v-gusman.

5. Globalized Construction and Ethnic Segmentation

1. Removal from the city center was driven in part by population loss, but also by the transition of downtown to tourism and entertainment establishments, by cutting through poor neighborhoods by highway projects, and by white flight in response to desegregation that inflated the populations of surrounding parishes (Brickford 1997; Passavant 2011). Further, public projects to drain swamps, construct levees, and build highways encouraged the population of previously uninhabitable areas, especially in New Orleans East (Campanella 2002; Baxter, Jenkins, and Kroll-Smith 2010).

2. Palm (1990) labels disasters "acts of capital," as they are the result of previous development decisions to protect against one threat while creating vulnerabilities to others. The levee system of New Orleans is a good example, as levees prevented flooding from the river but raised the risk of flooding from the lake and canals, which was what ultimately flooded the city (Barry 1997).

3. For "the evaluation, design and construction management of levees and floodwalls, special closure structures for protection of the communities adjacent to the Inner Harbor Navigation Canal, major pumping facilities and planning studies for improved levels of flood protection for New Orleans and southern Louisiana" (Arcadis, N.V. 2007).

4. Critics point to the lobbying efforts of Joe Allbaugh, a lobbyist for KBR and former FEMA director and campaign manager for President George W. Bush. "'This is a perfect example of someone cashing in on a cozy political relationship,' said Scott Amey, general counsel at the Project on Government Oversight, a Washington watchdog group. 'Allbaugh's former placement as a senior government official and his new lobbying position with KBR strengthens the company's already tight ties to the administration, and I hope that contractor accountability is not lost as a result.'" http://www.halliburtonwatch.org/news/hurricane_katrina.html.

5. Twelve of the seventeen members of the commission were businesspeople, one was the president of Tulane University who is on the New Orleans Business Council, and the others included the Catholic archbishop and two local musicians. Their first act was to contract with the Urban Land Institute, which offered a plan for a "smaller footprint" through "green spacing," meaning abandoning some of the people whose homes had been flooded (Arena 2012, 151). The public outrage triggered by this threatened expulsion forced the mayor to open the planning process to a more participatory Unified New Orleans Plan.

6. In addition to infrastructure funds, there was also significant capital introduced for remediation and home reconstruction. FEMA budgeted $9.8 billion for debris removal, and the federal Road Home program sent $8 billion in rebuilding grants to underinsured homeowners. Private insurers claimed to have paid out over $11 billion to homeowners (Eaton and Treaster 2007).

7. "As with Charity, LSU and Tulane have wrangled over the new hospital's governance. Like Long, Gov. Bobby Jindal hails the potential of a new teaching hospital. But unlike his famous Democratic predecessor, the Republican governor has focused more on economic development, medical education and research, rather than providing health care for the poor. And despite a $1.1 billion public investment, Jindal attempts to fit UMC into his philosophy of a government smaller than what Long fought for eight decades ago. So insistent are Jindal aides that the state is not building a 'Charity successor,' they do not even concede that UMC is a 'public' hospital" (Barrow 2012).

8. These actions were finally found to be illegal in 2012, though few teachers and staff had the wherewithal to see the judicial process through to its completion and receive a settlement (Eggler 2012).

9. For some this was a demographic as well as economic dividend: "The storm destroyed a great deal and made plenty of room to build houses to sell for a lot of money. Most importantly, the hurricane drove poor people and criminals out of the city, and we hope they don't come back" (Finis Shellnut quoted in Cedric Johnson 2011, 190).

10. The allocation of these funds was fraught with problems, including failure to provide funds for renters and the discriminatory and inegalitarian allocation of funds according to the pre-storm value of property (Reckdahl 2011).

11. Arena targets the Greater New Orleans Foundation, which collected funds from national foundations such as Rockefeller, Gates, and Bush-Clinton and directed them to compliant local nonprofits and activists (2012, 174). "Their incorporation into the nonprofit complex, including receiving funding from foundations directly involved in privatization, placed a restraint on what they could do" (2012, 213).

12. There had been about fourteen thousand public-housing units for low-income residents in the 1990s, but this number was cut in half by 2004 with the demolition and mixed-use reconstruction of the St. Thomas and the Desire projects (Arena 2012).

13. Only government employment held steady and continues as the largest single employment sector, while oil and gas employment was buoyed by rising oil prices since 2003.

14. While loosening employment verification requirements eased entry for undocumented workers, the deployment of 725 additional Immigration and Customs Enforcement (ICE) personnel and ICE raids even on Red Cross shelters indicated that immigrants would be welcomed for their labor but employers would have the power of the state behind them if they wished to target a worker (Shore 2005).

15. A recent study of these low-wage sectors in the three largest U.S. cities — New York, Chicago, and Los Angeles — found that 26 percent of the four thousand low-wage-sector workers surveyed had not been paid the minimum wage, 76 percent of those eligible for overtime had not been paid overtime, and 43 percent of workers who complained to their employer or attempted to organize a union experienced a form of illegal retaliation. The study further reported that only 8 percent of workers injured on the job filed claims for workers' compensation, and fully half of all immigrant workers who told their employers about an injury were reported to immigration, fired, or instructed not to file claims (Bernhardt et al. 2009).

16. Mayor Ray Nagin reflected the nativist response within the African American political elite when he asked, "How do I ensure that New Orleans is not overrun by Mexican workers?" (Mui 2010).

17. Additional data were gathered through a separate, non-random sampling strategy targeting Latinos, as well as qualitative interviews with specialists and observers. All results reported here are drawn from the population-based, random sample.

18. The database was created by merging the New Orleans Sewerage and Water Board dataset of addresses with water meters with data from the Census Bureau and the Geographic Information Systems Department of New Orleans, and it included all addresses in the City of New Orleans with geographic reference points and links to pre-Katrina demographic information. The sampling procedure was conducted with the support of the Emergency Operations Center of New Orleans.

19. Based on the minimum sample size formula, the minimum sample size was 97 if we assumed 95 percent confidence, a prevalence estimate of 50 percent, and desired precision of .10. To have sufficient sample size to stratify, we increased the minimum sample size requirement to 150. The minimum sample size formula is given by: $N \geq Z^2 \times (P)(1-P)/d^2$.

20. Surveyors made a spiral outward from the sample point until finding a construction site. On arrival, the surveyors would ask the closest worker to the left to participate in the study, moving sequentially leftward until a respondent was found.

21. There are several reasons responses might not have occurred. In some areas there was little construction occurring, and in other places no workers would agree to the survey. The difference in response rates from 2006 to 2009 could reflect the fact that residential housing reconstruction had tapered several years after the storm, as the immediate period of rebuilding was completed and there were fewer new returnees.

22. To minimize risk of worker discomfort, surveyors offered respondents information sheets and contact information for nonprofits active on worker rights and immigrant rights, and the study was submitted to review by the institutional review board of the author's university.

23. The concentration of Latinos and undocumented workers, in particular, in residential construction affirms segmentation in the allocation of projects, with native and documented immigrant workers drawn to the larger-scale commercial and infrastructure construction spurred by post-2008 stimulus spending and long-delayed FEMA and Army Corps of Engineers investment and Latino and undocumented workers in remaining residential reconstruction jobs.

24. To characterize these trends precisely, the analysis compares proportions of documented and undocumented workers experiencing different conditions across time periods using Pearson chi-squared statistics to test the significance of differences in group proportions. This table includes conditions for which there was no significant difference or for which the conditions were so low for all workers that it made sense to put them in the category of difficult conditions for all.

25. Both of these conditions had also been problematic for documented workers in 2006, but by 2009 their families had been reunited and they were no longer sharing their living arrangements with large numbers of roommates. This was not the case for undocumented workers.

26. In this case, significance tests used the t-statistic and accounted for the possibility that group means are non-homogeneous, as indicated by the Levene's test for equality of variances. Still, results are practically indistinguishable from those under the assumption that variances are equal.

27. Wages were also calculated using self-reported income per payment, frequency of payment, and average hours worked. There were some outliers in both groups, but results were robust to truncating the samples for outliers above 1.5 standard deviations above the mean. When outliers were truncated, undocumented

workers received a mean hourly wage of $10.75 and documented workers received a mean hourly wage of $15.80.

28. Income was calculated using self-reported income. Differences between undocumented and other workers were once again robust to truncating outliers at a maximum of 1.5 standard deviations above the mean. With outliers removed, undocumented workers received a mean salary of $1,536.20 and documented workers received almost exactly double that, $3,076.78.

29. This is consistent with the findings of a Department of Justice investigation of the New Orleans Police Department (Department of Justice Civil Rights Division 2011).

30. As for why the mistreatment accelerated faster for the native-born and documented, it is possible that undocumented workers were already being mistreated at such high rates that little more could be squeezed from them.

31. Wage theft was a problem in major infrastructure and large-scale projects, also. KBR was required to pay 2,600 workers in 107 different contractors for more than $1.4 million in unpaid wages (M2 Presswire 2007).

32. https://www.youtube.com/watch?v=XI2R0fstcvE.

33. Such agreements fall under the Housing and Urban Development (HUD) Act of 1968, which requires HUD-financed projects draw at least 30 percent of their workforce from low-income residents, ideally residents of housing projects.

6. Racial and Gender Segmentation in Tourism and Services

1. Corruption surrounding the land grant for the Harrah's eventually resulted in the conviction of then governor Edwin Edwards in 2000.

2. In questions of cultural evolution, this is contrasted with tourism from below, "the range of framing strategies, symbols, aesthetic codes, and other expressive resources that local people and groups create and use in everyday life to stimulate cultural invention, construct local authenticity, and promote tourism at a grassroots level" (Gotham 2007, 10).

3. Health care, with 11.2 percent, is the only sector that is larger (Bureau of Labor Statistics 2009).

4. The Brennans' host of restaurants are controlled by two corporations, the Brennan Restaurant Group and Dickie Brennan and Company, and includes the following high-end restaurants: Red Fish Grill, Jazz Kitchen, Ralph's on the Park, Café B, Heritage Grill, and Café NOMA, Commander's Palace, Mr. B's, Brennan's, Bourbon House Seafood and Oyster Bar, Dickie Brennan's Steakhouse, the Palace Café, and Tableau.

5. Examples include John Besh, Paul Prudhomme, and Emeril Lagasse, among others.

6. http://www.campaignmoney.com/political/contributions/ralph-brennan.asp?cycle=14.

7. http://204.196.0.52/cgi-bin/laimg/?_1073714+0.

8. http://www.opensecrets.org/pacs/pacgot.php?cmte=C00003764&cycle =2008. To return the favor, Louisiana politicians spent $1.5 million in restaurants, with locally branded high-end chains Ruth's Chris Steak House topping the recipients at $171,000 and Emeril's New Orleans Restaurant grossing $34,000 at its Shreveport location alone (Anderson 2014).

9. http://www.lra.org/lra/insurance/insurance.asp.

10. http://www.allbusiness.com/north-america/united-states-louisiana/4060925 –1.html.

11. http://www.lra.org/lra/members/membership_epli.asp.

12. http://www.allbusiness.com/food-beverage/restaurants-food-service/118 13583–1.html.

13. The distinction between traded and untraded services is an economic categorization for activities that serve external consumers (e.g., tourism) versus those that serve local consumers (e.g., hairdressers). The distinction is fuzzy, as locals might also frequent a tourist destination, but offers a rough distinction between external and internal markets.

14. Among other collaborations, the author and his students have participated in national surveys for the production of the annual ROC Diners' Guide over various years.

15. Data are from the 2012 Bureau of Labor Statistics Occupational Employment Statistics, https://www.bls.gov/oes/current/oes_research_estimates.htm. In Louisiana, the tipped minimum wage is $2.13 per hour and minimum wage for non-tipped workers is the federal minimum, as the state has no minimum wage law of its own. In the event that tips do not bring workers to a higher than minimum wage, employers are required to cover the difference to bring them to the federal minimum for hours worked.

16. The Economic Policy Institute calculates a living wage as that which "affords the earner and her or his family the most basic costs of living without need for government support or poverty programs" based on costs of housing, food, transportation, health care, taxes, and other basic necessities.

17. Other results show similarly dangerous conditions: 41.8 percent performed a job they were not trained to do, 23.8 percent report unsafely hot kitchens, 25.8 percent report fire hazards, 36.8 percent report missing floor mats, 28.1 percent report not receiving instruction or training about workplace safety, and 14.4 percent did something due to time pressure that might have harmed the health and safety of customers.

18. Quick-serve workers were the most likely to handle toxic chemicals (38.5 percent).

19. In the back of the house, by contrast, African American workers were 62.5 percent of the workforce and white workers only 21.7 percent.

20. Most African American workers were in quick serve (58.7 percent).

21. While the numbers of other non-white populations were not as large, qualitative interviews also revealed industry and job segmentation on the basis of national

origin. As one worker observed, "Definitely there are Hispanics working back there, and it's interesting because they are the ones in the back; they're the ones doing the hard work. This is a Mexican restaurant, but there wasn't a single Mexican or Hispanic server—All Caucasian, all college kids, all white, and uppity on top of that. . . . To them it's almost like a favor, 'Be grateful we even give you this job' kind-of-thing" (Schneider and Jayaraman 2014, 251).

22. Lack of mobility reinforced ascriptive segmentation. Of all workers surveyed who never received a promotion, 76.7 percent were workers of color.

23. According to a Sodexo flier, they employ "more than 120,000 people at 10,000 locations in North American."

24. Four percent were white and native-born, 4 percent were mixed-race, 4 percent were Latino, and 2 percent were white, non-Latino, foreign-born.

25. While rejection rates were not recorded, interviewers estimated that approximately two-thirds of workers who were approached declined participation, usually citing apprehension at reprisal from a supervisor. Interviewers were trained to explain that workers were being interviewed only on breaks or off-duty; that all people have a right to say what they wish when they are not at work; and that students and staff would defend any worker who wished to speak freely. None changed their mind.

26. The same proportion, slightly over one-third (36 percent), were between eighteen and twenty-five. The average number of children was 1.8, with a maximum of 7, and workers supported an average of 1.63 dependents. For slightly over half (56.9 percent), high school was the highest level of education completed, but one-third had completed college. A small percentage (3.9 percent) had completed only middle school.

27. This is 21.4 percent above $10 per hour.

28. Also, 41.7 percent earned between $200 and $300, and 19.5 percent earned between $300 and $400.

29. In addition, 4.7 percent had received public assistance, 3.1 percent received Social Security benefits, and 1.6 percent had received Family Health Plus.

30. Of those surveyed, 28.1 percent received a raise of 20 cents per hour, and 12.5 percent received a raise of over a dollar per hour.

31. Respondents reported working an average of 35.6 hours per week, with a maximum of 65, a minimum of 20, and the majority (60.8 percent) between 30 and 40.

32. In describing their work schedule, 82 percent reported working full-time and 18 percent part-time. In response to a question about how often their schedule changes, slightly under half (49 percent) reported that their schedule never changes, while 11.8 percent reported changes in schedule daily, 35.3 percent weekly, and 3.9 percent monthly.

33. Of those who had guaranteed sick days or earned them, the average was 5.4 days per year, with 17.6 percent reporting zero paid sick days, and approximately a third between zero and five (35.3 percent) and five and ten sick days (38.3

percent). With respect to vacation days, the average among the thirty respondents who answered was 3.3 days, with a maximum of 24, though half received no days and approximately a quarter (26.7 percent) received zero to 4 days.

34. There were also allegations of intimidation, assault, and sexual harassment, but these were not confirmed in court documents.

35. At one point the city took notice and investigated J'obert, finding that he owed over a million dollars in taxes. To make up some of the back taxes, they confiscated his $100,000 Bentley (Eggler 2011b).

36. Such cooperatives already exist in New York and in Detroit, under the name "Colors."

37. ROC has also sought to provide other services to members, including health insurance.

38. The workers at neighboring Loyola University also organized at the same time.

39. The types of activities suggested included music events, food, sports leagues, and speaking or film events.

40. The fact that the workers attempted to organize at all is significant, as outside the workplace they participated in very few organizations besides churches: 11.4 percent participate in a parent-teacher type of association, 8.9 percent in another organization, 5.7 percent in a neighborhood association, 5.7 percent in a sports league, and 2.9 percent in a community organization.

41. From Sodexo, Area Manager Ben Hartely wrote: "Sodexo believes that the decision to unionize or not is an important one for our employees. . . . We follow the National Labor Relations Board standards that call for open dialogue to ensure employees are fully informed before they make such a decision" (E. W. Lewis 2010, 3).

42. Author's communication with SEIU organizer Rob Harmon, August 15, 2011.

7. Deindustrialization versus Joined-up Workplace and Community Struggle

1. http://aapa.files.cms-plus.com/Statistics/2009US_PORTRANKINGS_BY_CARGO_TONNAGE.pdf.

2. Subsidies included construction and operating differential subsidies (CDS and ODS), in which shipbuilders could receive up to half the added cost of building a ship or operating it with U.S. workers instead of foreign ones (Unger 2012).

3. Focus groups were held with approximately ten workers invited by union leaders on the basis of their knowledge of the history of the shipyard, their role in the union, and their role as leaders in the community. Focus groups provided qualitative observations and helped design the survey instrument.

4. There was no significant difference across the survey methods in terms of the detail in the responses. We removed some of the more open-ended questions for application in person as respondents would not have the same time to consider and

write answers. The take-home surveys produced only thirty-eight responses, a low rate that offered an initial indication of the low morale and high levels of stress facing workers. To secure more responses, student workers and the principal investigator went to the gate of the shipyard when workers left their shifts. It was truly an experience. When the whistle blows, the one thousand workers ending their shift materialize over the levee, visible at first only as hard hats bobbing over the lip of the berm. As heads and bodies slowly materialized, an eventual sea of workers cascaded down the levee, hopping over guardrails and retaining walls to make their way to the gates where they punched out. Now within sight of the parking lot, they lumbered past, eager to get to their car and beat traffic home. Many smiled and waved as they went past, apologizing for some domestic obligation that prevented them from delaying, but a sufficient number paused to ask our business and/or agreed to respond to the survey.

5. Identities of workers were separated from their responses, and in the results below workers are identified only as "focus group participant" or "survey respondent."

6. The survey instrument was designed with the help of Ron Mancoske from the Southern University of New Orleans and Nick Unger from the AFl-CIO.

7. Much of the material on the history of the unionization campaign comes from Nick Unger, a veteran of multiple unionization campaigns, including the effort to save Avondale.

8. As one worker related during a focus group, "Winning the union was not easy. In fact, the hardest part was getting people together, getting them to feel like they didn't have to be afraid to stand up. The company would fire people, and lots of people lost their job around the time of the organizing. It was a way of scaring people." Another worker affirmed a similar feeling, "Lots of people were scared they'd lose their jobs. I wore my stickers, I went to the hearings, and I knew they couldn't legally fire me, and that knowledge kept me strong. Still, the company tried to divide us, bring us in one by one and offer us stuff. They made us targets, offered us better positions, like trying to make us foremen." "It wasn't just that," observed the first worker, "I think I must have taken fifteen urine tests in those days. You had to be clean; you had to be on time all the time; you had to know your job better than anyone and not make any mistakes. They were looking for an excuse to fire you if you were trying to help organize" (Focus Group, June 8, 2011).

9. A 2001 NLRB ruling cited Avondale for 141 labor law violations and mandated rehiring forty-nine people fired for union activity.

10. "When I think of the work we did, I'm proud. You look at the TV, and they used to have this show Hawaii 5-0. During the music, the opening part, when they show the ships in the ocean, the big Navy destroyers, those are ours. We made those ships. That was a good feeling. I made those, and everybody was seeing them." Another worker echoed, "I was in the military for twenty-six years, and every so often I'd get called up from work. One of those times, I was even assigned to a ship

that I had built. Imagine that, a boat I built and was then going to serve on" (Focus Group, June 8, 2011).

11. The average age of respondents was forty-eight, with a few younger than thirty and the bulk between thirty and seventy. Of the total, 47 percent of the workers were between thirty and fifty, and 38 percent of the workers were over fifty. The oldest worker surveyed was sixty-six. A majority of the workers (62 percent) were married, and workers shared their home with an average of slightly fewer than three family members, with the largest household comprising twelve family members. Exactly half of the workers were African American, with 28 percent white, 11 percent Latino, and 11 percent other. There was a small cohort of women workers, at 11 percent of the sample. Of the workers asked about their education, 8 percent of the workers had completed college, with 24 percent completing some college, 8 percent completing an associate's degree, 44 percent with a high school diploma or GED, and 16 percent with less than a high school education. These results reflect New Orleans metro averages, where 27 percent of the people completed college, 16 percent completed less than high school (Ortiz 2011), and functional illiteracy is between 24 and 32 percent. National Center for Education Statistics website, consulted November 19, 2011. http://nces.ed.gov/naal/estimates/StateEstimates.aspx.

12. Several explanations for these patterns came from the focus group discussions. The first was that Katrina disrupted work patterns for all workers, and because it had occurred six years earlier, in 2005, it may have depleted some of the workers who would have by now accumulated between eleven and twenty years. A second observation is that there was a lull in defense spending in the years prior to September 11, 2001, and the slowdown in military spending might have corresponded to lower levels of activity and hiring in the shipyard.

13. The youngest member of the focus groups, a recent hire who was twenty-one years old, explained that with the threat of closing, he was not given the same options: "They closed the credit union, and when I went to a bank for a car loan, they told me they couldn't be sure I'd be able to pay in the future" (June 8, 2011).

14. Workers reported shopping for food up to seven days a week, with an average of 2.3 trips, ate out on average 2.1 times and a maximum of 10 times per week, and visited the drugstore an average of 3.1 times per week and a maximum of 15 times.

15. The impending closure led him to comment, "Now, with the threat of closing, I see that it is inside Avondale that people are hurting. I minister to them here now" (Focus Group, June 8, 2011).

16. Data compiled from Federal Elections Statistics at http://elections.gmu.edu/Turnout.html, checked November 19, 2011.

17. "Insufficient training and experience contribute to the careless mistakes by workers, and that may have played a role in recent accidents. From what I can see, that probably is part of it" (Darce 2002).

18. In 2008 Northrup Grumman declared a $1.2 billion loss, traced in part to a $3.1 billion "goodwill impairment" charge that offset the value of Litton and

another company on Northrop's books, suggesting that the value had been inflated (Baxter et al. 2011, 7).

19. One of the workers in the focus groups had similar worries: "If wages are right, then a young man sees this as an opportunity. He'll get off the streets and go get his GED, get himself a job here. Avondale even trained people up, paid you to go to school full-time, get that engineering degree, and then you come back and work even higher. Without Avondale, what will be left? I'll tell you what, it's the street. You never get that kid off the street, and there you go, that's where you get problems. If there are no places with wages that are right, what choice do they have" (Focus Group, June 8, 2011).

ACIR (Advisory Commission on Intergovernmental Relations). 1964. *The Problem of Special Districts in American Government.* Washington, D.C.: ACIR.

Adelson, Jeff. 2015. "After Hurricane Katrina: How Federal Aid Helped Region Rebuild, Improve." *New Orleans Advocate,* June 20. http://gnoinc.org/news/region-news/after-hurricane-katrina-how-federal-aid-helped-the-region-rebuild-improve-advocate-staff-photo-by-john-mccusker-the-new-permanent-london-avenue-canal-pumping-station-is-under-construction-where.

Ahlers, Douglas, Allison Plyer, and Frederick Weil. 2008. "Where Is the Money?" January. http://gnocdc.s3.amazonaws.com/reports/HurricaneFundingGap.pdf.

Albright, Matthew. 2010. "Avondale Shipyard Employees Say They Saw Plant Closure Coming." *Times-Picayune,* July 14. http://www.nola.com/business/index.ssf/2010/07/avondale_shipyard_employees_sa.html.

Alexander, Michelle. 2012. *The New Jim Crow: Incarceration in the Age of Colorblindness.* New York: New Press.

Alston, Lee J., and Joseph P. Ferrie. 1999. *Southern Paternalism and the American Welfare State.* New York: Cambridge University Press.

Amin, Samir. 1976. Trans. Brian Pearce. *Unequal Development: An Essay on the Social Formation of Peripheral Capitalism.* New York: Monthly Review Press.

Anderson, Brett. 2014. "Top 100 Restaurants Louisiana Politicians Love." *Times-Picayune,* January 30. http://www.nola.com/dining/index.ssf/2014/01/do_louisiana_politicians_have.html#incart_special-report.

ANES. (Various years). *National Election Survey.* http://www.electionstudies.org/studypages/download/datacenter_all_NoData.php.

Arcadis, N.V. 2007. "ARCADIS, Bioengineering Win Contract New Orleans." *Infrasite.net,* January 4. http://archive.is/efK0o.

Archer, Robin. 2010. *Why Is There No Labor Party in the United States?* Princeton: Princeton University Press.

Arena, John. 2012. *Driven from New Orleans: How Nonprofits Betray Public Housing and Promote Privatization*. Minneapolis: University of Minnesota Press.

Arnesen, Eric. 1994. *Waterfront Workers of New Orleans: Race, Class and Politics*. Chicago: University of Illinois Press.

Aronowitz, Stanley. 2004. *How Class Works: Power and Social Movement*. New Haven: Yale University Press.

Arrighi, Giovanni. 2010. *The Long 20th Century*. London: Verso.

Associated Press. 2004. "New Orleans to Drop Privatization of Water and Sewer Systems." *Water and Waste Digest*, April 22. http://www.wwdmag.com/new -orleans-drop-privatization-water-and-sewer-systems.

Audubon Institute. 2008. *Comprehensive Annual Financial Report*. New Orleans: Audubon Institute.

Bankston, Carl L., and Stephen J. Caldas. 2002. *A Troubled Dream: The Promise and Failure of School Desegregation in Louisiana*. Nashville: Vanderbilt University Press.

Barrow, Bill. 2012. "Charity Hospital: The Times Picayune Covers 175 years of New Orleans History." *Times-Picayune*, February 1. http://www.nola.com/175years/ index.ssf/2012/02/charity_hospital_the_times-pic.html.

Barry, John M. 1997. *Rising Tide: The Great Mississippi Flood of 1927 and How It Changed*. New York: Simon and Schuster.

Baulch, Bob. 1996. "The New Poverty Agenda." *IDS Bulletin* 27 (1): 1–10.

Baumbach, Richard O., Jr., and William E. Borah. 1981. *The Second Battle of New Orleans: A History of the Vieux Carre Riverfront*. Tuscaloosa: University of Alabama Press.

Baxter, Vern, Pamela Jenkins, and Steve Kroll-Smith. 2010. "Urbanization: New Orleans Neighborhood Change after Hurricane Katrina." In *The New Encyclopedia of Southern Culture*, 15:111–20. Chapel Hill: University of North Carolina Press.

Baxter, Vern, Ted Quant, Patrice Sams-Abiodun, and Steve Striffler. 2011. "Avondale: The Uncertain Future of a Great American Shipyard." Manuscript. University of New Orleans.

Beitel, K. E. 2004. "Transforming San Francisco: Community, Capital, and the Local State in the Era of Globalization, 1956–2001." Ph.D. diss., University of California, Davis.

Bernhardt, Annette, and Siobhan McGrath. 2005. "Trends in Wage and Hour Enforcement by the U.S. Department of Labor, 1975–2004." *Economic Policy Brief* 3 (September): 1–2.

Bernhardt, Annette, Ruth Milkman, Nik Theodore, Douglas Heckathorn, Mirabai Auer, James DeFillipis, Ana Luz González, Victor Narro, Jason Perelshteyn, Diana Polson, and Michael Spiller. 2009. *Broken Laws, Unprotected Workers: Violations of Employment and Labor Laws in America's Cities*. Chicago: National Lawyers Guild. https://nelp.3cdn.net/e470538bfa5a7e7a46_2um6br 7o3.pdf.

Bernhardt, Annette, Martina Morris, Mark S. Handcock, and Marc A. Scott. 2001. *Divergent Paths: Economic Mobility in the New American Labor Market.* New York: Russell Sage.

Berry, Christopher. 2008. "Multi-level Government and the Fiscal Common Pool." *American Journal of Political Science* 52 (4): 802–20.

Berry, Jeffrey M. 1999. "The Rise of Citizen Groups." In *Civic Engagement in American Democracy,* ed. Theda Skocpol and Morris Fiorina, 367–95. Washington, D.C.: Brookings Institution Press.

Bobo, James R. 1985. *The New Orleans Economy: Pro Bono Publico?* New Orleans: Division of Business and Economic Research, University of New Orleans.

Bollens, John C. 1957. *Special District Governance in the United States.* Berkeley: University of California Press.

BondGraham, Darwin. 2010. "The Long Hurricane: The New Orleans Catastrophe Predates Katrina." *The Public Eye* 25 (3). http://www.publiceye.org/magazine/v25n3/the-long-hurricane.html.

———. 2011. "Building the New New Orleans." *Review of Black Political Economy* 38:279–309.

Bonilla-Silva, Eduardo. 1997. "Rethinking Racism: Toward a Structural Interpretation." *American Sociological Review* 62 (3): 465–80.

Borjas, George J. 1998. "To Ghetto or Not to Ghetto: Ethnicity and Residential Segregation." *Journal of Urban Economics* 44 (2): 228–53.

Boulard, Garry. 1998. *Huey Long Invades New Orleans.* Gretna, La.: Pelican Publishing.

Bousquet, Marc. 2011. "Big Brother on Campus." *Chronicle of Higher Education,* April 25. http://chronicle.com/blogs/brainstorm/big-brother-on-campus/3 4552.

Bowman, Kirk, Fabrice Lehoucq, and James Mahoney. 2005. "Measuring Political Democracy: Case Expertise, Data Accuracy, and Central America." *Comparative Political Studies* 38 (8): 939–70.

Boyle, Mark. 1999. "Growth Machines and Propaganda Projects." In *The Urban Growth Machine: Critical Reflections, Two Decades Later,* ed. Andrew E. G. Jonas and David Wilson, 55–73. Albany: State University of New York Press.

Brazile, D. L. 2006. "New Orleans: Next Steps on the Road to Recovery." In *The State of Black America,* 233–37. Washington, D.C.: National Urban League.

Brickford, Susan. 1997. "Anti-Identity Politics: Feminism, Democracy, and the Complexities of Citizenship." *Gender and Philosophy* 12 (4): 111–31.

Brown, Michael K., and Steven P. Erie. 1981. "Blacks and the Legacy of the Great Society." *Public Policy* 3:299–330.

Brox, Brian. 2009. "Elections and Voting in Post-Katrina New Orleans." *Southern Studies* 16 (2): 1–23.

Bruno, Andorra. 2015. "Immigration-Related Worksite Enforcement: Performance Measures." *CRS Report R40002.* Washington, D.C.: Congressional Research Service.

Brunsma, David L., David Overfelt, and J. Steven Picou, eds. 2007. *The Sociology of Katrina: Perspectives on a Modern Catastrophe.* Lanham, Md.: Rowman and Littlefield.

Brunsma, David, and J. Steven Picou. 2008. "Disasters in the Twenty-First Century: Modern Destruction and Future Instruction." *Social Forces* 87 (2): 983–91.

Buchanan, James M. 1965. "An Economic Theory of Clubs." *Economica* 32 (February): 1–14.

Bullard, Robert D., ed. 1989. *In Search of the New South.* Tuscaloosa: University of Alabama Press.

Bullock, Charles S. 2010. *Redistricting: The Most Political Activity in America.* New York: Rowman and Littlefield.

Bureau of Government Research. 2015. *Do the Tax Dedications in New Orleans Make Sense?* New Orleans: BGR.

Bureau of Labor Statistics. 2009. *National Occupational Employment and Wage Estimates.* http://www.bls.gov/oes/2009/may/oes_nat.htm.

———. 2010. *Union Affiliation Data from the Current Population Survey.* https://data.bls.gov/cgi-bin/surveymost?lu.

———. 2014. *State and Metro Area Employment, Hours, and Earnings.* http://www.bls.gov/sae/data.htm.

Bureau of National Labor Affairs. 2005. *Daily Labor Report,* October 21.

Burns, Nancy. 1994. *The Formation of American Public Governance.* New York: Oxford University Press.

Burns, Peter F., and Matthew O. Thomas. 2006. "The Failure of the Nonregime: How Katrina Exposed New Orleans as a Regimeless City." *Urban Affairs Review* 41 (4): 517–27.

———. 2015. *Reforming New Orleans: The Contentious Politics of Change in the Big Easy.* Ithaca: Cornell University Press.

Byrne, John. 2005. "WSJ: White Rich Elude Orleans Chaos, Don't Want Poor Blacks Back." *Rawstory,* September 8. http://www.rawstory.com/news/2005/WSJ_White_rich_escape_New_Orleans_chaos_dont_want_blacks_poor_0908.html.

Campanella, Richard. 2002. *New Orleans Then and Now.* Gretna, La.: Pelican Publishing.

Cangelosi, Robert J., and Dorothy G. Schlesinger. 1997. *New Orleans Architecture.* Vol. 7. Gretna, La.: Pelican Publishing.

———. 2000. *New Orleans Architecture: The University Section.* Vol. 8. Gretna, La.: Pelican Publishing.

Carville, James. 2009. *Tulane University/Democracy Corps Mayoral Survey.* New Orleans: Democracy Corps.

Castells, Manuel. 1983. *The City and the Grassroots.* Berkeley: University of California Press.

———. 1989. *The Informational City: Economic Restructuring and Urban Development.* New York: Wiley-Blackwell.

———. 1996. *The Rise of the Network Society*. Malden, Mass.: Blackwell.

Castells, Manuel, and Alejandro Portes. 1989. "The World Underneath: The Origin, Dynamics, and Effects of the Informal Economy." In *The Informal Economy: Studies in Advanced and Less Developed Economies*, ed. Alejandro Portes, Manuel Castells, and Laura A. Benton, 1–40. Baltimore: Johns Hopkins University Press.

Cerny, Philip G. 1997. "Paradoxes of the Competition State: Dynamics of Political Globalization." *Government and Opposition* 32 (2): 251–74.

Chang, Cindy. 2012. "Louisiana Is the World's Prison Capital." *Times-Picayune*, May 13. http://www.nola.com/crime/index.ssf/2012/05/louisiana_is_the_worlds _prison.html.

Charpentier, Colley. 2007. "Union Alleges Labor Laws Abused on Construction Site." *Times-Picayune*, August 15. http://blog.nola.com/times-picayune/2007/08 /union_alleges_labor_laws_abuse.html.

Chervenak, Edward, and Bogdan Mihoc. 2012. *2012 Quality of Life Survey*. New Orleans: UNO Survey Research Center.

Cho, Dong Sung, and Michael Porter. 1986. "Changing Global Industry Leadership: The Case of Shipbuilding." In *Competition in Global Industries*, ed. Michael Porter, 539–67. Cambridge: Harvard Business School. 1986.

Chomsky, Avi. 2008. *Linked Labor Histories: New England, Colombia, and the Making of a Global Working Class*. Durham: Duke University Press.

Christovich, Mary Louise, Sally Evans, Roulhac Toledano, and Betsy Swanson. 1995. *New Orleans Architecture*. Vol. 5. Gretna, La.: Pelican Publishing.

City of New Orleans. (Various years). *Annual Operating Budget*. http://www.nola .gov/mayor/budget.

———. (Various years). *Comprehensive Annual Financial Reports*.

City of New Orleans, Component Units and Unincorporated Public Entities. (Various years.) *Comprehensive Annual Financial Reports*.

Clark, Terry N., and Lorna Crowley Ferguson. 1983. *City Money*. New York: Columbia University Press.

CNN. 2005. "Military Due to Move in to New Orleans." September 2. http://www .cnn.com/2005/WEATHER09/02/katrina.impact.

Cobb, James C. 1994. *The Most Southern Place on Earth: The Mississippi Delta and the Roots of Regional Identity*. New York: Oxford University Press.

Cohen, Ariella. 2008. "Lawsuit Filed against Road Home with Allegations of Discrimination against Blacks." *New Orleans City Business*, November 12. http:// www.gnofairhousing.org/wp-content/uploads/2012/02/11-12-08_citybusiness_ Lawsuit_filed_against_Road_Home.pdf.

Coleman, James S. 1988. "Social Capital in the Creation of Human Capital." *American Journal of Sociology* 94:95–120.

Coll, Max. 2010. "SEIU Escalates Union Efforts: Workers and Students Present Demands to Regional Management." *Tulane Hullaballoo*, April 9. http://tulane .usas.org/files/2010/04/20100414_hullabaloo_april_12.pdf.

Collins, Gabriel, and Michael C. Grubb. 2008. *Comprehensive Survey of China's Dynamic Shipbuilding Industry*. Newport, R.I.: Naval War College.

Collins, P. H. 2000. "Gender, Black Feminism, and Black Political Economy." *Annals of the American Academy of Political and Social Science* 568:41–53.

Community Evaluation Commission. 2014a. "Community RFP Process." http://www.communityrfp.com/?page_id=2.

———. 2014b. *Findings*. https://drive.google.com/file/d/0B9ZruaacUroJY1JZbWNS Qzl0UW8/edit?pli=1.

Cook, Brian J. 2007. *Democracy and Administration: Woodrow Wilson's Ideas and Public Management*. Baltimore: Johns Hopkins University Press.

Cooper, Christopher. 2005. "Old Line Families Escape Worst of Flood and Plot the Future." *Wall Street Journal*, September 8. http://www.wsj.com/articles/SB112 614485840634882.

Corten, Renee. 2011. "Visualization of Social Networks in Stata Using Multidimensional Scaling." *Stata Journal* 11 (1): 52–63.

Cowen Institute. 2012. *The State of Public Education in New Orleans: 2012 Report*. New Orleans: Cowen Institute. http://www.coweninstitute.com/wp-content/up loads/2012/07/SPENO-20121.pdf.

Crain, Robert L. 1969. *The Politics of School Desegregation: Comparative Case Studies of Community Structure and Policy Making*. Garden City, N.Y.: Anchor Books.

Dahl, Robert. 1961. *Who Governs? Democracy and Power in an American City*. New Haven: Yale University Press.

Darce, Keith. 2002. "Job Deaths at Avondale Scrutinized: Three Fatalities in Two Months." *Times-Picayune*, December 29, A1.

Dean, Amy. 2014. "Will the Next Labor Movement Come from the South?" *Truthout*, May 20. http://www.guestworkeralliance.org/2014/05/a-new-labor -movement-born-in-the-south-saket-soni-in-truthout-may-2014.

Dees, J. Gregory. 1998. "The Meaning of 'Social Entrepreneurship.'" Reformatted and Revised, May 30, 2001. https://entrepreneurship.duke.edu/news-item/the -meaning-of-social-entrepreneurship.

Department of Homeland Security. 2005. "Waiver of Compliance with Navigation and Inspection Laws." Washington, D.C.: Department of Homeland Security. http://npga.org/files/public/Jones_Act_Waver_9–05.pdf.

Department of Justice Civil Rights Division. 2011. *Investigation of the New Orleans Police Department*. New Orleans: U.S. Department of Justice. http://www.jus tice.gov/sites/default/files/crt/legacy/2011/03/17/nopd_report.pdf.

De Toqueville, Alexis. (1832) 2001. *Democracy in America*. New York: Harper Perennial Press.

Devereaux, Steven. 2003. "Conceptualizing Destitution." *IDS Working Paper 216*. Brighton: IDS at the University of Sussex.

Domhoff, G. William. 2009. *Who Rules America? Challenges to Corporate and Class Dominance*. New York: McGraw Hill.

Downes, Lawrence. 2007. "In Forgotten New Orleans, Life and Hope Stir at the Bottom." *New York Times*, May 7. http://www.nytimes.com/2007/05/07/opin ion/07mon4.html?pagewanted=print.

Downie, Leonard. 1970. *Mortgage on America*. New York: Praeger.

Eaton, Leslie, and Joseph Treaster. 2007. "Insurance Woes for Hurricane Katrina Victims." *New York Times*, September 2. http://www.nytimes.com/2007/09/02/business/worldbusiness/02iht-orleans.4.7353442.html?_r=1&.

Economic Policy Institute. 2008. *What Families Need to Get By*. Washington, D.C.: Economic Policy Institute.

Eggler, Bruce. 2010. "Labor Concerns Presented to City Council Economic Development Committee." *Times-Picayune*, April 13. http://www.nola.com/politics/index.ssf/2010/04/labor_concerns_presented_to_ci.html.

———. 2011a. "Smaller Jail Is Approved by New Orleans City Council." *Times-Picayune*, February 3. http://www.nola.com/politics/index.ssf/2011/02/smaller_jail_is_approved_by_ne.html.

———. 2011b. "Bar Owner's Bentley Is Seized to Pay His New Orleans Taxes." *Times-Picayune*, May 4. http://www.nola.com/politics/index.ssf/2011/05/bar_owners_bentley_is_seized_t.html.

———. 2012. "Orleans Parish School Firings after Hurricane Katrina Were Contract Violations." *Times-Picayune*, June 20. http://www.nola.com/katrina/index.ssf/2012/06/orleans_parish_school_firings.html.

Elliott, Lauren, and Brian Ford. 2010. "Sodexo Workers on Tulane and Loyola's Campuses Walk Out of Work to Protest Unfair Labor Practices." *Louisiana Justice Institute*, April 29. http://louisianajusticeinstitute.blogspot.com/2010/04/lji-guest-column-sodexo-workers-on.html.

Engerman, Stanley L. 1971. "Some Economic Factors in Southern Backwardness in the Nineteenth Century." In *Essays in Regional Economics*, ed. John Kain and John Meyer, 276–306. Cambridge: Harvard University Press.

Fairclough, Adam. 1995. *Race and Democracy: The Civil Rights Struggle in Louisiana, 1915–1972*. Athens: University of Georgia Press.

Farmer, Paul. 2004. *Pathologies of Power: Health, Human Rights, and the New War on the Poor*. Berkeley: University of California Press.

Fine, Janice. 2006. *Worker Centers: Organizing Communities at the Edge of the Dream*. Ithaca, N.Y.: ILR Press.

Flaherty, Jordan. 2010a. "James Perry's Run for Mayor of New Orleans." *Colorlines*, January 28. http://www.colorlines.com/articles/james-perry%E2%80%99s-run-mayor-new-orleans.

———. 2010b. "The Incarceration Capital of the US." *Huffington Post*, November 9. http://www.huffingtonpost.com/jordan-flaherty/the-incarceration-capital_b_781150.html.

———. 2015. *No More Heroes: Grassroots Challenges to the Savior Mentality*. Chico, Calif.: AK Press.

Fletcher, Bill, Jr., and Fernando Gapasin. 2009. *Solidarity Divided: The Crisis in Organized Labor and a New Path toward Social Justice.* Berkeley: University of California Press.

Florida, Richard. 2003. *Cities and the Creative Class.* New York: Routledge.

Frymer, Paul. 2004. "Race, Labor, and the Twentieth-Century American State." *Politics and Society* 32: 475–509.

Fuchs, Ester. 1996. "The Permanent Urban Crisis." In *Breaking Away: The Future of Cities,* ed. Julia Vitullo-Martin, 49–73. New York: Twentieth Century Fund Press.

Fussell, Elizabeth. 2007. "Constructing New Orleans, Constructing Race: A Population History of New Orleans." *Journal of American History* 94 (December): 846–55.

———. 2009. "Post-Katrina New Orleans as a New Migrant Destination." *Organization and Environment* 22:458–69.

———. 2011. "The Deportation Threat Dynamic and Victimization of Latino Migrants." *Sociological Quarterly* 52 (4): 593–615.

Gabe, Thomas, Gene Falk, and Maggie McCarty. 2005. *Hurricane Katrina: Social-Demographic Characteristics of Impacted Areas.* Washington D.C.: Congressional Research Service, The Library of Congress.

Garrett, Geoffrey. 2004. "Globalization's Missing Middle." *Foreign Affairs* 83 (6): 84–96.

Gaventa, John. 1982. *Power and Powerlessness: Quiescence and Rebellion in an Appalachian Valley.* Champaign: University of Illinois Press.

Gendron, Richard, and G. William Domhoff. 2009. *Leftmost City: Power and Progressive Politics in Santa Cruz.* Boulder: Westview Press.

Gerharz, Barry, and Seung Hong. 2006. "Down by Law: Orleans Parish Prison before and after Katrina." *Dollars and Sense,* March/April. http://www.dollars andsense.org/archives/2006/0306gerharzhong.html.

Germany, Kent B. 2007. *New Orleans after the Promises.* Athens: University of Georgia Press.

Gibson-Graham, J. K. 2003. *The End of Capitalism (As We Knew It): A Feminist Critique of Political Economy.* Oxford: Blackwell.

Gill, James. 1997. *Lords of Misrule: Mardi Gras and the Politics of Race in New Orleans.* Jackson: University Press of Mississippi.

Gorman, Leo. 2009. "Latino Migrant Labor Strife and Solidarity in Post-Katrina New Orleans, 2005–2007." Master's thesis, University of New Orleans. http:// scholarworks.uno.edu/cgi/viewcontent.cgi?article=1930&context=td.

Gotham, Kevin. 2000. "Urban Space, Restrictive Covenants and the Origins of Racial Residential Segregation in a U.S. City, 1900–50." *International Journal of Urban and Regional Research* 24 (3): 616–33.

———. 2007. *Authentic New Orleans: Race, Culture, and Tourism in the Big Easy.* New York City: New York University Press.

Gotham, Kevin, and Miriam Greenberg. 2014. *Crisis Cities: Disaster and Redevelopment in New York and New Orleans*. New York: Oxford University Press.

Gould, Kenneth A., David N. Pellow, and Allan Schnaiberg. 2004. "Interrogating the Treadmill of Production." *Organization and Environment* 17 (3): 296–316.

Gramsci, Antonio. 1971. *Selections from the Prison Notebooks*. New York: International Publishers.

Greeley, Martin. 1994. "Measurement of Poverty and Poverty of Measurement." *IDS Bulletin* 25 (2): 1–15.

Greenhouse, Steven. 1998. "5 Years after Workers' Vote, Shipyard Holds Off a Union." *New York Times*, July 10. http://www.nytimes.com/1998/07/10/us/5-years-after-workers-vote-shipyard-holds-off-a-union.html.

Grimm, Andy. 2014. "Ray Nagin to Report to Prison Monday to Start 10-Year Prison Sentence." *Times-Picayune*, September 8. http://www.nola.com/crime/index.ssf/2014/09/ray_nagin_to_report_to_prison.html.

Guba, Egon G., and Yvonne S. Lincoln. 1989. *Fourth Generation Evaluation*. Thousand Oaks, Calif.: Sage.

Haas, Edward F. 1974. *DeLesseps S. Morrison and the Image of Reform: New Orleans Politics, 1946–61*. Baton Rouge: Louisiana State University Press.

Hall, Peter, and Rosemary Taylor. 1996. "Political Science and the Three Institutionalisms." *Political Studies* 44:936–57.

Harding, Alan. 1995. "Elite Theory and Growth Machines." In *Theories of Urban Politics*, ed. David Judge, Gerry Stoker, and Hal Wolman, 33–53. London: Sage.

Harrison, Mason. 2014. "Black Majority Regained on New Orleans City Council." *Louisiana Weekly*, March 31. http://www.louisianaweekly.com/black-majority-regained-on-new-orleans-city-council.

Harvey, David. 1973. *Social Justice and the City*. Baltimore: Johns Hopkins University Press.

———. 2007. *A Brief History of Neoliberalism*. Oxford: Oxford University Press.

———. 2012. *Rebel Cities: From the Right to the City to the Urban Revolution*. London: Verso.

Hensman, Rohini. 2011. *Workers, Unions and Global Capitalism*. New York: Columbia University Press.

Hill, Mark Lamont. 2016. *Nobody: Casualties of America's War on the Vulnerable, from Ferguson to Flint and Beyond*. New York: Atria Books.

Hirsch, Arnold R. 1983. "New Orleans: Sunbelt in the Swamp." In *Sunbelt Cities: Politics and Growth since World War II*, ed. Richard M. Bernard and Bradley R. Rice, 100–137. Austin: University of Texas Press.

———. 1992. "Simply a Matter of Black and White: The Transformation of Race and Politics in Twentieth-Century New Orleans." In *Creole New Orleans: Race and Americanization*, ed. Arnold Hirsch and Joseph Logsdon, 262–320. Baton Rouge: Louisiana State University Press.

Hirschman, Albert O. 1958. *Strategies of Development*. New Haven: Yale University Press.

Humphrey, John. 2001. "Governance in Global Value Chains." *IDS Bulletin* 32 (3): 3.

Huntington, Samuel P. 1981. *American Politics: The Promise of Disharmony*. Cambridge: Harvard University Press.

———. 2004. *Who Are We? Challenges to America's National Identity*. Boston: Simon and Schuster.

IBIS *World*. 2012. "Staying Afloat: Despite a Decline in Commercial Orders, Military Shipbuilding Will Thrive." Industry Report 33661a, July.

Jamieson, A. G. 2003. *Ebb Tide in the British Maritime Industries: Change and Adaptation, 1918–1990*. Exeter: Exeter University Press.

Jenkins, S. 2002. "Organizing, Advocacy, and Member Power." *Working USA* 6 (2): 56–89.

Jessop, Bob. 1983. "Accumulation Strategies, State Forms, and Hegemonic projects." *Katipalistate* 10/11:89–112.

Jindal, Bobby. 2011. "Governor Signs Bills into Law." http://www.knoe.com/home /headlines/Gov-Jindal-signs-bills-into-law-309379441.html.

Johnman, Lewis, and Hugh Murphy. 2005. *British Shipbuilding and the State since 1918: A Political Economy of Decline*. Exeter: University of Exeter Press.

Johnson, Calvin, Mathilde Laisne, and Jon Wool. 2015. "Criminal Justice: Changing Course on Incarceration." *New Orleans Index at Ten*. New Orleans: The Data Center.

Johnson, Cedric. 2011. *Neoliberal Deluge: Hurricane Katrina, Late Capitalism, and the Remaking of New Orleans*. Minneapolis: University of Minnesota Press.

———. 2016. "An Open Letter to Ta-Nahesi Coates and the White Liberals Who Love Him." *Jacobin*, February. https://www.jacobinmag.com/2016/02/ta-nehisi -coates-case-for-reparations-bernie-sanders-racism.

Joyner, James. 2007. "New Orleans City Council Now Majority White." *Outside the Beltway,* November 19. http://www.outsidethebeltway.com/new_orleans_ council_now_majority_white_.

Kaplinsky, Raphael. 2005. *Globalization, Poverty and Inequality*. London: Polity Press.

Karnig, Albert, and Susan Welch. 1980. *Black Representation and Urban Policy*. Chicago: University of Chicago Press.

Katz, Michael B., Mark J. Stern, and Jamie J. Fader. 2007. "The Mexican Immigration Debate: View from History." *Social Science History* 31 (2): 157–89.

Katznelson, Ira. 1976. *Black Men, White Cities: Race, Politics, and Migration in the United States, 1900–30, and Britain, 1948–68*. Chicago: University of Chicago Press.

Kendall, John. 1922. *History of New Orleans*. Chicago: Lewis.

Kerner Commission. 1968. *Report of the National Advisory Commission on Civil Disorders*. http://www.eisenhowerfoundation.org/docs/kerner.pdf.

Kirby, Alicia. 1990. *Nothing to Fear: Risks and Hazards in American Society*. Tucson: University of Arizona Press.

Klein, Naomi. 2006. *Shock Doctrine: The Rise of Disaster Capitalism*. New York: Picador.

Klinenberg, Eric. 2002. *Heat Wave: A Social Autopsy of Disaster in Chicago*. Chicago: University of Chicago Press.

Kurtz, Michael L. 1971. "The Demagogue and the Liberal: A Study of the Rivalry of Earl K. Long and DeLesseps Morrison." Ph.D. diss., Tulane University.

Kurtz, Michael, and Morgan D. Peoples. 1991. *Earl K. Long: The Saga of Uncle Earl and Louisiana Politics*. Baton Rouge: Louisiana State University Press.

Lambert, S. 2009. "Passing the Buck: Labor Flexibility Practices That Transfer Risk onto Hourly Workers." *Human Relations* 61 (9): 1203–27.

LaRose, Greg. 2015. "What Should Be the Economic Development Priorities for Louisiana's Next Governor?" *Times-Picayune*, October 27. http://www.nola.com/futureofneworleans/2015/10/what_should_be_the_economic_de.html.

Lay, J. Celeste. 2009. "Race, Retrospective Voting, and Disasters: The Re-Election of C. Ray Nagin after Hurricane Katrina." *Urban Affairs Review* 44 (5): 645–62.

Lenin, Vladimir I. (1902) 1969. *What Is to Be Done?* New York: International Publications.

———. (1917) 2011. *Imperialism, the Highest Stage of Capitalism*. Hartford: Martino Books.

Lewis, Edmund W. 2010. "Tulane Part of Effort to Support Better Working Conditions for Sodexo Employees." *Louisiana Weekly*, April 12. http://tulane.usas.org/files/2010/04/20100414_louisiana_weekly_april_12.pdf.

Lewis, W. A. 1954. *Economic Development with Unlimited Supply of Labour*. Manchester: The Manchester School.

Lincoln, Yvonna S., and Egon Guba. 1986. "But Is It Rigorous? Trustworthiness and Authenticity in Naturalistic Evaluation." *New Directions for Program Evaluation* 30 (Summer): 73–84.

Lipton, Michael. 1997. "Editorial: Poverty: Are There Holes in the Consensus?" *World Development* 25 (7): 1003–7.

Liu, Amy, Matt Fellowes, and Mia Mabanta. 2006. *Katrina Index: Tracking Indicators of Post-Katrina Recovery*. Washington, D.C.: Brookings Institution Press.

Liu, Amy, and Alison Plyer. 2010. *Katrina Index: Tracking Variables of Post-Katrina Reconstruction*. Washington, D.C.: Brookings Institution Press.

Liu, Baodong. 2006. "Whites as a Minority and the New Biracial Coalition in New Orleans and Memphis." *Political Science and Politics* 39 (1): 69–76.

Liu, Baodong, and James M. Vanderleeuw. 2007. *Race Rules: Electoral Politics in New Orleans, 1965–2006*. Lanham, Md.: Lexington Books.

Logan, John R. 2006a. "The Impact of Katrina: Race and Class in Storm Damaged Neighborhoods." Manuscript. Brown University.

———. 2006b. "Population Displacement and Post-Katrina Politics: The New Orleans Mayoral Race, 2006." Manuscript. Brown University.

Logan, John R., and Harvey Molotch. 1987. *Urban Fortunes: The Political Economy of Place*. Berkeley: University of California Press.

Logan, John R., Rachel B. Whaley, and Kyle Crowder. 1997. "The Character and Consequences of Growth Regimes: An Assessment of 20 years of Research." *Urban Affairs Review* 32 (5): 6303–30.

Lorenz, E. H. 1991. "An Evolutionary Explanation for Competitive Decline: The British Shipbuilding Industry, 1890–1970." *Journal of Economic History* 51 (4): 911–35.

Louisiana Legislative Auditor Office. 2010. *Compliance Audit: City of New Orleans*. Baton Rouge: Louisiana Legislative Auditor.

Louisiana Restaurant Association. 2006. *Initial Quarterly Report*, February. http://lra.louisiana.gov/assets/docs/searchable/reports/FiNAL_QP2006_FEB_06_revised.pdf.

Luckey, John R. 2005. "Emergency Contracting Authorities." *CRS Report RS22273*. Washington, D.C.: Congressional Research Service.

Lukes, Steven. 1974. *Power: A Radical View*. New York: Macmillan.

Luxembourg, Rosa. 1971. *The Mass Strike, the Political Party, and the Trade Unions*. London: Harper Torchbooks.

——. 2003. *The Accumulation of Capital*. New York: Routledge.

M2 Presswire. 2007. "KBR, Inc. Katrina Workers Due $1.4 Million in Back Wages." *M2 Presswire*, June 26. http://callcenterinfo.tmcnet.com/news/2007/06/26/2740356.htm.

MacDonald, Ian. 2014. "Beyond the Labor of Sisyphus: Unions and the City." *Socialist Register* 50:247–82.

MARAD (Maritime Administration). 2013. *The Economic Importance of the Shipbuilding and Repairing Industry*. Washington, D.C.: MARAD. http://www.marad.dot.gov/wp-content/uploads/pdf/MARAD_Econ_Study_Final_Report_2013.pdf.

Marglin, Stephen, and Janet Schor. 1990. *The Rise and Fall of the Golden Age*. Oxford: Clarendon Press.

Martin, Naomi. 2014a. "New Orleans Tax Proposal to Fund Jail Backed by Sheriff Marlin Gusman, Mayor Mitch Landrieu." *Times-Picayune,* October 8. http://www.nola.com/crime/index.ssf/2014/10/new_orleans_tax_proposal.html.

——. 2014b. "New Orleans Voters Reject Law Enforcement District Tax." *Times-Picayune,* November 4. http://www.nola.com/elections/index.ssf/2014/11/law_enforcement_district_tax_e.html.

Martin, Nathan C. 2014. "Building Homes and a Multi-Racial Construction Industry in New Orleans." *Next City,* March 31. https://nextcity.org/daily/entry/race-labor-racism-new-orleans-construction-katrina.

Marx, Karl. (1894) 1993. *Capital*. 3 vols. New York: Penguin Classics.

——. (1898) 1974. *Value, Price and Profit*. New York: International Co.

——. 1976. *The Poverty of Philosophy*. In *Marx and Engels Collected Works: Volume 6: Marx and Engels, 1845–1848*. New York: International Publishers.

Marx, Karl, and Friedrich Engels. (1847) 2012. *Manifesto of the Communist Party*. New York: Penguin Classics.

Massey, Douglas S., and Nancy A. Denton. 1993. *American Apartheid: Segregation and the Making of the Underclass*. Cambridge: Harvard University Press.

McClendon, Robert. 2014a. "Aviation Board Vows to Complete Terminal on Time." *Times-Picayune*, June 9. http://www.nola.com/politics/index.ssf/2014/06/aviation_board_vows_to_complet.html.

———. 2014b. "New Orleans Is 2nd Worst for Income Inequality in the U.S., Roughly on Par with Zambia, Report Says." *Times-Picayune*, August 19. http://www.nola.com/politics/index.ssf/2014/08/new_orleans_is_2nd_worst_for_i.html.

Media Matters for America. 2012. "Hannity Labels Sandy Aftermath 'Obama's Katrina.'" Video. *Media Matters*, November 1. http://mediamatters.org/video/2012/11/01/hannity-labels-sandy-aftermath-obamas-katrina/191074.

Mikell, Ray. 2007. "New Orleans Recovery Case Study." Manuscript. New Orleans: University of New Orleans.

Miura, Hirotaka. 2012. "Stata Graph Library for Network Analysis." *Stata Journal* 12 (1): 94–129.

Mock, Brentin. 2015. "How New Orleans Stopped Making Jailing a Business." *City Lab*, June 18. http://www.citylab.com/crime/2015/06/how-new-orleans-stopped-making-jailing-a-business/396188.

Molotch, Harvey. 1976. "The City as a Growth Machine: Toward a Political Economy of Place." *American Journal of Sociology* 82:309–32.

———. 1979. "Capital and Neighborhood in the United States." *Urban Affairs Quarterly* 14 (3): 299–312.

———. 1988. "Strategies and Constraints of Growth Elites." In *Business Elites and Urban Development: Case Studies and Critical Perspectives*, ed. Scott Cummings, 25–47. Albany: State University of New York Press.

———. 1999. "Growth Machine Links: Up, Down, and Across." In *The Urban Growth Machine: Critical Perspectives Two Decades Later*, ed. A. E. G. Jonas and David Wilson, 247–65. Albany: State University of New York Press.

Moore, Barrington. 1966. *Social Origins of Dictatorship and Democracy*. Boston: Beacon Press.

Morris, Tim. 2009. "William Jefferson Verdict: Guilty on 11 of 16 Counts." *Times-Picayune*, August 5. http://www.nola.com/news/index.ssf/2009/08/william_jefferson_verdict_guil.html.

Morrison, DeLesseps. 1965. *Latin America Mission*. New York: Simon and Schuster.

Moses, Norton H. 1997. *Lynching and Vigilantism in the United States: An Annotated Bibliography*. Westport, Conn.: Greenwood Publishing Group.

Moskowitz, Peter. 2015. "Destroy and Rebuild: A Q&A with One of New Orleans' Biggest Developers." *Gawker True Stories*, February 16. http://truestories.gawker.co/destroy-and-rebuild-a-q-a-with-one-of-new-orleans-bigg-1684973590#.

Mossberger, Karen, and Gerry Stoker. 2001. "The Evolution of Urban Regime Theory." *Urban Affairs Review* 36 (6): 810–35.

Mt. Auburn Associates. 2005. *Louisiana: Where Culture Means Business.* http://www.mtauburnassociates.com/pubs/Louisiana_Where_Culture_Means_Business.pdf.

Mui, Ylan Q. 2010. "Five Years after Katrina, New Orleans Sees Higher Percentage of Hispanics. " *Washington Post,* August 21. http://www.washingtonpost.com/wp-dyn/content/article/2010/08/20/AR2010082005636.html.

Mumphrey, Anthony J., and Pamela H. Moomau. 1984. "New Orleans: An Island in the Sunbelt." *Public Administration Quarterly* 8 (Spring): 91–111.

Myrdal, Gunnar. 1944. *An American Dilemma: The Negro Problem and Modern Democracy.* New York: Harper & Bros.

New Orleans Business Alliance. 2016. *Transportation, Trade, and Logistics Overview.* New Orleans: NOBA. http://www.nolaba.org/wp-content/uploads/2016/03/Tansportation-Trade-Logistics.pdf.

New Orleans City Council. 1954. *Home Rule Charter.* New Orleans: City Council.

New York Times. 2005. "Barbara Bush Calls Evacuees Better Off." September 7. http://www.nytimes.com/2005/09/07/national/nationalspecial/07barbara.html.

Nolan, Bruce. 2010. "Sodexo Workers Stage One-Day Walkout at Tulane, Demand Better Wages." *Times-Picayune,* October 7. http://www.nola.com/education/index.ssf/2010/10/cafeteria_workers_walk_out_at.html.

Nossiter, Adam. 2007. "Whites Take Majority on New Orleans City Council." *New York Times,* November 20, A14. http://www.nytimes.com/2007/11/20/us/nationalspecial/20orleans.html.

Nussbaum, Martha, and Amartya Sen. 1993. *The Quality of Life.* New York: Oxford University Press.

OECD (Organisation for Economic Co-operation and Development). 2007. *Factors Affecting the Structure of the World Shipbuilding Industry.* WP6. Paris: Council Working Party on Shipbuilding. November.

OIG (Office of the Inspector General). 2013. "Review of New Orleans Security Taxing Districts." http://www.nolaoig.org/uploads/File/OIG%20Review%20of%20Security%20Taxing%20Districts%20130924.pdf.

Omi, Michael, and Howard Winant. 1994. *Racial Formation in the United States: From the 1960s to the 1980s.* New York: Routledge.

Ortiz, Elaine. 2011. *Who Lives in New Orleans and the Metro Area Now? Brief and Data Tables.* New Orleans: Greater New Orleans Community Data Center.

OSHA (Occupational Safety and Health Administration). 2006. "OSHA Resuming Regular Enforcement along Most of U.S. Gulf Coast." https://www.osha.gov/pls/oshaweb/owadisp.show_document?p_table=NEWS_RELEASES&p_id=11805.

Palm, Risa. 1990. *Natural Hazards: An Integrative Framework for Research and Planning.* Baltimore: Johns Hopkins University Press.

Parent, Wayne. 2006. *Inside the Carnival: Unmasking Louisiana Politics*. Baton Rouge: Louisiana State University Press.

Park, Robert E. 1928. "Human Migration and the Marginal Man." *American Journal of Sociology* 33 (6): 881–93.

Parkinson, Caroline, and Carole Howorth. 2008. "The Language of Social Entrepreneurs." *Journal of Entrepreneurship and Regional Development* 20 (May): 285–309.

Passavant, Paul A. 2011. "Mega-Events, the Superdome, and the Return of the Repressed in New Orleans." In *Neoliberal Deluge: Hurricane Katrina, Late Captialism, and the Remaking of New Orleans*, ed. Cedric Johnson, 87–130. Minneapolis: University of Minnesota Press.

Passel, Jeffrey S. 2006. *Size and Characteristics of Unauthorized Migrant Population in the U.S.* Pew Research Center, March 7. http://www.pewhispanic.org/2006/03/07/size-and-characteristics-of-the-unauthorized-migrant-population -in-the-us.

Pastor, Manuel, and Enrico Marcelli. 2003. "Somewhere over the Rainbow? African Americans, Unauthorized Mexican Immigration and Coalition Building." *Review of Black Political Economy* 31 (1–2): 125–55.

Persky, Joseph J. 1991. *Burden of Dependency: Colonial Themes in Southern Economic Thought*. Baltimore: Johns Hopkins University Press.

Peterson, Paul E. 1981. *City Limits*. Chicago: University of Chicago Press.

Piketty, Thomas. 2014. *Capital in the Twenty-First Century*. New York: Belknap Press.

Piore, Michael. 1976. "Immigration, Work Expectations, and Labor Market Structure." In *The Diverse Society: Implications for Social Policy*, ed. Pastora San Juan Cafferty and Leon Chestang, 109–27. Washington, D.C.: National Association of Social Workers.

———. 1980. *Birds of Passage: Migrant Labor and Industrial Societies*. New York: Cambridge University Press.

Piore, Michael, and Charles Sabel. 1986. *The Second Industrial Divide: Possibilities for Prosperity*. New York: Basic Books.

Piven, Frances Fox. 2006. "Response to *American Democracy in an Age of Inequality*." *Political Science and Politics* 39 (1): 43–46.

Piven, Frances Fox, and Richard Cloward. 1978. *Poor People's Movements: Why They Succeed, How They Fail*. New York: Vintage Books.

Plyer, Allison. 2008. "Four Years after the Storm: The Road Home Program's Impact on Greater New Orleans." *Congressional Testimony before House Subcommittee on Housing and Community Opportunity*. August 20. http://archives .financialservices.house.gov/media/file/hearings/111/plyer.pdf.

———. 2015. "Facts for Features." http://www.datacenterresearch.org/data-resources /katrina/facts-for-features-katrina-recovery-2.

Plyer, Allison, Elaine Ortiz, and Ben Horwitz. 2011. *Housing Development and Abandonment in New Orleans*. New Orleans: Greater New Orleans Data

Center. http://www.datacenterresearch.org/reports_analysis/housing-development
-and-abandonment.

Plyer, Allison, Nihal Shrinath, and Vicki Mack. 2015. *New Orleans Index at Ten: Measuring Greater New Orleans' Progress toward Prosperity.* New Orleans: Greater New Orleans Data Center.

Porter, Douglas. 1992. *Special Districts: A Useful Technique for Financing Infrastructure.* Washington, D.C.: Urban Land Institute.

Postel, Charles. 2009. *The Populist Vision.* New York: Oxford University Press.

Powell, Lawrence. 1990. "A Concrete Symbol." *Southern Exposure,* Spring:40-43. http://katrinareader.org/sites/katrinareader.org/files/Concrete_Symbol.pdf.

Putnam, Robert. 1994. *Making Democracy Work.* Princeton: Princeton University Press.

———. 2000. *Bowling Alone: The Collapse and Revival of American Community.* New York: Simon and Schuster.

Quigley, Bill. 2015. "New Orleans Katrina Pain Index at 10: Who Was Left Behind." *Huffington Post,* July 20. http://www.huffingtonpost.com/bill-quigley/new-or leans-katrina-pain_b_7831870.html.

Rainey, Richard. 2015. "Pressure Rebuilds over New Orleans Jail Size: Live Coverage of City Council Meeting." *Times-Picayune,* July 7. http://www.nola.com/ politics/index.ssf/2015/07/pressure_rebuilds_over_new_orl.html.

Ramakrishnan, S. Karthick, and Thomas J. Espenshade. 2001. "Immigrant Incorporation and Political Participation in the United States." *International Migration Review* 35 (3): 870–909.

Rana, Aziz. 2010. *Two Faces of American Freedom.* Cambridge: Harvard University Press.

Ranis, Gustav. 2006. "Is Dualism Worth Revisiting?" In *Poverty, Inequality and Development: Essay in Honor of Erik Thorbecke,* ed. A. Janvry and R. Kanbur, 371–88. New York: Springer.

Reckdahl, Katy. 2011. "Road Home Settlement Will Benefit 1,500 Homeowners." *Times-Picayune,* July 6. http://www.nola.com/katrina/index.ssf/2011/07/road_ home_settlement_will_bene.html.

———. 2015. "10 Years after Katrina, New Orleans Public Housing Still in Limbo." *Next City,* June 15. https://nextcity.org/features/view/10-years-after-katrina-new -orleans-public-housing-still-in-limbo-iberville.

Reed, Adolph, Jr. 1993. "The Battle of Liberty Monument—New Orleans, LA White Supremacist Statue." *The Progressive,* June 1. https://www.thefreelibrary.com/ The+battle+of+Liberty+Monument.-a013773324.

———. 1999. *Stirrings in the Jug: Black Politics in the Post-Segregation Era.* Minneapolis: University of Minnesota Press.

———. 2013. "Marx, Race, and Neoliberalism." *New Labor Forum* 22 (Winter): 53–54.

———. 2015. "From Jenner to Dolezal: One Trans Good, the Other, Not So Much." *Common Dreams,* June 15. http://www.commondreams.org/views/2015/06/15/ jenner-dolezal-one-trans-good-other-not-so-much.

———. 2016. "The Post-1965 Trajectory of Race, Class, and Urban Politics in the United States Reconsidered." *Labor Studies Journal* 41 (3): 1–32.

Reich, Robert. 1992. *The Work of Nations.* New York: Vintage Books.

Ridlen Ray, Marcella. 1999. "Technological Change and Associational Life." In *Civic Engagement in American Democracy,* ed. Theda Skocpol and Morris Fiorina, 297–330. Washington, D.C.: Brookings Institution Press.

Rivlin, Gary. 2015. *Katrina: After the Flooding.* New York: Simon and Schuster.

Robertson, Campbell. 2014. "Mitch Landrieu Is Re-elected Mayor of New Orleans." *New York Times,* February 2, A19.

Robertson, D. Osei. 2008. "Property and Security, Political Chameleons and Dysfunctional Regime: A New Orleans Story." In *Seeking Higher Ground,* ed. Manning Marable, 39–63. New York: Springer Books.

Robinson, William I. 2004. *A Theory of Global Capitalism.* Baltimore: Johns Hopkins University Press.

ROC (Restaurant Opportunities Center). 2009. *Behind the Kitchen Door: Inequality, Instability and Opportunity in the Greater New Orleans Restaurant Industry.* New Orleans: ROC–NOLA.

Rodriguez, Maya. 2009. "Day Laborers, Huge Task in Region for Wage Theft, Ask Council for Help." June 30. http://nowcrj.org/2009/07/02/63009-wwltv-day -laborers-huge-task-in-region-for-wage-theft-ask-council-for-help.

Ross, Robert J. S. 2011. "Is New Orleans a Rust Belt City?" *Metropolitics,* July 6. http://www.metropolitiques.eu/New-Orleans-as-a-Rust-Belt-City.html.

Rothschild, Matthew. 2010. "Tulane Graduation Marred by Crackdown." *The Progressive,* May 14. http://www.progressive.org/mc051410.html.

Rudowitz, Robin, Diane Rowland, and Adele Shartzer. 2006. "Health Care in New Orleans before and after Hurricane Katrina." *Health Affairs* 25 (3): 393–406.

Sakakeeny, Matthew. 2013. *Roll with It: Brass Bands in the Streets of New Orleans.* Durham: Duke University Press.

Sassen, Saskia. 1991. *The Global City: New York, London, Tokyo.* Princeton: Princeton University Press.

———. 2001. *The Global City: New York, London, Tokyo.* Rev. ed. Princeton: Princeton University Press.

Sayre, Katherine. 2014. "Home Prices in New Orleans Metro Area Continue Steady Climb, Report Says." *Times-Picayune,* February 3. http://www.nola.com/busi ness/index.ssf/2014/02/home_prices_in_new_orleans_met.html.

Schick, Alan. 1966. "The Road to PPB: Stages of Budget Reform." *Public Administration Review* 26 (4): 243–58.

Schlozman, Kay Lehman, Sidney Verba, and Henry Brady. 1999. "Civic Participation and the Equality Problem." In *Civic Engagement in American Democracy,* ed. Theda Skocpol and Morris Fiorina, 427–60. Washington, D.C.: Brookings Institution Press.

Schneider, Aaron. 2016. "Social Entrepreneurship, Entrepreneurship, Collectivism, and Everything in Between: Prototypes and Continuous Dimensions." *Public Administration Review* 76 (5): 421–31.

Schneider, Aaron, and Saru Jayaraman. 2014. "Ascriptive Segmentation between Good and Bad Jobs." In *Working in the Big Easy: History and Politics of Labor in New Orleans,* ed. Thomas Adams and Steve Striffler, 237–72. Baton Rouge: Louisiana State University Press.

Schumpeter, Josef. 1918. "The Crisis of the Tax State." Reprinted in Richard Swedberg, *Joseph A. Schumpeter: The Economics and Sociology of Capitalism,* 101. Princeton: Princeton University Press, 1991.

Seelos, Christian, and Johanna Mair. 2005. "Social Entrepreneurship: Creating New Business Models to Serve the Poor." *Business Horizons* 48:241–46.

Sen, Amartya. 1985. *Commodities and Capabilities.* New York: Elsevier Press.

———. 2000. *Development as Freedom.* New York: Oxford University Press.

———. 2005. "Human Rights and Capabilities." *Journal of Human Development* 6 (2): 151–66.

Sen, Rinku, and Fekkak Mamdouh. 2008. *Accidental American: Immigration and Citizenship in the Age of Globalization.* San Francisco: Berrett-Koehler Publishers.

Shallat, Todd. 2001. "In the Wake of Hurricane Betsy." In *Transforming New Orleans and Its Environs: Centuries of Change,* ed. C. E. Colton, 121–37. Pittsburgh: University of Pittsburgh Press.

Shore, Elena. 2005. "Katrina Victims Denied Aid and Face Deportation." *New America Media,* September 28. http://news.newamericamedia.org/news/view_alt_category.html?page=14&first=130&last=139&category_id=371.

Shoup, David. 2011. "SODEXO Responds to Report of Human Rights Abuses." *Tulane Hullaballo,* February 25. http://issuu.com/hullabaloo_online/docs/the_tulane_hullabaloo__02.25.2011_.

Sims, Robert T. 2010. *2010 Quality of Life Study.* New Orleans: UNO Survey Research Center.

Singer, H. W. 1999. "Dual Economy." In *The Social Science Encyclopedia,* ed. Adam Kuper and Jessica Kuper, 202. 2nd ed. London: Routledge.

Sisco, Annette. 2009. "Justice Elusive in Katrina Contractor Fraud." *Times-Picayune,* July 31. http://blog.nola.com/guesteditorials/2009/07/point_of_view_justice_elusive.html.

Smith, Michael P., and Marlene Keller. 1983. "Managed Growth and the Politics of Uneven Development in New Orleans." In *Restructuring the City: The Political Economy of Urban Redevelopment,* ed. Norman I. Fainstein and Susan S. Fainstein, 126–60. New York: Longman.

Smith, Preston H., II. 2012. *Racial Democracy and the Black Metropolis: Housing Policy in Postwar Chicago.* Minneapolis: University of Minnesota Press.

Smith, Stanley C., John White, and Patrick Dobard. 2012. *Superintendents' Report.* New Orleans: Orleans Parish School Board. http://lrsd.entest.org/Superintendent_s%20Report%20%20for%20December%202012%20_2_.pdf.

Smith Kendall, John. 1922. *History of New Orleans.* Vol. 2. Chicago: Lewis Publishing Company.

Souther, J. Mark. 2003. "Into the Big League: Conventions, Football, and the Color Line in New Orleans." *Journal of Urban History* 29 (6): 694–725.

———. 2006. *New Orleans on Parade: Tourism and the Transformation of the Crescent City.* Baton Rouge: Louisiana State University Press.

SPLC (Southern Poverty Law Center). 2006. "Broken Levees, Broken Promises: New Orleans Migrant Workers in Their Own Words." https://www.splcenter.org/sites/default/files/d6_legacy_files/downloads/brokenlevees.pdf.

———. 2009. *Under Siege: Life for Low-Income Latinos in the South.* Montgomery: SPLC.

———. 2013. *Close to Slavery: Guestworker Programs in the United States.* Montgomery: SPLC.

Stanonis, Anthony. 2006. *Creating the Big Easy: New Orleans and the Emergence of Modern Tourism.* Athens: University of Georgia Press.

Steinmo, Sven. 2008. "Historical Institutionalism." In *Approaches in the Social Sciences: A Pluralist Perspective,* ed. Donatella della Porta and Michael Keating, 118–38. Cambridge: Cambridge University Press.

Stokes, P. 1997. *Ship Finance: Credit Expansion and the Boom-Bust Cycle.* London: LLP Limited.

Stoll, Michael A., Edwin Melendez, and Abel Valenzuela. 2002. "Spatial Job Search and Job Competition among Immigrant and Native Groups in Los Angeles." *Regional Studies* 35 (2): 97–112.

Stone, Clarence N. 1976. *Economic Growth and Neighborhood Discontent.* Chapel Hill: University of North Carolina Press.

———. 1989. *Regime Politics: Governing Atlanta, 1946–1988.* Lawrence: University Press of Kansas.

———. 1993. "Urban Regimes and the Capacity to Govern." *Journal of Urban Affairs* 15 (1): 1–28.

———. 2005. "Looking Back to Look Forward: Reflections on Urban Regime Analysis." Urban Affairs Review 40 (3): 309–41.

Stone, Harold. 1934. "Confusion in Our City's Ranks." *Bureau of Governmental Research Collection.* New Orleans: BGR.

Stopford, M. 2009. *Maritime Economics.* New York: Routledge Press.

Story, Louise, Tiff Fehr, and Derek Watkins. 2016. "Explore the Data." *New York Times,* December 1. http://www.nytimes.com/interactive/2012/12/01/us/government-incentives.html?_r=0-LA.

Strath, B. 1987. *The Politics of De-Industrialization: Contraction of West European Shipbuilding Industry.* London: Croom Helm.

Taylor, Shaquille, and Mat Freimuth. 2011. "Shaq and Mat." *Tulane University Peace Action Committee,* February 5. http://tulane.usas.org/2011/02/05/shaq-and-mat.

TCA (Total Community Action). 2001. *A History of the Community Action Movement in New Orleans, 1964–2001.* New Orleans: TCA. http://www.tca-nola.org/userfiles/2011/04/tca-history.pdf.

Thompson, E. P. 1966. *The Making of the English Working Class*. New York: Vintage Books.

Thompson, Richard. 2012. "Energy Industry May Play a Part in Future of Avondale Shipyard." *Times–Picayune*, December 18. http://connect.nola.com/user/richardthompson/posts-8.html.

Thompson, Shirley Elizabeth. 2009. *Exiles at Home: The Struggle to Become American in Creole New Orleans*. Cambridge: Harvard University Press.

Tiebout, Charles. 1956. "A Pure Theory of Local Expenditure." *Journal of Political Economy* 64:416–24.

Times-Picayune Staff. 2011. "5 NOPD Officers Guilty in Post-Katrina Danziger Bridge Shootings, Cover-up." *Times-Picayune*, August 5. http://www.nola.com/crime/index.ssf/2011/08/danziger_bridge_verdict_do_not.html.

Todd, Daniel, and Michael Lindberg. 1996. *Navies and Shipbuilding Industries: The Strained Symbiosis*. Westport, Conn.: Praeger.

Tulane USAS. 2011. "Labor Standards for Tulane University Contracts." http://tulane.usas.org/files/2010/11/20101102_laborcodeofconductdoc.pdf.

UNDP (United Nations Development Program). 1990. *Human Development Report*. New York: UNDP.

Unger, Nick. 2012. "SOS Avondale." Manuscript. New Orleans.

UNO (University of New Orleans). 2013. "Job Approval Ratings for Mayor Landrieu and Orleans City Council." http://www.uno.edu/cola/political-science/doc uments/2013-Job-Approval-Ratings-for-Mayor-Landrieu-and-Orleans-City -Council.pdf.

U.S. Census Bureau. 2002. *Census of Governments*. http://www2.census.gov/govs/cog/2002COGprelim_report.pdf.

———. 2010. *2010 Census*. http://www.census.gov/2010census/.

———. 2013. *MSA Business Patterns*. http://censtats.census.gov/cgi-bin/msanaic/msasect.pl.

Varela, Raquel, and Marcel Van der Linden. 2011. *In the Same Boat*. https://in thesameboatproject.wordpress.com/international-meetings-and-conferences.

Vega, William A., William M. Sribney, and Ijeoma Achara-Abrahams. 2003. "Co-occurring Alcohol, Drug, and Other Psychiatric Disorders among Mexican-Origin People in the United States." *American Journal of Public Health* 93 (7): 1057–64.

Vinck, Patrick, Phuong N. Pham, Laurel Fletcher, and Eric Stover. 2009. "Inequalities and Prospects: Ethnicity and Legal Status in the Construction Labor Force after Hurricane Katrina." *Organization and Environment* 22 (4): 470–78.

Wacquant, Loic. 2001. "Deadly Symbiosis: When Ghetto and Prison Meet and Mesh." *Punishment and Society* 3:95–134.

Walton, Hanes, Jr. 1972. *Black Politics: A Theoretical and Structural Analysis*. Philadelphia: Lippincott.

———. 1973. *The Study and Analysis of Black Politics*. Metuchen, N.J.: Scarecrow Press.

Walton, Hanes, Jr., and Robert Smith. 2000. *American Politics and the African American Quest for Universal Freedom.* New York: Longman.

Walzer, Michael. 1992. *What It Means to Be an American.* New York: Marsilio.

Wasem, Ruth Ellen. 2005. "Hurricane Katrina–Related Immigration Issues and Legislation." *CRS Report for Congress RL23091.* Washington, D.C.: Congressional Research Service.

Weber, Max. (1922) 1968. *Economy and Society.* Berkeley: University of California Press.

WGNO Web Desk. 2015. "Parking and More for the Indy Grand Prix of Louisiana." http://wgno.com/2015/04/06/parking-and-more-for-the-indy-grand-prix-of-louisiana.

Whelan, Robert K. 1987. "New Orleans: Mayoral Politics and Economic-Development Policies in the Postwar Years, 1945–86." In *The Politics of Urban Development,* ed. Clarence N. Stone and Heywood T. Sanders, 216–29. Lawrence: University Press of Kansas.

Whelan, Robert K., Alma H. Young, and Mickey Lauria. 1994. "Urban Regimes and Racial Politics in New Orleans." *Journal of Urban Affairs* 16 (1): 1–21.

Whittaker, William G. 2005. "Davis-Bacon Suspension and Its Legislative Aftermath." *CRS Report for Congress RS22288.* Washington, D.C.: Congressional Research Service.

Wildavsky, Aaron. 1964. *Politics of the Budgetary Process.* New York: Little, Brown.

Witte, Griff. 2005. "Prevailing Wages to Be Paid Again on Gulf Coast." *Washington Post,* October 26. http://www.washingtonpost.com/wp-dyn/content/article/2005/10/26/AR2005102601706.html.

Woodward, C. Vann. 1981. *Origins of the New South.* Baton Rouge: Louisiana State University.

Wright, Erik Olin. 1997. *Class Counts: Comparative Studies in Class Analysis.* New York: Cambridge University Press.

Wright, Gavin. 1986. *Old South, New South: Revolutions in the Southern Economy since the Civil War.* Baton Rouge: Louisiana State University Press.

Youngman, Nicole. 2011. "Swamped: Growth Machines and the Manufacture of Flood Risk in Mid-Twentieth Century New Orleans." Ph.D. diss., Tulane University.

Zhou, Min. 1997. "Segmented Assimilation: Issues, Controversies, and Recent Research on the New Second Generation." *International Migration Review* 31 (4): 975–1008.

Zhou, Min, and Carl L. Bankston. 1998. *Growing Up American: How Vietnamese Children Adapt to Life in the United States.* New York: Russell Sage Foundation.

(continued from p. ii)

AARON SCHNEIDER is Leo Block Chair of International Studies at the Josef Korbel School of International Studies at the University of Denver and author of *State-Building and Tax Regimes in Central America*.